DECADE IN EUROPE

BARRETT McGURN

Barrett McGurn

DECADE
IN
EUROPE

E. P. DUTTON & CO., INC.

NEW YORK, 1959

McGurn, Barrett. Decade in Europe. ₜ1st ed.₎ New
York, Dutton, 1959. 288 p. illus. 22 cm. 1. Europe—Hist.—1945— 1. Title. D1051.M3 940.55
59–5822 ‡ Library of Congress

Map on pages 6-7 by James MacDonald

CONTENTS

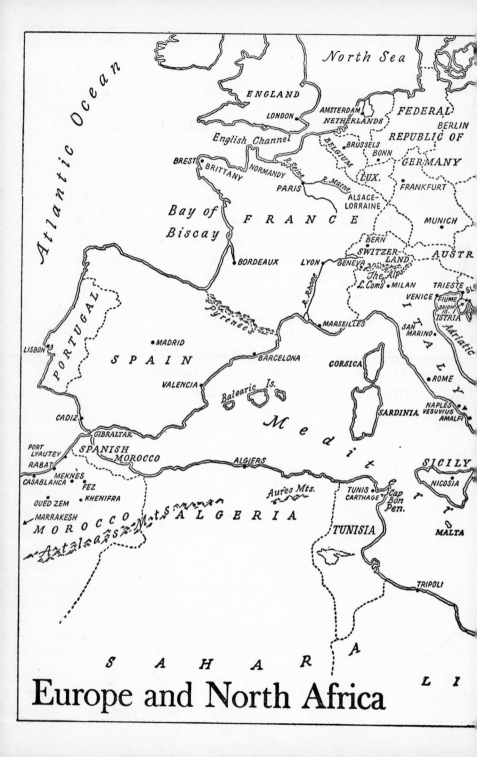

Europe and North Africa

I

NORTH AFRICA IN FLAMES

Meknes in the middle fifties of the twentieth century looked very much as it must have two centuries earlier in the time of Sultan Moulay Hassan. Cinnamon-colored walls with bulbous pointed arches surrounded the densely crowded native quarter in which three quarters of the city's population lived. Along the narrow streets of the Arab quarter artisans plying biblical trades crouched in shops no bigger than packing cases. Little was changed, except that there was no new Moulay Hassan to preside over an army of 100,000 men, a horse troop of 10,000, a harem of 500, a slave corps of 30,000, and a special construction force of 3,000 Christian prisoners. Now a sultan of far milder pretensions occupied the throne in Rabat, one hundred miles distant. The other significant change in Meknes was the European quarter on a hill opposite the native district. The foreigners living in the new quarters numbered only one sixth of Meknes' 140,000 inhabitants, but most of the wealth and almost all the political power were in their hands. Most of them were French, immigrants and descendants of immigrants who had come to Morocco during the half century since the soldiers of Paris opened the mysterious, closed sultanate to the Western world. A few were Europeans from other countries, notably Spanish and Italians.

The town was only one hundred miles from the Mediterranean and five hundred miles from France, but all the distance between the old continental imperialist mentality and the new anti-colonialist psychology of Africa and Asia separated Meknes from France on the evening of July 25, 1955, when I visited it.

That month many American correspondents in Europe had gathered in Switzerland to cover the sterile "summit" conference attended by Nikita Khrushchev and Nikolai Bulganin of the Soviet Union, President Eisenhower of the United States, Prime Minister Sir Anthony Eden of Great Britain, and Premier Edgar Faure of France. A discerning foreign editor had sent me, instead, southward from my base in Paris, to check what was happening in the North African colonies on Europe's doorstep. While the government leaders talked emptily, history was being rewritten on the Continent's threshold. The communism of "B. and K." was not the only hostile foreign force threatening the ruin of France, America's chief continental ally. Anti-colonialism, unrepresented at the Geneva meeting, but nonetheless dangerous, could work disasters, too.

A new French resident general, Gilbert Grandval, had been appointed to Morocco. In obedience to custom, he was making formal visits to the main cities of the sultanate. In his white military uniform as number-one representative of the French "protector," he was expected to call at each principal Moroccan community to accept the traditional Arab offering of a sip of sweet white almond juice and a date or two, and make a little speech about lasting French-Moroccan friendship.

In the past many other new residents general had made this polite round with no untoward happening to mar the outward amenities. This time, with nationalism in full force, it was different. Police scrutinized me as I walked through the exit from the railroad station. They were watching for nationalist hotheads from Casablanca, where shootings and sabotage had been going on for months in an effort of newly educated native youths to throw off the imperialist yoke of Paris. As a Westerner I passed muster, for the officials said nothing as I went through.

My first call was on the French general commanding at Meknes. His palm-shaded headquarters were on the lip of the European hill looking across the ravine to the native town. Eight finger-slim, cool, green prayer towers of Meknes mosques probed above the skyline visible from the officer's window. The general was calm but concerned. Banners hailing Grandval had been discovered in native hands and confiscated by the police. Ironically, the existence of such banners was a bad sign, for Grandval was generally considered a liberal, one of the French officials willing to make concessions to a new era. That implied that the freshly named resident was against the existing rigid French domination. A cheer for him by a Moroccan was thus a demand for a new dispensation, perhaps even for the expulsion of France from Morocco—something that neither Grandval nor many other French liberals would advocate.

Beyond this, the general told me, Meknes had been comparatively quiet, though it had been necessary to ban intermissions at the motion-picture theaters. The breaks during which audiences took a breath of air had lent themselves all too conveniently to the depositing under the seats of time bombs set to hit those who returned for the second half of the program.

Grandval's ceremonial arrival in the square before the main archway in the old walls of the native quarter was scheduled for 9 A.M. I joined the local newspapermen in pushing my way through the crowded streets to the square half an hour early. It was well that we did, for the day's tragic events already were rushing forward to a bloody climax. There was intense excitement as mobs jammed every inch of space in the square, behind the lines of the police. The police evidently wanted as few spectators present as possible, for they pressed back close to the surrounding buildings. Even so, thousands of Moroccans managed to crush in behind them. Overhead loomed the fine Moorish archway, built, one could presume, by Christian slaves. The music of a band all but drowned out the first few cries of "Grandval!" But the military tunes added to the tension. I noticed that the cheeks of police officials were quivering with nervousness. I had never seen policemen so moved.

The emotional cloud did not take long to release its lightning. There was still a wait of a quarter of an hour for the new resident general when shouts were heard below the square. For a few seconds the rising wave of angry voices rolled closer and then there were gunshots. For the eternity of a minute I listened as rifles fired volley after volley. I pushed through the crowd. Bodies already had been lifted up by survivors. A dozen heelless native slippers lay on the pavement, pitiful symbols of the vulnerability of the weak flesh and bones they had covered.

The official count was three dead and six wounded, all natives. Police said that young men in a little group had thrown a stone and perhaps even fired a few shots. In the West, tear gas or fire hoses would have been used. The Meknes police, perhaps from nervousness, perhaps in order to "teach a lesson," had squeezed their triggers within a matter of seconds.

When Grandval arrived in the square, he stayed, to my surprise, for less than two minutes. His speech could wait until he got back to the European quarter. He tasted a spoonful of almond juice, gulped a date, and climbed back into his car. By now the blaring of the band no longer drowned out the cries of the crowd. I watched one slim youth pumping an arm up and down like a cheerleader as he directed yells of "Long live Grandval!" with ever shorter pauses between cries and a constantly mounting passion. Dozens of Moroccans slipped under the arms of the police on the pretext that they had to cross to the other side. The officers' lines slowly dissolved. Veiled Moslem women wailed the *"you-you,"* a weird, thin cry produced by a rapid vibration of the tongue, a double-purpose call calculated to heighten the joy at festivities and to arouse the male fighting spirit in battle.

A police jeep swung into line behind Grandval's limousine. I sprawled into it sideways and a moment later was glad of the quick decision. The police lines collapsed, the crowd filled the narrow street, and shouts of spurious approval for Grandval changed instantly into screams of rage against all the Westerners and native collaborators in the Grandval cortege. Our jeep was the last car through. The mob blocked the rest, smashed windows, spat in faces, and reached in to gash the cheeks of officials. Police fired two more volleys. At last the crowd fell back and the rest of the Grandval party emerged, many with blood running from cuts in their faces.

A policeman waved down our jeep. A prisoner was thrust in between me and the driver. He was a boy of ten. His tiny wrist was no bigger than an American twenty-five-cent piece, but with it he had stoned the police. The child wept piteously. The driver pushed on the gas. Nothing was better calculated to provoke a new attack than the sight of our diminutive captive. What would happen to the boy? Perhaps a scolding and an "ear-boxing," I was given to understand, but cases of children such as he serving prison terms of many weeks had been reported in the conscience-troubled parliament in Paris.

Back in the European quarter Grandval made his speech. It was optimistic, as expected, but the words were covered by "you-you" cries shrilling from the native village a quarter of a mile away. With a few other reporters in a jeep I dashed back into the Arab town. It was out of bounds by then to all Westerners, but police let us through. Beside a sacked shop thousands of cigarettes were strewn in the street. Tobacco taxes were used by the French as an important source of revenue, so the underground nationalist movement had forbidden smoking. The police gunfire had sent enraged bands on a rampage through the native quarter. One of their first targets had been the cigarette shops. The street before this one was deserted, but a hundred yards farther on a throng watched beneath the balcony of a burning frame house. Someone, perhaps the owner, was at work alone dropping valuables from the second floor. The flames gained rapidly. There were no firemen. A young man glanced in our direction in surprise, paused, and then gesticulated to us to come forward and get out. Perhaps our neutrality as journalists, accepted by the police who had let us pass their lines, would be recognized by the mob, but perhaps it would not. I remembered the week in Salonika in Greece during which I covered the trial of the alleged murderers of my friend George Polk, an American journalist killed apparently by communists as he tried to cross the lines to "get both sides of the story" in the Greek civil war. George had been a fighter pilot in World War II, but his full devotion in postwar months had been to the news. He had acted as if all the world shared his reverence for the facts, for objectivity, and for the neutrality of the open-minded journalist. I told the driver to back up and around as quickly as the narrow alley would permit and to return to the European town. With quick lunges the squat machine twisted around and, moments later, we were back through the tank-guarded valley and on our way up the European hill. I noticed, as we drove, a "For Sale" sign on a comfortable European villa. Why the occupants were leaving was clear. Who would replace them was not so plain.

The official toll, rarely on such occasions an underestimate, was nineteen natives killed, mostly by police gunfire, one law officer in critical condition from a rock blow, fifteen other policemen injured, and more than forty-five natives seriously hurt. As usual in those first weeks of the critical summer of 1955 in Morocco, the ill-armed Arabs had paid the heavier price.

The Moroccans had lost more than the French, and yet, had they? The deaths in Meknes brought to 100 the number of natives killed in the few weeks since Grandval's arrival in the protectorate and the start of his official tour. So far he had visited North Africa's principal city, Casablanca, and southern Morocco's feudal main community, Marrakesh. One important town remained for Grandval to visit—Fez, a thousand-year-old Moslem holy city where a pretendant to the sultanate had been fed to the royal lions only fifty years earlier. One hundred had died in riots at Fez a year earlier on the first anniversary of the deposition by the French and their feudal native collaborators of the nationalistic sultan, Mohammed V. Fez, the reporters speculated, might well top the Casablanca-Marrakesh-Meknes fireworks with something more garish. I went there to await Grandval, but there was relief among both the French and the pro-European natives when the resident general "postponed" the visit to Fez for what proved to be forever.

Another day's slaughter had been averted. How high would be the price in terms of encouragement to the occult nationalists none cared to think, but within days the cost was plain. Grandval's liberal policy calling for the removal of the pro-French puppet sultan, Moulay ben Arafa, but not for the restoration of Mohammed V to the throne, proved not good enough as a compromise. Mohammed V would have to return, whatever the cost to continental prestige on the shore of Africa nearest Europe. One more surrender to nationalism in Europe's overseas colonial area was inescapable. The Continent's humane code demanded it. Police could not go on shooting men who cried "Grandval!" and arresting boys who were scarcely out of their babyhood. If the salutary influence of Europe was to continue, with all that it meant in terms of the ideals of twenty-five post-Athenian, Christian, and liberal centuries, it would have to be in the form of voluntary collaboration and no longer in that of a military domination. It was plain that it was in no one's interest that a new Moulay Hassan should organize slave troops and huge harems. But in those days of mid-1955, as the pendulum moved, it was unclear whether it was swinging forward toward a democratic new world, in which continental values would be honored and prosperity would be shared, or back toward the chaos and savagery of pre-French Morocco. Much the same was true throughout all French North Africa and all of Europe's former colonial holdings in the Dark Continent and in the Orient. What was happening would help to determine the future of America's continental ally, and of the West and of the world.

Until then, in three years of covering the news in Paris, from 1952 to 1955, I had been able to follow the painful turning point in Europe's colonies only through news-agency dispatches from France's lost war in Indo-China. Now, with the events of Meknes and what followed them in all three parts of French North Africa—Morocco, Algeria, and Tunisia—it was possible to cover both the Continent and its overseas crisis simultaneously. For the next three years I was to shuttle back and forth across the Mediterranean and gradually make out four main contenders in the North African struggle. They were the Americans, who had become the often unwitting participants in every world quarrel; the French civilian settlers; the men of very different mentality who were the soldiers of France; and the overwhelming native majority. Among them they were deciding fundamental history.

The Americans, for the most part, were to be found at our four long-range strategic air bases in Morocco and at the Navy installation there. Ten thousand servicemen and perhaps as many wives and children were there on permanent assignment. The Americans were doing their best to stay out of social quarrels between the indigenous French and the natives, but it was somehow never possible to do so. In Marrakesh, American officers who were the sons or grandsons of penniless European emigrants accepted the invitation of the medieval Thami el Glaoui, baron of southern Morocco, to use his private golf course. Every time they stepped on a green they identified themselves, however unintentionally, with the antique ruling class and invited the antagonism of the ragged, barefooted or slipper-shod native majority in whom nationalism was awakening.

The bases were little Americas. As always, the Navy was living best. The shopping center at the sailors' compound at Port Lyautey was lifted bodily out of one of the smarter New York suburbs. There was even a lawn, a precious possession in bleak, parched Morocco. The Strategic Air Force, too, was doing what it could to bring modern comforts to its half-billion-dollar chain of atomic bomber bases, but at the base at Ben Guerir airmen were using a half stick of dynamite to blast a hole for the roots of each tree.

"It will be World War IV," they said, "before we get this place fixed up."

At Nouasseur base the S.A.C. was doing better. Baseball teams in bright green and blue uniforms were playing beside one of several post chapels, and 200 men, their young wives and their children were at a swimming pool. *Ma and Pa Kettle in Hawaii* was the attraction of the day at the post theater. The good-natured, mild-mannered ballplayers and swimmers were the men who would carry the atomic bomb to Moscow if the "balloon went up."

At the first sign of new trouble after the Meknes riots American military authorities placed more than half of Morocco out of bounds to the servicemen. They banned even French restaurants, where a native might throw a bomb. Post radios omitted all local news in deference to the French, who feared that United States anti-colonialism might be stirred into such broadcasts. I was amazed to find that my own stories of Moroccan violence later that summer were all that many of the service families had to keep them informed. They could not understand the local French papers and had to wait a day or two until my reports came back in my newspaper's Paris edition. A knowledge of French was so rare an accomplishment among the atomic base officers that one friend of mine, hired for "intelligence" work, found that his job was merely to translate the local press. The Americans were leaning so far backward that one of the highest-ranking officers confided that his own secret intelligence weapon was his chauffeur, a young native who spoke Arabic, French, and English. Each day the officer asked the driver what he heard from the grapevine. That way, by his account, he kept up with Morocco's powerful undercover nationalist movement.

The American attitude scarcely could have been more gingerly, and yet a recurrent story I handled was of the sacking by French mobs of American consulates and libraries. I was to be struck particularly by the wrecking of the American diplomatic mission and reading room in Tunis in the spring of 1956. I flew to Tunis from Rome to see the damage. A French throng, enraged at American doubts about colonialism, had smashed wash sinks with crowbars, ripped pages out of hundreds of books, and even bashed in walls. Thirty thousand dollars' worth of damage was done in fifteen minutes while French police looked on without interfering. Yet what impressed me, too, was what happened to the ten-year-old son of an attaché,

one of the few Americans in the consulate at the time. Not un-
naturally, the boy wept with terror.

"Oh, don't be afraid," the mob leader told him gently and
even affectionately. "I was with the American army during the
war. Nothing will happen to you."

The wreckers were our allies!

In the most profound sense it was true. The best friend the
French population of Tunisia had was the United States. Any
hope the West had of preserving a foothold in the country
lay in the financial, military, and, to some extent, philosophical strength of the Americans. In desperation at the rise of the
natives, the settlers were turning against their main supporters
in a hysterical effort to get additional help.

"You Americans killed the Indians; at least we let the North
Africans live," Frenchmen constantly repeated to representatives of the United States. One consular officer heard this so
often that he sent to Washington for statistics to show that
there were more "redskins" in the United States in the mid-
twentieth century than there had been in 1492. The data did
no good, of course. The real argument underlying the words of
the French was that the settlers of the Wild West had in effect
committed partial genocide in the nineteenth century and that
the United States accordingly should compromise its moral
position in the mid-twentieth century in order to give the
North African French all-out support against the natives, who
outnumbered them ten to one. As they argued, the fact that an
act of a century earlier was a crime justified another one now!
If, as a result, the free world's struggle for the friendship of
Africa and Asia should be lost, it was worth it. All this was implied. Yet despite the words no Frenchman really believed any
such nonsense, so the attacks on American offices were merely
momentary acts of passion quietly made good on the morrow
by the transfer of the policemen who had stood by idly, and by
financing repairs.

The mob that wrecked the American diplomatic offices in
Tunis was made up of one type of North Africa European. The
variety among the settlers was vast, but common to them all was

their effort to maintain their "presence" on Africa's northern shore.

Some sought only spiritual "presence." A Jesuit conducting a school for boys in the open countryside of one of the North African territories showed me how he required the sons of planter families to work in the gardens with their own hands so as to acquire respect for their future employees; how he had walled his classrooms with glass in order to accustom his charges to the open and to impress on them that moral restraints of the future would have to come from within themselves and not from opaque classrooms or priestly supervision; and, finally, how he had arranged for 10 per cent of the school's students to be Moslems, since it was so important to accustom the Christians to living in peace with North African sons of Islam. "But," the priest admitted, "this could all end in massacres."

More typical of the French was Jacques Soustelle, governor of Algeria in 1955, who offered over lunch at his Moorish-type official residence to arrange a one-thousand-mile, ten-day tour of his territory for me if I would promise to look at the good as well as the bad, at the modern farms, dams, and Sahara oil rigs, as well as the battlefields of the Algerian native war for independence, then just beginning. A brilliant original Dufy looked over the shoulder of the intensely intellectual young governor as the ashes from his cigarette sprayed unnoticed down the front of his blue serge suit.

I disliked the implication that an American reporter would not normally give a balanced picture, but I agreed with alacrity and for the next week and a half probed every corner of Algeria. I went deep into the Sahara Desert, where Netherlanders, on contract from France, were working eight-hour heavy labor shifts in a mid-August heat of 150 degrees Fahrenheit (so hot we rolled up automobile windows to keep in the relative cool of our own body temperatures). I went up into the mountains of the Kabylias where a dam rose impressively in what had been corsair country little more than a century ago. The dam, however, was not so striking as to obliterate the effect of what we saw just below it: tribesmen breaking stones by hand to sell as gravel at starvation pay. Finally I saw the fine farms and factories—where the wealth unfortunately was almost exclusively in European hands—and toured a string of combat areas where the most modern arms of the Atlantic Alliance were proving ineffectual against persistent native rebels who lacked even machine guns.

A type whose number was legion was one rancher who graciously invited me for lunch beside his terrace swimming pool. He owned two three-mile holdings in Morocco and another fine home in Paris. On the ranch I visited were twenty native servant families. They tended their master's 150 cattle and 1,000 sheep.

The puppet Ben Arafa was still on the throne at Rabat. Riots like that at Meknes had not yet restored Moroccan independence as they would within a year.

"This country," said my host as a white-jacketed native servant waited on us, "is like an adolescent. When we started it was a child. Now you might say it is seventeen or eighteen, nearly grown but still needing guidance."

We strolled to the quarters of the Arab employees—shacks of brush only three feet high at the sides. A tall man crept out from under one of them. He pointed to an infected eye.

"How do you expect it to heal, with that dirty handkerchief?" the proprietor demanded. "Go on up to the house and see my wife!"

His wife, he explained, was ranch nurse, doing a job many other plantation mistresses performed during their stays at their properties.

Pay for the native workers, said the owner, was sixty-five cents a day plus the right to keep a cow, two donkeys, a sheep, a goat, and some chickens. Whenever the floorless brush huts got too dirty they were shifted.

"I pay partly in grain," he explained, "and give it to them every eight days. If I paid monthly and all in cash they'd be starving by the end of four weeks. Their tongues would be hanging out!"

The native foreman of the plantation occupied a small concrete house. He had served in Italy during the war, married an Italian woman, had a son by her, deserted his little family, and returned to take up with a new native wife back on the plantation. With his freshly acquired European manners, he had been an asset and the owner had ushered him into the newly built house of concrete. After a few days the foreman was back in a brush shack.

"My new wife," he explained, "is afraid of the electricity."

"Go back to the concrete house or I'll burn down your brush home as a fire hazard," the proprietor had threatened.

This benevolent violence had worked, but violence it was. Men such as the foreman cooperated in later weeks to end the French protectorate and restore Moroccan liberty.

The difference between the soldiers of France and the settlers, a gulf so great that it made the army a separate factor in itself, had been typified for me in the personality of Colonel André Gribius, who had taken me one day rebel hunting through the hills of Tunisia. That was in late 1954. Like the Morocco of Ben Arafa, the Tunisia of that year was still a French "protectorate." European control was complete so far as the laws of the land were concerned, but as we drove over the central Tunisian mountains it was plain that French dominance was shaky at best. We rode into the sun-baked hamlet of Bit el Arbi as the several hundred French soldiers accompanying us, in single file and carrying two-way radios and automatic rifles, closed in on the community from either side. The hamlet seemed lifeless except for a youth in his early twenties who watched sullenly from a doorway and two men in the monklike native cowls and robes who approached from the largest house in the village and politely invited us to have some coffee.

The French colonel grimaced. "You don't know where the rebels are?" he inquired. "You haven't been up in the hills with them yourselves?"

Both Arabs grinned in amusement. One of them went for some moth-eaten easy chairs.

"It's always like that," the colonel said helplessly. "Their code of hospitality. They'd take time out from the fighting to be hospitable."

We drank the coffee and left. Our hosts undoubtedly had been rebel collaborators. Living exposed on that hill with 200 insurgents on the ridges overhead, they could not have survived had they not been. But how could the colonel shoot down possibly innocent men? There was always the chance that they were not involved, and in any case it was probable that they were poor men who knew nothing of politics and yearned only to survive in the pitiful way they always had.

The day's bag was zero. It was an all-too-familiar experience.

"My good Bretons take half an hour to climb what these rebels go up in five minutes," Colonel Gribius said. "They see us coming on these open hills. They are remarkable! To hear my men tell it you'd think the natives could jump a six-yard chasm."

On their home ground, the insurgents easily were keeping the Europeans at bay. A day or two earlier they had kept up a hot fire for ninety minutes from one village. In another all-day battle the French had shot down twenty-seven of them.

I listened that night as Colonel Gribius gave his orders for the next day's operation.

"Go back to the hills and give them a new combing," he instructed. "Let's not miss a day. Before we know it we'll get reverse commands from Paris."

The remark touched on another bitter division. There was really a third Frenchman in North Africa, the invisible, distant man of the Paris government, who changed his ideas from premier to premier, twice a year on the average, as the mercurial combinations in parliament supported "hards" in office one day and Leftist compromisers the next. Some of Gribius' officer associates had had the unnerving experience of arresting Tunisian politicians one year and commanding their guards of honor after their restoration to greater power a year or two later.

It was what the commander of a French Army division told me in 1955 in the mountains of the Kabylias.

"My greatest single wish? That the Paris government make up its mind once and for all what it wants and then stick to it —in all three parts of North Africa. You can't give to natives in Tunisia and Morocco what you deny to Algeria. A firm policy followed by one of concessions is worse than never having tried to be stern at all."

I did not recognize it then, but it was the beginning of the revolt of the colonels and generals which was to threaten France with civil war in mid-1958. It was the start of the army rebellion which put General De Gaulle in power as a moderate authoritarian in Paris.

By and large the army officers were liberal. They knew war from Indo-China and had no taste for wanton slaughter.

"I could put down the Aurès revolt if I were just to go in and kill natives as I found them," General Gaston Parlange told me over a good wine and well-prepared lunch during the trip arranged for me by Soustelle in 1955. We had met in the general's villa at Batna at the edge of the Sahara in eastern Algeria.

"The natives give the rebels food and information," he went on, "but to crush the revolt that way I might have to kill 30,000 . . . 40,000 . . . maybe even 100,000."

One hundred thousand was the total population.

This attitude did not mean that the French soldiers were not aggressive and courageous. Parlange sent me up under a fifty-man escort (Foreign Legionnaires, mostly young yellow-haired Germans) to see Commandant Jean Nivelgioni, the Aurès regional commander. The barren, abrupt heights were where the Algerian war had started on November 1, 1954, with the killing of two bus passengers, a young French schoolteacher on his way to take over a mountain school, and a caid, one of the Moslem local officials who were condemned by the rebels as French collaborators. When the revolt had started there were only three French administrators and twelve policemen to look after the 100,000 natives in the region. Under a law enacted after World

War II, the people of the Aurès were all Frenchmen, but not more than a handful of them knew it. By declaring Algeria part of France and its 9,000,000 natives French citizens, moral grounds had been provided for continuance of the privileges enjoyed by the 1,000,000 European settlers. The latter retained French rather than special Algerian citizenship and among them they had half of Algeria's wealth and income, even half of the parliamentary representation. Sometimes the French, with straight faces, called it a fifty-fifty relationship, but on a person-to-person basis it meant that the average native had one ninth the income and one ninth the political weight of the average European, if that.

The result of their scant numbers had been that the French officials in the Aurès whizzed through their territory in their jeeps, paying no calls on some hamlets for years at a time. The Berber natives stayed in their primitive mud villages on the hilltops, remained illiterate, and cultivated the traditions of freedom which had made it impossible for the Roman legions, or any successive invasion in the subsequent two thousand years, fully to conquer them. Finally, in the fifties, the natives had begun listening to the call of Arab nationalistic revolt coming from Radio Cairo and from the communist Radio Budapest.

That evening in his headquarters in the mountain village of Arris, Commandant Nivelgioni used a blackboard to show me how he was meeting his problem. The Aurès, he said, "like Europe," was split up into what were in effect several little nations. Nation B's neighbors, A and C, were allies against the B both of them knew well, although A and C were not well acquainted with one another. Nation D, on the far side of C, was B's support against the tribe between them. Under Nivelgioni was a hastily expanded force of 3,000, many of them Legionnaires, some of them troops from other colonial areas whose peoples felt no tie as yet to the rebels in the Algerian part of the dissolving French empire. To supplement his main and direct force of 3,000 men, Nivelgioni was making use of the old intertribal enmities. Aurès natives were being enrolled in

a *Group Mobile de Police Rurale*—auxiliary units useful against
the various members' traditional foes. The natives, so inept
in the French language, called themselves, to the amusement
of their continental officers, the *Jean-Pierres*. It was their
version of "zhay-em-pay-air," the French pronunciation for
G.M.P.R. When word got around that Commandant Nivelgioni was giving guns to Jean-Pierre volunteers, all too many
stepped forward. I was with Nivelgioni's aides as they refused
some such requests, at least for the time being. The trouble
was that no one could be sure which way a Jean-Pierre gun
would point.

My briefing by Nivelgioni was interrupted by an aide who
whispered a message to the commandant. Nivelgioni's face
flushed. There had been an incident in the night-blackened
outskirts of Arris. A twelve-man G.M.P.R. squad had vanished
with their arms. Perhaps they had been captured and taken
off to be slain. Perhaps they had gone over in a body with their
French-issued weapons to join the insurrection. The latter
seemed the more probable. The Jean-Pierres were no surely
successful formula.

Three years later, despite all Commandant Nivelgioni's brave
efforts and General Parlange's open-handed deployment of
forces, the Aurès would still be rife with ambush traps and
France would not yet have won.

The portrait of the fourth man in the North African ring,
the native who represented the vast majority, was unprepossessing if painted by French military or civilians.

"Some natives have even become officers with us, commanding some of our finest troops," one general in Algeria reminded
me, "and then after a little while back in their villages, after
marrying, have relapsed. We had a case near here. The man
came back bringing a modern bedroom suite. You know, these
native women cook on the floor without stoves. Well, he went
home one night to find that his wife had started the fire for
the supper right in the middle of the bed. He pitched the furniture out and now you couldn't tell the difference between
him and any other *indigène*."

The natives of Algeria would never be absorbed into French life as true citizens until their women unveiled, as a first step toward intimate contact with the French settler life around them, many French were convinced. But by mid-1958 psychological pressure on the women to take the step was still having only slight effect.

The native, met face to face as an equal, was far more understandable than the caricatures the French sketched of him. I dined one night with a turbaned chieftain of the Moroccan Atlas Mountains. France had exiled him to the ocean-shore cities to break his hold over his semi-savage tribesmen. The Moor was illiterate, but a man of immense dignity and evident courage. We squatted on the floor of a modern European apartment in Rabat and, from a common bowl, ate couscous, the traditional grain-and-meat dish of North Africa. Warm water, soap, and a towel were passed occasionally as we dipped in with the three right-hand fingers which serve the North African as knife, fork, and spoon. We might have been in a tent in the Atlas except for a child's one roller skate forgotten in a corner.

What the Moors needed from the United States, the chief told me, could be summed up in a single word: guns. They would be weapons to use against America's French ally, to be sure. I told him it was impossible, but the daring old man had his way anyway. Months later I was to see him at the palace of Sultan Mohammed V, no longer a prisoner but now elevated to the rank of high counselor to the restored monarch of a free Morocco. Stones in the hands of the Meknes crowds and knives in those of other natives had been enough.

Besides that brave, unlettered man there was another who symbolized much of emerging native-ruled North Africa. He was Habib Bourguiba, who in 1955 and 1956 became president and prime minister of the former protectorate of Tunisia, now a free republic. I watched Bourguiba through repeated interviews as he evolved from a captive in French hands in Paris to become one of the strong men of North Africa.

Bourguiba was, in effect, the man Gribius was really fighting in the hills around Bit el Arbi in Tunisia. A Paris-educated lawyer with a French wife, Bourguiba had organized the Tunisian nationalist movement in the 1920's and had been an exile or French prisoner for the better part of a generation.

The nationalist's spirit was unbroken when I lunched with him in a Paris hotel suite during his final days as a semi-captive in 1955. In the hotel lobby police kept watch on his callers, and I had reason to believe that Bourguiba had few secrets from the French, even those he protected as his most personal ones. But the Tunisian was uncowed as he blurted out his ideas. The eternal splits among the egotists of the French Parliament were opening the way to Tunisian autonomy, he was sure.

I asked him whether he would be "reasonable" in permitting some sort of continuing French foothold in Tunisia if his jailers were to let him return there.

"The French themselves are never reasonable," he snorted. "They leave a country only when force is raised against them. It takes Dien Bien Phu." (The reference was to the disastrous last battle of France's lost war in Indo-China.)

Using his fingers, Bourguiba picked lettuce leaves from the bowl between us. He speared a butter patty with his fork. It was patent as he talked that he meant to yield not an inch.

"What will you do if you are outflanked by extremists?"

"I will out-extreme them."

If the French-hating rabble rousers went to work Bourguiba would be able to match them with worse anti-Paris diatribes. I could interpret the leader's remark in no other way.

A single word stood out as we talked: "humiliation." Bourguiba, his father, and his grandfather had been humbled under both the native ruler, the Bey of Tunisia, and the foreign "protector." The humiliation had to be expunged, whatever the cost. How high that price could be had been indicated that same winter in Tunis where it was widely reported that militant nationalists had slashed away the lips of natives for violation of the underground's ban against smoking, that habit which yielded revenue to France.

"We have time yet," Bourguiba went on. "I am waiting until

world opinion is crystal clear. We want independence—the right to leave the French Union if we choose. We would accept a status like that of Pakistan or India. Otherwise we'll fight. How? The function forms the organ. Circumstances will decide."

I hesitated to publish some of Bourguiba's remarks in our Paris edition. In loyalty to one who had spoken frankly—though "on the record"—I hesitated to expose him to the violence of the probable reaction in Parliament. No Frenchman wanted to hear such words on the eve of freeing the nationalist. But Bourguiba understood what I did not. The rebellion had already won. France had no choice but retreat.

Half a year later, in the fall of 1955, Bourguiba took me with him on a victory tour through the Cap Bon Peninsula, south of the all-but-obliterated ruins of ancient Carthage. The sparse stone remains of the city vanquished by Rome survived as a symbol of one European victory over the people of North Africa. Bourguiba's ride that afternoon represented the reverse.

Not a Western face was to be seen. Thousands of screaming Arabs jammed the narrow streets of the white-walled villages to welcome the conqueror. In one town an avenue of cut evergreens had been erected along the sides of the dusty road to provide the cool colors the sun-haunted Arabs love. Within moments of our arrival all the trees were gone, trodden under by the running throng. Bourguiba seemed to float weightlessly out of the jeep seat in front of me as many hands reached under to lift him to men's shoulders.

I had thought at lunch in Paris, as I watched Bourguiba's fierce, staring gray eyes; his broad, protruding jaw like that of the late Italian dictator, Mussolini; the myriad indignant, theatrical shapes of his wide mouth; and the dodging and twisting of his chunky body, like that of a pugilist, that he must be masterful before a native crowd. He was. He said everything three times: first in the rarely-used classical Arabic, then in his own natural middle-class language, and finally in gutter dialect. The educated understood him all three times, but no man was so humble that he could not comprehend at least once. Youths

fired repeated salutes from rifles which doubtless came from
caches concealed from the French during the time when Gribius
and I had the frustrating cup of coffee together a year earlier at
Bit el Arbi. A pretty Girl Scout of ten twisted her kerchief
across her snub nose and little mouth, playing at being already
a grown veiled woman. Her female elders, phantomlike in
black robes and shawls concealing all but their eyes, looked
down from rooftops and wailed the hysterical "you-you." The
native tide was high. So was Bourguiba's—though that did not
mean, in tumultuous Tunisia, that he had perfect personal security. A week later, at another rally, an assassin shot down
his bodyguard.

In Paris, Bourguiba had been a rumpled man, with a line
of pens and pencils poking from his coat pocket. His clothes,
especially his handsome blue tweed coat, were better now, but
their colors clashed in a haberdasher's nightmare: brown socks,
black shoes, gray shirt, and blue suit. When I was to see him
next, late in 1957, Bourguiba would be wearing the silver tie
and impeccable garb of a statesman. Then he received me both
at his bright-tiled Arabian-style office, where young, smartly-
uniformed soldiers saluted with fixed bayonets, and at his
home, the Hollywoodian former residence of the secretary general of the French Protectorate.

Bourguiba had many reasons by then for satisfaction. The
American consulate which a French mob had wrecked not so
many months ago was a full-fledged embassy now in tribute to
Tunisia's free status, and was conducting a language course
elegantly named The Bourguiba School of English. The tree-
shaded, very French main thoroughfare of Tunis was now
Bourguiba Boulevard. The Mussolinian jaw jutted out now
from pictures on the country's postage stamps.

But Bourguiba was no more relaxed than ever. The French
had told me what had happened when the olives ripened a
year or two before. Starving nomads, riding their camels and
carrying their dromedary-skin tent homes with them, had come
north out of the desert like locusts and had taken the harvest
for themselves. The French had sent out troops but the hungry

horde had walked into the guns. No one was harsh enough to order a massacre and the troops had withdrawn. The day had been a victory for the Arabs. Now that Bourguiba, the number-one native, occupied the French secretary general's fine home and office as premier-president and virtual dictator of Tunisia, the question was what he could do for his olive-stealing, famished nomads.

The United States had to help more, Bourguiba told me. Some economic and military aid had come, but far too little. America feared giving the French the impression it was replacing them, but real friendship for Paris demanded it, Bourguiba insisted.

"The French," he said, "still have big investments to protect here."

I asked about Russia as a new factor in Tunisia.

"They will never consider me an acceptable bargaining partner. I have always taken a position too much opposed to them. But they are working in the best possible way, by the force of the example of what they have done economically and militarily for Syria. That is a way to influence my public opinion."

What would he do if his public deserted him?

"I will always be with my public opinion."

What Bourguiba's words seemed to mean was: where my people go I will go. They may turn to Russia; then the question will be whether Russia will agree to deal with me. But Russia had negotiated even with Hitler. I was less sure than Bourguiba that he would be "unacceptable," at least in early discussion stages. A few months later, in fact, Bourguiba was to announce that he would let the Russians open an embassy in Tunisia—their farthest outpost in strategic western North Africa.

First the illiterate chief from the Atlas Mountains who wanted American guns; then Bourguiba, the subtle, French-educated master of shaky Tunisia—the list of natives I met gradually grew longer. Some were even more violent; a few sided at least tactically with France, but everywhere it was clear that the native world of French North Africa at last was awake to the nationalistic changes running through all the rest of Africa and Asia.

I asked one Tunisian college graduate if he would not admit that France had brought modern civilization, with its roads, its shops, its comfortable buildings, and its concepts of social welfare, to the medieval beylic of a century earlier.

"Yes, I'll admit that," he said in the superb French he had polished in Paris. "I'll add all that to the balance—and it brings the scale up to zero."

Tunisia, in his view, owed France nothing.

Others who typified the diverse attitudes of the North African natives were four men in Morocco: el Glaoui, whose golf course was used by the American officers in Marrakesh; Si Mohammed el Mokri, more than a century old, who was premier of Morocco in early 1955; Si M'bareck Ben Mustapha el Bekkai, who succeeded el Mokri as head of the sultanic government; and a lower-ranking native, in this account nameless, in the French service in Morocco.

El Glaoui was a man out of the Dark Ages. He had been a young tribal leader in the southern Atlas when the French invaded Morocco in the first decade of the present century. He had been one of the first to take the side of France, and the French had been grateful. He became the master of Marrakesh, keeping order by tough-fisted methods. When nationalists ordered shopkeepers to close their establishments in political lockouts, el Glaoui's police smashed the stores open again. On the eve of Grandval's visit, el Glaoui's criers had warned that for anyone to shout "Long live Grandval," or for that matter anything else, might be treated as a capital offense. Guards in priestlike robes sprawled in the dirt of the road in front of el Glaoui's baronial palace. The daggers at their belts spoke eloquently to any who might attempt to storm the home of France's number-one ally in southern Morocco.

I attended a reception held by el Glaoui in the main hall of his palace, with its intricately carved cedar ceiling soaring high above us. The mahogany-colored, withered, octogenarian Glaoui nodded unsmilingly to the hundred members of our party, mostly French who were in Morocco for the dedication of a new power dam in the Atlas behind Marrakesh. A silver stiletto hung at el Glaoui's side, but near him loomed a stout Negro bodyguard wearing a .45-caliber pistol. This forbidding functionary doubled as major-domo, directing with words and glances a corps of waiters and their captains. Rank was indicated by footwear or lack of it. The waiters, who brought us hot mint tea, almond juice, and tasteless Arab cookies, were barefoot; their captains wore socks but no slippers; and el Glaoui's guard, as he oversaw everything, stepped about proudly in stockings and heelless shoes.

We asked el Glaoui, who had been one of the main organizers of the deposition of the independence-minded Sultan Mohammed V two years earlier, his formula for peace in nationalism-torn Morocco.

More power should be restored to the local chiefs, the old man said instantly. I knew what that meant from my talks with the local French. El Glaoui could not understand why it took more than a year to exhaust all the legal processes leading up to the execution of an offender. Quick, stern justice, he felt, was what his people understood.

When Grandval called on him one afternoon in July 1955 el Glaoui had made his views plain. His quarrel with the newly educated youth of Marrakesh was more than the usual one between the generations. It spanned a gap of one thousand years. When el Glaoui drove in his Rolls-Royce through the swarming native quarter during an intermission in his talks with the new resident general, a crowd blocked his way. He dispersed them with a wave of the chromium-plated tommy gun an American general had given him during the World War II liberation. Later in the day other crowds fell back with less docility. The police killed at least ten and wounded twenty-seven others.

Within a year el Glaoui was to die, a broken-spirited man, and the nationalists he had fought were to take over, hideously slaughtering many of el Glaoui's allies and appropriating much of his wealth.

El Mokri was another French collaborator. Owing to the difference in length between the Arab and the European year and to carelessness with birth records before the French era, no one, not even el Mokri himself, knew how old he was. Some thought he was one hundred and twelve; all agreed that he was at least one hundred and six. His best clue to his age was that in his early twenties he had been present as envoy of the Moroccan court at the opening of the Suez Canal in 1869. El Mokri's father had made a fortune in the mid-nineteenth century as the Sultan's director of public works and had introduced his promising son at court. Another who had taken the French side from the start, el Mokri had been useful to Paris even before its twentieth-century invasion of Morocco. Already a middle-aged man, he had sat in as the Sultan's designee at the meeting at Madrid in 1880 where Europe laid the first groundwork for the conquest of Morocco. In 1906 he had represented Morocco at the Algeciras Conference, at which France made diplomatic preparations for the penetration. El Mokri was premier of Morocco when the French protectorate was set up in 1912. The sultan had abdicated, but el Mokri stayed on and aided in the takeover. His children had been just as successful as their father. One daughter had married two successive sultans. Another was the wife of the main threat to the sultans, el Glaoui. Two of el Mokri's sons served successively as pasha or native governor of Casablanca, the Moroccan metropolis.

As one sultan went out and another in, el Mokri stayed on. In midsummer of 1955, as riots like those in Marrakesh and Meknes showed that the puppet Arafa would have to abdicate, a grotesque controversy involved el Mokri. The French said they would agree to a three-man regency to replace Arafa, but they insisted both that the docile and cooperative el Mokri be in the regency and that he be flanked by a representative of the conservatives. A nationalist could have the third place, the French conceded. The leaders of the independence movement turned down the offer. At one hundred and six, el Mokri was so safely "conservative," they argued effectively, that that current of opinion needed no additional representation. The argument fizzled out in the face of events. Soon the nationalists got everything. I would see the stoop-shouldered, doughty old el Mokri for the last time when he went to the airport to welcome Grandval's successor, General Boyer de la Tour, who was to arrange the restitution of Mohammed V to the throne in an almost complete surrender to the independence movement. For even that switch in policy el Mokri was ready, but his long day was over. He, too, soon died.

El Mokri's successor was a good example of the best for which France and Europe could hope in the new North Africa. He was a wooden-legged forty-eight-year-old war hero and lieutenant colonel in the French Army who had resigned his post as pasha of one of the cities in the Atlas foothills, in protest when Mohammed V was ousted by el Glaoui and the French. Of all the pashas in Morocco, Bekkai had been the only one to make the gesture.

Bekkai's tattoo-faced mother looked on uncomprehendingly as her son told me why the feudal age must go.

"The prestige of France must be protected here—I agree to that," the former officer said. "But there must be changes. The France of the 1789 revolution has been maintaining an absolute dictatorship here. They have been keeping Morocco in feudalism. Any pasha can put anyone in jail arbitrarily for up to two months. There has been total lack of liberty: no freedom of assembly, speech, or press." Even to sing on the streets a song in favor of the exiled Mohammed V, he pointed out, was a two-year jail offense.

Morocco, in Bekkai's view, had to have more of France's own splendid civil liberties internally, and more freedom as a nation.

"We are, after all," he pointed out, "a people with thirteen and a half centuries of independence behind us. Sometimes there was good administration and sometimes bad, but over all it has been a beautiful history."

Remembering the lion-eaten pretender to the throne of a half century earlier, I could not agree that all Morocco's free history had been handsome, but the patriotism of the former pasha and his devotion to much that was finest in France were transparent. The old woman beside him must have sensed with pride much of his meaning.

When I talked with Bekkai in mid-1955 he was a barely-tolerated visitor in Arafa's realm. Within months he was back as premier of the new regime of the restored Sultan Mohammed V.

The last of these half-dozen typical natives was one Moroccan functionary who kept a picture of French Premier Pierre Mendès-France on his office wall even after the latter was overthrown in Paris. To the French the picture seemed to say: "I honor a Frenchman." To the natives it surely communicated: "The Frenchman for me is the one who gave Bourguiba and Tunisia their freedom and may follow the same conciliatory line with us." On his office wall was no picture of the compromised reigning puppet Arafa.

At home this official's front door was guarded permanently by police. As one collaborating with the French, he needed much protection. His house had two stories. On the lower one his guests sat on the floor and dined Moorish fashion. To them this first floor looked native indeed, with its picture of the ousted Mohammed V and framed excerpts from the Koran. On the second floor all the furnishings were French. There were chairs instead of floor cushions. A powerful radio brought the news of the world. It was there that the Moor and his French wife passed much of their time. It was a life of all things to all men, but what little of the hopeful I found in it was that in the final analysis, in his upper-floor retreat, the loyalty in that man's case was to the West.

It was of all these groups and of each of these individuals, the American general with the linguistically accomplished native chauffeur, the French planter with his unflattering ideas of a "teen-age" Morocco, the brave and frustrated French officers, and such natives as Bourguiba, Bekkai, el Mokri, and el Glaoui that I thought as the 1955 summer rushed to a Moroccan climax foreshadowing events in next-door Algeria and the sure future of many other European colonies elsewhere.

"You are arriving in Casablanca," the Air France hostess had told us as we circled over empty city streets at 6 A.M. of a mid-July morning in 1955. "Enjoy your stay."

There was no irony in her tone. Rather, there was warmth. It was one of those moments when humans in trouble feel the closeness they so often forget. It was an hour of test for France and the West, for Casablanca was under martial law, a curfew had emptied the streets, and dozens during the previous seventy-two hours had died in street fighting. What was going on in Casablanca was a warning of what could happen everywhere in the remaining colonies of Europe unless continental ingenuity found a constructive new form of relationship with Europe's former subjects.

The Casablanca rioting had started three days earlier, on July 14, the French national holiday. On that day everywhere under the French tricolor crowds had sipped *apéritifs* at sidewalk cafés and had danced in the streets. In Casablanca the holiday had started the same way, but pleasure had exploded into a massacre when a time bomb in a bicycle basket killed a half-dozen French citizens as they sat at the outdoor tables of a bar. The July 14 holiday commemorated the taking of the Bastille in Paris during the French Revolution, the revolt of the subjugated. But for Morocco's nationalists the message of the day was not pro-French, but rather one of violent self-liberation, and that fact murderously had been borne in on the European celebrants.

For hours in retaliation, European mobs had raged in the center of highly modern Casablanca, killing every native they found. Since five sixths of the city population of 600,000 were Arabs and Berbers, they found many.

Even as far away as Paris I had seen the fury of the day rising. There in the French capital I had covered two July 14 parades, one on the magnificent Avenue des Champs Elysées, the symbol of French glory, the other at the site of the long-since razed Bastille. The first of the parades was the official national celebration. Beside pale young officers from the military academy, still so frail as to seem mere boys, were the marchers the French highly prized—swarthy colonials in turbans, Moslems still loyal to the Paris Republic. While they and their swords were on France's side there was still hope for the old order.

The other parade was staged by the Communists. Most of its marchers were housewives out for some fresh air, but among them one delegation of 2,000 stood out as different. They were Algerians. Their cheeks were sunken and their eyes even wilder than Bourguiba's.

"These," I thought, "are real soldiers for revolution."

I ducked under a café awning for coffee during a sudden downpour and ten minutes later, when I caught up with the parade, found I had missed the event of the day. There had been a scuffle with police and a half dozen of the Algerians were dead. Even in slow-shooting Paris, the bullets of the police were taking toll.

Now, having driven into downtown Casablanca from the airport, I asked the French authorities to take me through the city's *bidonville*, literally the "village of tin cans." I had seen the shanty slum a few weeks earlier and knew what a pool of misery and nationalist agitation it was. The one-room houses, some twelve feet square, were made of flattened United States Army oil cans and even in one case, I was told, of tediously collected sardine tins. All lacked water or electricity, but about one house in every twenty had a battery-fed radio capable of picking up anti-French propaganda from Middle Eastern and communist stations. A man living in such misery joined nationalist terror groups if only to have a sense of belonging, one French reporter told me.

There was an evil mood in the bidonville, though when I rode there with Captain André de la Porte des Vaux, of the Casablanca Native Affairs Office, on that first trip through the quarter, I noticed how the sullen expressions on the faces of the gutter loungers relaxed when the officer addressed them in Arabic. At least some of the trouble was because of the language barrier. I observed also how the officer shifted his jeep into second gear at each corner, so that if need be we would have the power to burst through a sudden crowd.

This new trip was different: now the French sent me in a patrol of two weapons carriers. Black ribbons were tied to the muzzles of the soldiers' rifles. The guns were in mourning for a slain policeman. If new trouble developed, it was clear that the weapons would awaken out of their grief and would know how, in their own turn, to cause suffering among native rebels.

Now the menace I had felt in the atmosphere on my first visit had been fully realized. A European who had attempted to drive through the bidonville had been beaten to death in his automobile. Trees and telephone poles were chopped off at the ground. Scores of shops gaped open, their goods lying strewn and charred inside. Fire licked at the American Kodak sign at the "Photo Moderne," presumably some European's property and therefore a target.

"Whatever it is, even a tree, they see it as the government's, and so they're against it," my accompanying officer said. "It is pure revolt."

At each stop our escort of soldiers hopped out and crouched in a circle in firing position watching the upper windows and rooftops. In the middle of the streets black troops from Senegal lay sprawled behind sandbags. A clatter of shots drew us into a side street. One of the colonial soldiers still loyal to France was gray with fright. A hole the size of half an orange was gouged out of the plaster beside him.

"A bullet just whizzed by me," he said.

"Get back!" another called to me. "It came up that alley there where you're standing."

I moved obediently around the corner, though one row of empty windows looked the same as another. An Indian file of soldiers was formed to patrol the alleys. They found nothing.

"It's a game of hide-and-seek and we're basically impotent," the officer confessed.

In the following days quiet was slowly restored in the bidonville, but throughout the region rebellion still seethed. I attended a reception given by Sultan Arafa at his block-square cream-and-green palace. The sultan's Negro bodyguards, with their brilliant red and blue uniforms and ornate earrings, were a spectacular sight beneath the eternally serene blue sky of the capital (a clue to why the United States Strategic Air Command wanted the area for its atomic bases against Moscow). But there was no joy in the reception. After two escapes from assassinations, Arafa no longer left his palace compound even for the annual ceremonial slaughter of two rams on the Moslem feast celebrating Abraham's Old Testament sacrifice. Arafa did the sheep-knifing in a mosque a few hundred feet outside his palace gate and even as he rode those few yards in a Victorian crystal-walled carriage, his guards, I could see, were stiff with nervousness. None knew where Arafa's killer waited.

At the palace reception the French spokesman wished the bent, wispy-bearded old man a long life but omitted reference to an extended reign. The aged puppet mumbled something unintelligible and an aide stood erect to assure us all in easy French phrases that the incomprehensible mutter meant that the monarch thanked us in his own name and in that of his kingdom. But it was not to be his realm much longer.

The day of history's decision was August 20, 1955, the second anniversary of the deposition of the rightful ruler. For days many of us reporters had warned our readers to expect the worst, and some French settlers temporarily had left the protectorate, going to Spain to wait out the anniversary. Latecoming newsmen who had been slow to spot the developing North African story teased some of us who were already veterans of a month of gloomy copy.

"You'll be sorry," they predicted with no doubt a bit of tongue in cheek. "It's all quiet here in the hotel and on the sidewalk, except for the soldiers at the corners. Nothing will happen here tomorrow. You've made a lot of predictions and you'll see that they won't stand up."

That night, at the comfortable bar of the El Mansour Hotel, it seemed as if they might prove right. Perhaps our gloom had been too deep.

Next morning, a calm Sunday in downtown Casablanca, on the spur of the moment I joined two other journalists, Raymond Vanker, of the Paris illustrated weekly *Radar,* and Alain de Prelle, representing a string of Belgian newspapers, for a trip to Khenifra, due east of Casablanca in the Atlas foothills, where there had been shooting the night before. A half-dozen persons, French and natives, had been killed. If nothing else, we would have an account of Khenifra's excitement for the morning papers the day after the long-heralded anniversary.

Outside our hotel we engaged a baby-blue taxicab whose driver, Charles Moraly, was parked at the curb awaiting business, and set out. We were not many miles outside Casablanca when we saw that the anniversary was a special day, after all. There was still the same calm we had observed in the city. The trouble was that there was too much of it. Except for a ragged Moor plowing a field behind a camel, no one was to be seen for miles. The road was ours.

At Venet Ville we flashed through a community of brush huts with only one European building, a concrete cubicle labeled in French "French-Moslem school."

Farther on was a town where a few natives sat on the curbs staring as we went by. I smiled and waved but there was no answering sign. There were no Europeans in sight. In a small square the colorful figure of a tribesman sat astride a white horse, like a monument. He could have modeled a picture of Sitting Bull before the Custer slaughter if only a few of his Berber characteristics had been altered.

We were getting to the far side of the Moroccan plain. Ahead and to one side tall columns of smoke stood in the still air.

"Pretty bad natives in this area," Moraly remarked conversationally. "Never been completely put down . . . but they're all right."

The road turned and the smoke was straight ahead.

"That's Oued Zem," Moraly said casually.

It was the last time any European in Morocco would mention the name so easily.

Two miles from the town barefoot women in the discordantly colored, ankle-length dresses of the Berber tribes, and men in gowns and the twisted cloth headgear of Mahometans, were running toward Oued Zem in gradually converging lines on both sides of the highway. A knot of a hundred clustered beside the route where it dipped into the village. A truck blocked our side of the road. Two native cyclists, weaving unsteadily, took up the other. Moraly did not hesitate. He stepped on the gas, clamped his hand on his horn, and drove for the two men on bicycles. They were not daydreaming. Evidently half-ready for such a maneuver, they hopped lightly aside and let us through. A hundred feet farther on a fallen telephone pole blocked most of the road. Another native crowd clustered beside it. Moraly shot around that obstacle, too.

Ahead of us in the town smoke boiled up from a half-dozen raging fires. The city looked lifeless save for a plane diving, climbing, and spearing down again. There was no sound of strafing or bombs. If the plane was attempting to intimidate rebels, it was not yet using its ultimate arguments.

I recommended that we turn back. Morocco was living up all too well to our earlier journalistic predictions.

The others in our little party saw it differently. Pointing to a tent and truck by the road ahead, Vanker and De Prelle argued confidently that they obviously belonged to a French counterattacking force. We drove the few hundred feet farther forward, but the truck in front of the tent was aflame. The canvas shelter had apparently belonged to a road gang. There was no French detachment, no European at all in sight. The others agreed to go back.

Moraly's motor hesitated and almost died as we started back up the slope. His gas tank, last filled in Casablanca, was almost empty. To my relief the engine caught on again. Back at the fallen pole the crowd was ready for us. A patriarch with a long white beard raised a silver-encrusted heirloom rifle which looked like a trophy from the wall of someone's den. The gun fired, but there was no whistle of a bullet; lethal accuracy, it appeared, was fortunately not one of the weapon's virtues. The crowd pinched in so close that the taxi glanced off the tip of the pole, but Moraly's stout American tires held. Never was I so grateful for the sturdiness of American "name-brand" products. At the top of the rise the second ambush had dispersed.

Twenty miles back down the road Vanker stopped us to give word to an approaching column of Foreign Legionnaires. Like us, they had intended to go to Khenifra. They had heard nothing of Oued Zem. For the second time Moraly made a U-turn and with our sky-blue taxi an incongruous addition to the middle of the line of tanks and troop trucks, we drove a second time toward Oued Zem.

The eyes of the young German Legionnaires shone with excitement. They lit up last cigarettes, put bullets in their rifle chambers, helped set up light machine guns at the back of each truck, unplugged the armored car cannon, and unlocked machine-gun turrets.

"Don't split off from me," the driver of the first tank called back as his only request. The big metal vehicles, I knew, were a terror to the enemy if a few ground troops protected them, but their crews were apt otherwise to be at the mercy of attackers on foot.

"I'll be right behind you," the lieutenant in command shouted his promise.

This time on the edge of Oued Zem we met a few Europeans armed with rifles. I heard something that sounded like "must be taught a lesson," then the excited civilians turned on us. No newspapermen were allowed. We would have to go back to Casablanca.

The cabdriver did the talking.

"Impossible! A day like this on a road like that? And anyway, I have no more gas."

The Europeans had other worries. They forgot about us for the moment and the Legionnaires suggested a compromise. We could not stay in the center of the column, but we could tag on behind the rear guard. That was the way we entered what had once been a lovelier-than-average French village inside the Moroccan interior.

Rocks filled the streets beside the pole we had twice passed. A few dozen yards beyond it, just the other side of the work tent, a truck stood in the street, perhaps the same one around which we had curved. The rocks by the pole may have stopped it. The driver lay dead on his back, emasculated.

The town was a shambles. Fallen poles lay in so hopeless a tangle that we had to mount one sidewalk and then the other to steer a way through. Five men lay dead in the service station of an American gasoline company. Even the pumps had been shoved from their sockets.

The Legionnaires swung down into the native quarter. We could see native men fleeing at its farther side. The European civilians turned back on us. This, they said determinedly, was as far as we could go. We could not watch the Legion at its work. If we wished we could go to the makeshift fort at the city hall, where the European survivors were assembling.

The adventurer-mercenaries, a decent-looking young group withal, rolled down into the native section and shooting began immediately. We heard it for more than an hour from a few blocks distant.

At the city hall we were told the horrifying story of what had happened. It had been market day in the native area, but all had been quiet until about 9 A.M., when suddenly hundreds, perhaps thousands of the local Arabs had surged into the prosperous Little France quarter in which the European residents lived.

"You know, Monsieur X's grandson?" one woman almost casually inquired of her neighbor. "They slit him up like this." Her hand moved across her abdomen as if she were closing a zipper.

"I was down in the post office when they came through, and we locked the doors," an elderly woman said. "We were in there for two hours. My packages are still down there." Like many of the others, the woman still could not grasp what had happened.

A man carried in soft drinks commandeered from an abandoned grocery store. A young woman took a bottle of orange drink. Before she could raise it to her lips, a sobbing friend threw herself into her arms.

"They killed my brother!"

For an instant the first woman dangled the soft drink behind her bereaved friend's back. On a hot, foodless day like that, when no one knew what the evening would bring, the soft drink would have tasted good. Soon the supply would be gone. The young woman clutched the bottle for another instant, then waved to others to take it away.

Slowly we pieced together what had occurred. Eighty-eight Europeans had been knifed to death. One victim was a child who had been slain in his mother's arms. A dozen other children, including even a baby of two months, had been struck down. The crowd had devastated the hospital, killing all six patients and the doctor, and even beheading the physician's rabbits and disemboweling his pigeons. All the doctor's plants had been cut off at the ground. His money was left strewn on the pavement. Not larceny but total extermination of everything French had been the objective.

In one house I found even the electric refrigerator dismembered. Its inner wall had been torn out, exposing the insulation. A car outside the hospital, stalled at right angles to the street as if it had been caught turning around, was filled with rocks. The dashboard had been ripped out, all the paint had been burned off and, for good measure, ax blows had been driven into the hood. What must have been the frenzy of anti-European and, I supposed, anti-Western hatred that inspired such cruelty and devastation!

For our own little party, too, the anniversary day ended with tragedy. I rode in the front seat as we drove back at sixty miles an hour almost bumper to bumper with the circulation-department car of a Casablanca newspaper. The distributor had agreed to make his rounds even on that critical day, but only if a rifle-armed policeman accompanied him. To be as near as possible to the armed car ahead, our taxi stayed too close. Moraly could not maneuver quickly enough when a military relief column suddenly filled the road ahead of us. Our cab spun to the left in a U-turn and a tank crushed in our rear end, gravely injuring Vanker and mortally wounding the gallant young De Prelle.

On the far side of Oued Zem even worse happened. Natives waiting in ambush stopped three French newspaper colleagues of ours, who had reached Khenifra, our objective of that day, by another road. The mob tore up the reporters' calling cards and then stabbed them to death with so many wounds that even their feet were punctured.

The struggle of the summer was over. The natives were victorious. I was at Rabat airport when a fat passenger plane curved over the horizon, with silvery fighter planes escorting it like a shark's pilot fish. It was something the French had said they would never permit. Mohammed V was returning to his throne.

"See what Allah has wrought," a pious Arab said at my elbow.

For weeks Mohammed V tried to calm the delirious crowds, but I was a helpless witness a few days later when a mob of grinning Moors burned one of their own number alive in the sultan's compound. The wretched, barelegged, and shaven-headed man, presumably some French collaborator's body-guard, ran thirty or forty feet with flames standing five yards above him and then sank to an elbow as the crowd closed around him. Evidently he had been drenched in gasoline. Miserable Moors for whom life rarely provided such circuses pushed forward to share as spectators in the fiendish fun.

I interviewed the restored sultan. Word had just come that the 990 political prisoners in the French jail in Casablanca were rioting and that four, perhaps even twenty, had been killed. The monarch was shaken. He sat a step above me on the easy chair that was his throne and waved me to a comfortable place at his feet. He spoke at first in Arabic, through an interpreter, but finally switched to direct conversation in French.

All the 400,000 Europeans "in the country now," he said, were welcome to stay to "enrich and develop" the realm. The American bases, he declared, had "as their objective the strengthening of peace" and his government was "not against them." The phrases promised something but did not pledge all. Implied was the end of mass immigration by the French. Clear was the discontinuance of total control by Paris. Not being "against" the American bases did not necessarily mean a willingness to sign long-term commitments which would stand up even if agitators went to work against them as a disturbance to "peace." I was not surprised at the monarch's caution. I was not at all sure that he could guarantee his people's disciplined obedience to his future demands.

Europe, the fount of so much that was noblest in the West, was in crisis in its colonies. What happened there would affect the fate of the Continent and indirectly that of America. The answer to the question of the future of Western Europe as an ally of America would come from three zones: from the Continent itself, of course; but also from such colonies as those in North Africa, and from the nations of the Soviet bloc. In a dozen years as a reporter in Europe I was professionally privileged to cover all three.

II

YANK IN THE PACIFIC: AMERICA AND A CHANGING COLONIAL WORLD

My assignment to "cover" the news of postwar Europe came out of a mixed background as a New York college graduate, a half-dozen years as a Times Square-based "feature" reporter, and many months as a World War II correspondent.

To understand and interpret Europe to Americans at a time when the United States had assumed such a sudden and enormous responsibility for aiding the endangered Continent, the cradle of Western values, called for the talents and achievements of a philosopher, a student of political systems, a linguist, an aesthete, a sociologist, and an economist. Admittedly I was accomplished in none of these fields. For what negative comfort was to be drawn from it, few others seemed to have the needed preparation either.

A single news story, accurate or not, I soon found, could cause crises inside the foreign offices of the world. Presently I met fellow newspapermen who had the reputation of having provoked the collapse of French cabinets. That was perhaps not necessarily the stuff of the most significant history, for Paris premiers were "falling" on an average of twice a year, with or without shoves from journalists, but even so it was evident that an impressively great deal often was at stake when an American correspondent sat down at his typewriter in the Europe which followed World War II. If he were not suspected of being a spy the reporter often was seen at least as a State Department agent. On one occasion when I wrote that the United States should provide a fund for resettling French farmers from one of the most badly undermined parts of North Africa I was astonished to see the story denounced by one of France's most eminent southern Mediterranean experts as proof that the Washington government was planning to replace France in North Africa. The idea actually had come from another Frenchman, one of those most competent to judge the tormented North African policy.

The American reporter in Europe after World War II was a personality of sorts, invited occasionally to give talks and interviews to European groups, and sometimes accorded the intense form of attention which consisted in expulsion proceedings. In a dozen years covering the Continent and its periphery I had even that form of highly special treatment. Egypt, in 1957, expelled me.

The reason the American reporter found himself "making the news instead of covering it," something few journalists like to do, was varied. Part of it was that the words written by many American reporters were reproduced instantly all over the globe. News-agency men had audiences of more than one thousand newspapers on every continent. In the tense new era of the atomic rocket an error or, worse, a truth could have electrifying consequences within moments. Accuracy was at least as objectionable as error, I found, for much of Europe and its periphery in an age of communist propaganda and anti-colonialist excitement lived in dream houses whose opaque but unsubstantial walls were contrived by government propagandists. Whether it was an Egypt fostering a myth of power and felicity in a land of frightful poverty and weakness, or a Western European government attempting to create an atmosphere of business confidence in an ocean of threats and uncertainties, the reporter attempting the modest task of recording facts was likely to find himself in the headlines of controversy.

Except for a six-week assignment to Rome in 1939 to help cover the election of the new Pope, I had not seen Europe before landing at the acting military airport of Ciampino, resurfaced by the Americans, outside Rome in 1946. I was accompanying a party of four American archbishops who had been summoned to Rome by Pope Pius XII to be hatted as cardinals, thus raising the American membership in the Sacred College to the highest proportion it had ever reached: 7 per cent of the College membership. This contributed to reducing the proportion of Italian cardinals to less than half for the first time since the Middle Ages. It was one more indication of the American advance in all fields, even in that of the Church to which more than half of Europe's population belonged. America's involvement with Europe, and America's responsibilities with regard to the preservation of so much that was most spiritual and noble in the Continent, were again underlined.

I stepped down onto the rattling metal strips of the army-repaired airfield with excitement at seeing the land where so much of Western civilization had originated, but with few of the preparations I considered valuable. My college French would not stand up under a conversation of more than a few sentences. I had no Italian. Education in New York Catholic schools had given me a certain degree of technical preparation for covering the Vatican, but my knowledge of the history of Athens and of ancient Rome, however slight, was not matched by a similar understanding of what had been going on inside the battered Continent in recent decades.

Mostly what I had to bring to my work was an enthusiasm for learning about the Europe from which so much of the United States had come.

Also—and I was to find it more valuable than I realized on that February day—I had a degree of understanding of my own so suddenly important country, an understanding deepened during fourteen months as a *Yank* magazine correspondent in the Pacific in World War II.

I knew that Americans were not warlike, but that they had done a good job on the battlefields of the war, however unhappily and worriedly.

I knew that social injustice was not absent inside the American democracy, although I was also sure that progress was being made toward diminishing it.

I had seen the advance of the war fronts bringing the twentieth century to near-naked, semi-savage Melanesians, upsetting Europe's old colonial relationships on the world's far side, and raising questions of moral responsibilities toward the island populations.

The Pacific months had provided a bitter taste, too, of the mid-century violence which was not to be begun by the rampaging Moroccans or by the retaliating Legionnaires of Oued Zem.

I had grown up in one of the corners of America nearest to Europe, in the quiet promontory of Bay Ridge, Brooklyn, behind the Coast Artillery guns of Fort Hamilton, which protected the Narrows linking New York Harbor with the gray ocean. Bay Ridge small fry in those days collected glimpses of "four-stackers"—quadruple-funneled, mammoth ocean liners—the way other boys saved stamps or accumulated cards from radio hams around the world. My dream was to go out over the horizon where the four-stackers or even the little freighters went.

My first long trip out was in the opposite direction, however, and from the other side of America, in an unescorted little Liberty ship on a twenty-six-day journey in 1943 from San Francisco to the French South Pacific island of New Caledonia. It was a more exciting voyage than I had counted on, for we had no protection in that ocean of Japanese submarine and surface warfare other than that provided by small-bore guns aft and on the sides of our vessel and the common defense provided by the Allied war effort, which was gradually spreading out from New Caledonia in the south and from revived Pearl Harbor in Hawaii.

The ocean was cobalt blue, radiant, and empty, brilliantly beautiful but wiltingly hot and, it seemed, dangerous. Like all the other writers of *Yank*, the 2,000,000-circulation weekly magazine of the American Army, I was an enlisted man, a corporal then, later a staff sergeant. The mission of our ship was to carry cargo, but two dozen of us G.I.'s ("government issues") were bedded down in sheds amidship on deck.

It was a typical American cross-section. "Sparks," the radio operator, was a man of middle age with some breadth of reading and some intellectual interests. He agreed to copy what snatches of news he could from the air if I would type up a daily ship paper. I did, and the news-minded Americans of the journey seemed to appreciate it. Nick Gill, the third assistant engineer, was growing a beard and was doing well with it. Chris Doloff, the boatswain, liked to talk about his shipwrecks. He had had five, and once had been adrift for twenty-eight days. The important thing in a lifeboat, he liked to repeat, was to be sure to bring cigarettes.

A few old hands arranged a rather lewd and clumsy "induction" for the rest of us into King Neptune's realm as we pollywogs became shellbacks by crossing the Equator, but most G.I. time was passed with endless games of dominoes. I read Alexis Carrel's dissertation on the human mystery, *Man the Unknown*.

Our introduction to Pacific combat came three weeks out as spots of land appeared on the horizon. The captain was in a fury about a G.I. who had puffed a cigarette on deck in the black of the previous moonless night, and there had been six general alarms in the course of the day. A black bomber circled us lazily and then came down the alley from a quarter of a mile astern. We G.I.'s assumed that it might be a drill arranged by light signal, but it was a moment of uncertainty and tension when our rear guns opened up with an ugly stutter like a pneumatic drill on a New York pavement. Swift curves of light—our tracer bullets—swept under the plane. The great vulture wings embraced us close overhead for a moment but no little black eggs dropped, and the plane curved off. The ship's bells rang the All Clear, but some went to bed that night with their clothes on. Volunteers had been requested for a special lookout: a Japanese submarine was reported in the area.

The warning signs were not illusory. Most of us were asleep at midnight when something struck like an automobile hitting a wall at fifty miles an hour. The single difference was that there was no tinkle of breaking glass. We struggled into our clothes and pulled on life jackets. By the time we got to the small boat stations there was a second crash and then a third. The captain stopped the ship, ordered a search for torpedo holes, found none, and then ordered a swift resumption of speed on a zigzag course. In New Caledonia we found three round dents in the hull, evidently the nose marks of torpedoes which had not gone off. Japan's war effort, we were told, mercifully had an important proportion of duds. Perhaps the submarine had fired inside the minimum range, too close for the projectile to arm itself, a protection for the undersea boat. Whatever the explanation, my friends of the domino games, of the King Neptune induction, and of Sparks' news bulletins had had a war test and had passed it quietly and well. There had been no panic, although I had felt my cheek muscles tighten and voice pitches had seemed a degree higher. Chris Doloff's first act had been to get a carton of cigarettes. Nick Gill, just inside the thin metal wall into which the first projectile had rammed, had calmed the others in the dangerous underwater engine room with a remark later posted in a mess hall as "famous last words."

"Don't get excited, boys," Nick had told his men in an unfamiliar voice. "It's only a torpedo. Stand by your stations. We're just sinking slowly."

There were chuckles and leg-pulling out of that but Nick's key part of the ship had not failed. We all had coffee in bowlfuls and went back to bed.

There were many occasions later, when potential danger was fully realized and when shells exploded all too effectively, but the reaction was the same. Some men were more heroic, some cracked under the pressure, but most doggedly pushed on with the awful business. The G.I.'s were neither the military supermen nor the war-thirsty ruffians many propagandized Europeans considered them to be. On the other hand, they had reason for pride, however alien it is to the American character to glory in the martial. The sights and sounds of many moments of testing soon were fixed in my memory. The G.I.'s took it and fought on. There were, for instance:

The night off Bougainville, on a raid by two small American Navy torpedo boats, when a Japanese bomber strafed us twice, his tracers spilling down in the light of a full moon like the sparks of a welder's torch;

The many nights on Bougainville—"Bogan's Ville" to the American soldiers—when "Washing Machine Charlie," the small Japanese bomber, would chug over in the bright light of a lover's moon for his dive (a rising crescendo of the motors, zzz-ZZZ aaaaAAAA AHH), and the whistle of his bombs (wah-wah-wah-WAH baumph!);[1]

The nights of our own terrifying artillery counterattacks, such as the one on Bougainville when 100 Japanese shells were repaid with 2,000, the nearby cannon firing swiftly like machine guns (barum, barum, barum, barum), the shells shooshing out close overhead with a shove of air against us, like the last car on a fast train, or like thunder rumbling in a straight line through a long cloud;

The day on a hilltop outside the Bougainville lines when support from our own 155-millimeter cannon on the beachhead came in on nearby targets with a crackling sound like the tearing of many thicknesses of newspaper.

There was also the taste of what it was like to be hit and the inside glimpse of the hospital machinery through which casualties went.

We were twenty-five yards from some Japanese dug in under a tree on a Bougainville hilltop. A homemade flame thrower was being tested by soldiers of the Americal division (the "Miracle" division, "A miracle if we ever get back home," it was called by some members of the hastily-assembled Pacific-born unit).[2] The device consisted of cans of gasoline flung in flames from a grenade launcher. The Japanese sat silent for a few moments and then fired back with a knee mortar shell. The missile burst fifteen feet from us. I saw a sudden black bush of smoke around a brilliant blossom of red-orange flame and felt

[1] There were record nights of six raids on Bougainville and twenty at General MacArthur's first Philippine headquarters at Tacloban in Leyte.

[2] The division was organized in the South Pacific, in New Caledonia, hence its hybrid name suggesting "Americans of New Caledonia."

what seemed like the smash of a baseball bat across my chest. Seventy tiny fragments had gone in, one a fraction of an inch from the heart, where probing surgeons later had to abandon it.

Twenty of us were given beds in a ward a mile or two behind the front line, a collection point for emergency treatment and for preparation for evacuation farther to the rear. There I watched another side of the drama of the Pacific war. A husky Negro opposite me lay silently for four hours, under oxygen, as eleven bottles of plasma were emptied into his veins. His intestines had been riddled. Sand filtered down on us as cannon hammered in a continuation of the fighting. Pillows turned brown until orderlies tacked khaki blankets to the ceiling to cut off the gritty shower. Doctors clustered around the bed of the Negro, studied him briefly, and ordered the tent removed. It was evidently all over for him. He was carried out on a stretcher, his face covered. A broad bloodstain marked where he had been.

Chatter in the ward was still only for moments. The eternal talk of women, sports, and women resumed. The dead for all our immediate practical purposes were gone, the living got on with the necessary task of living.

There may have been little philosophizing in that ward, but it was not inhumane. The oxygen tent was removed from the bed next to me, that of an abdomen shrapnel case. The intellectual-seeming young man looked across to the taut cord holding the stump of a yellow-skinned new amputee.

"Give him my light," the abdomen case told an orderly. "He needs it more than I do."

Another Negro was brought in. He had held a grenade too long and his hand had been blown off. The accident had just happened and the black-skinned soldier was sunk in despair.

"Oh, hell, oh!" he moaned and rolled.

His fellow casualties watched him and then went to the work of consoling him.

"You gotta figure you're lucky," one said with a voice betraying that he was not quite sure of what he was saying. "Your

Jap-hunting days are over! You'll be back in the States in a couple of months—drinking beer!"

"They have mechanical hands they put on now," suggested another. "They attach them and they work like fingers . . ."

The man's voice droned on and the Negro hid his face.

"Would you like some ice cream?"

"No," the stricken Negro told the orderly, and then "Yes." Visions of beer in America were something a mutilated man could reject in his anguish, but ice cream in those torrid islands was something only the deepest despair could refuse. The handless man sat up, took his spoon awkwardly in the unfamiliar left hand, and began to eat. Three times he lay back exhausted before he could finish.

"What'd they do, cut your whole hand off?" the orderly asked casually, as if such disasters were nothing startling.

"A ——— hand grenade," the Negro said.

It was his first conversational reply. Repair of the wreckage had begun.

The scene was one I was happy to remember when America's moral position was challenged in Europe. Certainly postwar America needed all the intellectual and spiritual aid it could draw from the Continent as it assumed the leadership of the free world which was the inevitable consequence of its immense physical strength, but the progress I saw in that front-line hospital in the march toward assimilation and equality for the American Negro was comforting.

On the same island, earlier, I had observed another phase of America's minority problems, that of the Niseis, the sons of immigrants from Japan. At almost every turn in the Pacific war I found someone whose job I considered grimmer. The Niseis certainly had one which ranked high on the list of the unenviable. Their task was to question the few Japanese who surrendered. Added to the common combat tension and the psychological strain of serving their new country against that of their forefathers was the imminent danger that they would be mistaken by quick-shooting G.I.'s. A marine had captured one Nisei while he bathed alone nude in a stream and had marched him back to camp triumphantly. "Look at the Jap I found who speaks English!" After that none of the Nisei inter-preters had moved from their tent area after dark and none went to wash in the river alone.

The Niseis invited my Yank artist teammate, Sergeant Rob-ert Greenhalgh, and me to have a New Year's Eve dinner with them "on the Emperor" and we dined over soy-savory meat from captured Japanese rations cooked over Tokyo canned heat. The coffee had been twice "liberated." It had been seized by Japanese raiders and then won back.

The Niseis, Greenhalgh summed it up later, were wholly American in their griping. The Japanese Army allowed no grumbling, the Niseis told us, but over enemy delicacies Ameri-can freedom in that regard was exploited that night to the fullest. The Niseis complained that even while they were serv-ing abroad their families were treated as unreliable. They said they had passed many months on garbage-truck duty and on other low "details" absurdly out of relationship with the Phi Beta Kappa keys many owned. But as they groused they smiled, too. One said that he had been the blocking back of his high-school football team. "You know, the unsung hero!" Buxom Lana Turner, a Hollywood star of the moment, was a great charmer, all agreed. And those girls in Missouri and Min-nesota where the Nisei soldiers had trained!

"We had a professor," mused one, "who said that mixing the races brings out superior beauty in the children!"

Another approvingly followed up this idea, agreeing that the Midwest, with its much more lenient attitude toward assimilation of the Asiatics, was the place to move after the war.

"We may not get it for ourselves, but I have faith enough in the American people to believe that justice will go to our chil-dren," said a twenty-year-old Nisei. It seemed to sum up the conclusions of the bull session.

Just as the Pacific war offered an opportunity to study the character of my own so suddenly important fellow Americans, so did it give me a glimpse into the awakening world of Europe's once relatively placid colonies. I accompanied a G.I. fresh-fruit mission into the back islands of the New Hebrides and especially noticed one handsome black girl of twenty, clad only in a few strings, hiding shyly behind a tree trunk in the jungle market place. She seemed to know that the other world from which we came had different ideas of dress. However right I was in the interpretation, there was no question but that the march of modern America through the South Pacific islands was opening a new century to its nearly naked people, a century of hope for advancement but also, probably, of terrible new struggles in the course of change.

The New Hebrides had British-French "condominium," or "pandemonium," as it was called locally. Whatever one European partner wanted the other seemed to veto, and consequently little seemed to be accomplished. But imperceptibly an alteration in native minds and hearts was going on.

One sergeant was the local "G.I. ambassador." In Texas his desire for "culture" had taken the form of a fascination with the French language. After he had reached the point, largely self-taught, where he could read Paris novels in the original, the army in the New Hebrides had given him the job of maintaining contact with the local French planters. It was still the days of the German occupation in the French homeland and the Army felt that it was worth a noncommissioned officer's time to keep in touch with what the planters were thinking and doing.

The sentiments of the Gallic émigrés around the edges of the new bases seemed eminently pro-Allied and so the sergeant's life was just about idyllic. I accompanied him on a call on one planter. We were served lunch on the top of stacks of a half-dozen plates, slowly working our way down through the gradually peeled-off pile.

The atmosphere in the planter's grove seemed peaceful, prosperous, and comforting, until as we walked away the sergeant recounted a tale told about one old French farmer of the area.

"When he came years ago he raided one of the other islands for slaves and came back with a group including two young mothers and their babies. The little ones cried all the way and the other prisoners looked restless, too. Finally the planter taught everyone his lesson. He snatched up the babies by the heels and dashed out their brains on the deck. It was quiet after that and everyone knew who was boss."

Whether there was truth in the horrible story I could not know. Certainly these had been islands of hideous violence. Cannibalism had been practiced until recently and probably would return despite years of effort by missioners and the European-organized police, if the colonial masters of the islands were to withdraw. That was a common European opinion and it convinced me.

I saw the work of the missionaries of the West at Tangarare on the northern tip of Guadalcanal. I had heard some cynics say that missionaries had brought nothing but disease and prudish Western ideas of modesty, but at Tangarare I saw something of which I felt Europe could be proud.

I passed a night there at the mission of Father Emery Le Klerk, a Dutch Catholic priest. With the fervor of Holland's large Catholic minority the young man had gone to Rome to study for a life as a missioner, and had been able to see his mother often there, for she had followed him to the Eternal City for those final extra months together. At last one day he went to her with the news of his assignment.

"I am going to Guadalcanal!"

The name was to take a high place in World War II history as the first big Japanese-American battlefield but in those years in Rome it was unknown to all but a few prelates in the Vatican's Sacred Congregation for the Propagation of the Faith.

"Where is it?" the mother asked.

The priest didn't know, but he had a theory: somewhere off the lower tip of South America. Mother and son got out the atlas and finally found it an ocean and a quarter of the world away, at the edge of Asia.

With humor, courage, piety, and liberal use of Western intellectual advances, the good European was being all things: a father, a teacher, a doctor to the extent that he could find

answers in the German disease manual which took a proud
place beside his mass book as a mission essential, and even
sometimes a hunter. On one recent occasion he had hurried
out into the bush to help an Allied pilot downed in a crocodile
swamp.

I attended vesper service at the mission. Just as women
leaving a Western church might pull off their hats in the vesti-
bule, Father Le Klerk's ladies slipped out of their blouses at
the chapel exit, denuding themselves to the waist.

How evolved were his scantily-clad converts? Father Le Klerk
was not sure. There was some special quality, it seemed, in the
frenzy with which his congregation fell on a cattle carcass after
the priest had taken the filets, legs, and liver. The neo-Catholics
would dance until dawn, seemingly intoxicated by the animal
shreds, which they would scorch and swallow bit by bit until
everything had been eaten. They danced in two long opposing
lines, men on one side, women on the other, the two never
meeting.

Cannibalism seemed to have died out in the Tangarare area
a century earlier, when the white crew of a coastal boat had
disappeared, presumably the last victims. For years British
administrators with sturdy, shirtless native "police boys" had
tracked down eaters of human flesh as common murderers.
Fear of the police and the appeals of the missionaries had begun to lift the scourge which had made life a terror for all:
for parents who dreaded that their children might die in
neighbors' hands, for victors who were terrified that they
might have done unto them what they did to others.

One missionary friend of Father Le Klerk's, thirty years
earlier, had dined on "pork" in a jungle village, only to hear
later that it had been a man. A European traveler fifteen years
previously, in 1928, had accepted a package of "fresh meat"
wrapped in banana leaves—a man's forearm. But except perhaps for the delirious cattle roasts, even vague memories of
such days seemed to be gone from Tangarare.

I met only one islander who recalled the European-fought
plague of cannibalism. He was Mikaele, an employee of the

British on nearby Malaita, an island even more retrograded than Guadalcanal. Some natives in the interior of Malaita went entirely naked; Mikaele wore a rubber slipper on one foot because it was leprous. In embarrassment he scratched designs in the dust with his rubber-covered toe as he answered questions about man-eating. As a child, he said, he had been horrified by the sight of a man baked in leaves in a stone pit. The biceps, thighs, and shoulder blades were especially favored, but as for the hips, "I never heard good news about that part."

That occasion was the last and, as Mikaele had felt then, he hoped it would never be repeated.

On Florida Island, another in the Guadalcanal-dominated Solomon group, I visited the thatch house of Chief Patrick, head man for 1,500 natives in seventeen villages. The bare-bosomed women of Patrick's main village ran as we pushed ashore in a small boat, but later the chief's rather handsome young wife, uncovered to the waist, sat quietly on the mat-covered floor at one side of her single room as we talked to her husband. She puffed a pipe and was silent. Her naked five-year-old son Jackson coughed beside her on a cigarette. Three-year-old Salome, sucking an unlit pipe, hid under a khaki-colored army mosquito net Patrick had snagged from the passing flood of American equipment.

Two worlds were in every corner of the chief's little home. His own dress was of the West, a battered gray felt hat of the sort American trout fishermen commonly fancy, an American sailor's undershirt, and dungaree shorts. Prehistoric wood implements for grinding food lay beside a safety razor, a spool of thread, a can of tooth paste, a twelve-inch ruler, and a war club, the last doubtless shaped not for combat on Florida Island, but for sale for a native's pay for a month—$5.00—to an American G.I. The fact that there was a base a few hundred yards distant was no doubt the reason why the women, unlike the naïve ladies of remote Tangarare, were so shy. Those of Patrick's village knew by then how odd they seemed to the Western eye in their semi-nudity. A psychological change had come; no great one, to be sure, for Florida styles were still the same, but one of a myriad modifying the old colonial world.

Patrick, as a pillar of the established order, had little dissatisfaction to report, but as my teammate Greenhalgh and I did sketch-and-text interviews with a dozen natives of the Guadalcanal area we found many signs of new thought.

Duga, a husky boy at nine, told us that as he stood in the back row at the free movies at the American camps he was consumed with envy for the lucky children of the West who had such marvelous homes. His mind wandered from the plot to the settings. His dream, he said, was to have a house like those with a staircase "to run up and down!"

Suru, a dashing buck with a sailor's white cap over his forehead and a cigarette behind an ear, said that he, too, had been carried away by the world of the American movies. What he would like to see was clothing for the Solomon Island women. The women, he added, felt the same way. Those who lived in the Garden of Eden were convinced that there was more beauty and dignity outside it.

Would you like anything changed, Greenhalgh asked "Tigi."

"No like anything here," the Melanesian youth answered in very sad words indeed.

Tigi wanted to go to school. He had been depressed when American marines, arriving for the battle against the Japanese, had been unable to understand his brand of English. Tigi wanted to go after the war "in big boat see United States, see America." Tigi's friends were dissatisfied with the British masters of their area for not teaching them "to build houses like they have in the movies" and for not telling them "how to make big boats." The islanders with their tattooed faces, their black hair dyed orange, and their ear lobes punctured and enlarged to take discs two inches in diameter, were at last aware that their traditional canoes, high sterned like Venetian gondolas in reverse, were incapable of taking them to the wonder world below the horizon.

The old days when coconut planters had had to invent needs

to induce the natives to work, "telling them, for instance, that every man really had to have a hat, and then keeping up the price of hats so that they'd toil for one," were evidently over. But the new day promised to be no less difficult.

"Until recently they didn't want to come to school," said a British administrative officer, answering the charge that the Europeans had done too little to lift the islands from the Stone Age. "Only now they have begun to understand the value of education."

How well they comprehended even what was put before them was still a question. In one Guadalcanal village a pious Christian native congregation showed me their chapel bell, drilled by a bullet in a strafing and silenced. They wanted a replacement. Behind them as they spoke was a goblet made from a human skull, its eye and ear holes plugged. Their pagan forebears had made the vessel, the Christians explained. They were not guilty, it was true, but it was also plain that they still had not given the ill-fated ancient's brain box the grace of a Christian burial.

Had Europe's role in the islands been for better or worse? Surely the planters had given high consideration to the profits of London soap companies which exploited the palms and cheap labor of the former cannibal islands. Certainly the islanders were centuries behind the Europe and America of which they were becoming enviously aware. On balance it seemed to me, however, that Europe had a right to be proud. The Magellan who had found the islands four centuries earlier had opened the way to a far better world. It was well that Mikaele was forgetting cannibalism and that he was reluctant to dredge back what fading recollection remained. But it was also clear that G.I.'s from my own Brooklyn and from the rest of the United States who had been shocked at the tiny monthly wages of the natives and had preached the message of high American salaries, had planted revolutionary ideas which, in any case, would have been inculcated by the mere sight of the rich American military world rolling through the Pacific islands to victory in Japan.

The old colonial world of the Pacific could never be the same after what Duga, Tigi, Sugu, Mikaele, and even Chief Patrick had seen: the men of the Stone Age knew their misery now for what it was.

Unwittingly the American defense against Japan had weakened one of the foundation stones under America's European allies. Restoring peace in the colonies in Oceania would not be easy. It meant, it seemed to me, another responsibility added to the preposterously heavy list already weighing on my fellow G.I.'s of the near-torpedoing; on the Niseis of Bougainville, so quickly being assimilated; on the handless Negro of the front-line hospital; and on all the rest of my fellow Americans.

It was a responsibility both to help the Europe which had mothered America and to assist in holding open the doors to hope and progress through which the Melanesians of Guadalcanal and the colonial populations of a score of other areas had peered during the tumult of World War II.

On the threshold of Asia at the end of World War II I was attracted as a journalist by the lure of that billion-population continent which surely held within it much of the future of the world. Even greater, though, was the fascination for me of Europe, the continent which had been for twenty-five centuries the core of the Western past, and which, despite reverses, was sure to keep contributing major history for years to come. It was with keen anticipation that, the war over, I went early in 1946 to become my New York paper's correspondent in Rome.

III

ITALY RUINED:
THE CROWDED STREETCAR

One of the first words I learned in Italian in the late winter of
1946 I read on walls in letters five feet high: *"Pane,"* Bread.
The southern European member of the Berlin–Tokyo–Rome
axis had been reduced to that abject cry.

In those first days as a reporter in the Europe I had craved
to know I was obsessed by the poverty. There was no end to it
and no limit to its variety. Part of it, of course, was specifically
Italian. The sunny but otherwise not very richly endowed
peninsula which had been the heart of the Roman Empire
was no bigger than California but had a population of nearly
50,000,000, more than a fourth that of the United States.

The ruin, physical and to some extent moral, was so thorough and had been piled atop such original indigence that I
wondered how Italy could play a role in Western life again.

Covering the Italian crisis, like charity, began at home. The
American embassy was encouraging reporters to call for their
families. With the help of the United States Army stores (the
P-X's or "post exchanges") and with what was variously called
the black or "free" market, it was possible to get along. It was
Washington policy to cling to Italy in the face of the Communist tide rolling in from the East, and so it was embassy
counsel for Americans in Italy to resume normal lives, whatever the inconvenience.

Luckily, I heard of one diplomat who was being transferred
just as $200 worth of hams, canned foods, and other household
supplies that he had ordered arrived in Rome. I bought the
shipment sight unseen and for many months we stared at the
cans piled nearly to the ceiling in one of the children's rooms.

Everything eventually found a use, but the attaché's twenty-four bottles of furniture polish lasted eleven years!

With the food cache two more things were necessary, an apartment and a maid. Everyone assured me that although we had no servant in the States we would need one or more in a city not only upset by recent wreckage but many years behind the times in household devices and shopping efficiency. The advice was excellent. When my wife, Mary, arrived with our three-year-old son, Bill, she found that she had to shop at as many as twenty sidewalk stalls a day. Farmers came in to town to sell one or two items they had raised themselves. Even to get a full range of meats, to buy poultry, pork, lamb, beef, liver, and sausages, meant doing business with at least five different businessmen. No one sold them all.

Inflation, which had destroyed 98 per cent of the value of the Italian lira, was harassing Italian businessmen. A single cigarette—cigarettes were sold one at a time then and even a decade later—cost what would have been the equivalent of $2.00 or $3.00 in prewar lire.

Getting a maid was not difficult. I advertised that I would pay $10.00 with room and board for six days' work a week. The ad was short, but I had to take my interpreter, Gino Zaccardi, off other chores to interview the army of applicants who descended on us. Seventy-five replied and six were so superb that Zaccardi said he could not choose among them. One had cooked for ill-starred Claretta Petacci, Mussolini's mistress who was slain with him. Another was a half-Austrian girl from Trieste on the North Italian frontier, the region whose people had, in Italy, the best reputation for industry and cleanliness. I chose these two. For a while we were to have the luxury, unthinkable for most Americans, of two maids. We were to try, and like, a recipe the dictator's paramour had favored (eggplant soufflé).

It was to be luxury for us, but with an unhappy other side to it. The family of one of our maids lived on the edge of Rome in a shanty little better than a cave. As servants' salaries rose and household conveniences increased we were to drop out of the two-servant class, but for the sake of the maids, whose living conditions improved, Mary was to feel better about it.

Finding an apartment was difficult. Rents were frozen at a few dollars a month, but to get into a flat often required an under-the-table payment of *buon uscite* ("good exits"—key money), sums running to many hundreds of dollars. Woe to those who tried to get government help in requisitioning squatter-occupied premises, including even those which had been leased to one's own paper prior to the wartime evacuation by Allied nationals. If adequate *buon uscite* were not paid, a blight would strike the property. Even the water faucets would be cemented shut!

Our housing problem was solved by a man who had been high enough in fascism to lease a full floor in a modern apartment house but obscure enough to escape postwar prosecution. He was glad to surrender the better half of his floor. A gentle, quiet man, he turned out to be so unlike my mental picture of the "enemy" that I became convinced that all wars are fratricidal. We walked as mourners in his funeral procession a few years later.

I telegraphed for my family. My wife was amazed on her first night in Rome. The American Air Force invited us to an anniversary dinner and the party was handsome. There were corsages for the ladies, delicately prepared food and twice too much of it, a charming view of the yellow-orange tiled roofs and cupolas of the Eternal City, and only slightly seedily-attired waiters to lavish attention on us.

It was the reverse of "starving Europe." Had continental need been exaggerated, or were the victorious Americans beginning to live richly and callously like the rest of history's conquerors? To raise the question may have been ill repayment of the kindness of our hosts, but it seemed unavoidable.

The truth was a bit of all. S. M. Keeny, head of the United Nations relief mission, had no quick answer when a reporter from an isolationist New York newspaper challenged him to name a single Italian hamlet where there was true starvation. On the other hand, a United States senator from the Middle

West, another foe of "internationalism," was wrong when he told a flabbergasted group of Italians and of American embassy employees at a cocktail party in my home a few years later, "The fact is these people over here live better than we do at home. I'm proud that I've voted against every Marshall Plan (American Aid) appropriation."

For the sliver of Italian life the senator saw, a slice with which the remnants of the American armed forces and the beginnings of a postwar American civilian colony soon were identified, what the legislator said was possibly true. But as an observation on which to base a Senate vote it was appallingly false. Happily for my faith in democracy, the senator remained in the minority in Washington and finally lost his seat in the upper house. In postwar Rome one could not "believe his own eyes" and in most cases had to take the word of experts. The fact was that almost every Italian, probably starting with the cadaverous premier, Alcide De Gasperi, who was receiving the equivalent of $75 a week, was underfed.

There was another side to the life of the Americans who went to live amid the magnificence of subdivided Renaissance palaces. Often in the first months after the war in Italy, and even in the 1950's in Paris, such places were the only available near approximations of American middle-class housing.

"The congressman thinks I live in luxury because I have a painting on the wall," one embassy attaché complained, "but my bathroom doesn't work, it's always cold, and I can't get a decent refrigerator or stove."

The result was that officers such as our Air Force dinner hosts and a good share of the rest of the postwar American colony drifted toward at least the appearances of luxury amid need. Princes and princesses showed up at middle-class American cocktail parties. The story was told of Prince X, who "was exhausted at the time of the liberation of Rome, giving farewell parties to so many departing Germans one week and welcomes to so many Americans the next." It was the story of Marrakesh's feudal golf course once again, the sons of the American democracy hobnobbing with the people of privilege.

It was disturbing, and I was glad for the sake of American morals when the occupation forces in Europe, including our goodhearted Air Force hosts of my wife's arrival night, were to a large extent withdrawn.

Their removal meant, by default, an increase of the Soviet Communist threat against Europe. That was undoubtedly worse, but certainly a high price was worth-while to avoid the corruption a long and general American occupation of Western Europe apparently would have meant.

The Rome in which we set up housekeeping in early 1946 was the capital of a country in ruins. As a Catholic I had looked forward to Rome as a second home, a city of lofty values whose people were somewhat, but not too much, less than angels. Nineteen centuries at the core of Christianity surely mattered for something. It had, as I was gradually to learn after years of life among the humane Italians, but at first sight there was only disillusion and chaos.

How Italy was to be reclaimed as a useful member of the Western community baffled me. I was to hear later that many of the British, unlike the Americans, wanted Italy excluded from the anti-Soviet defensive alliance. There was, responsible Britishers argued, "not enough room under the umbrella" of Western resources; broken ex-Fascist Italy would have to take its chances in the "rain." The idea was overruled at American insistence and I watched the work of salvaging the land of Michelangelo and St. Francis, of Caesar and Mussolini, of Augustus and Columbus, of the Borgias, Nero, Macchiavelli, Da Vinci, Cellini, Galileo, and the labor-helping Popes Leo XIII and Pius XI, of the noble and ignoble, of sinners and saints, but of so many who had joined in creating the West from which America had drawn almost the whole of its intellectual formation.

In the first weeks in postwar Italy 80 per cent of each day went to keeping alive. Only the remaining tag end one fifth could go to collecting news.

The people of our house put us face to face with one emergency by refusing to chip in for coal for central heating. They could not afford it. Each of us had to heat his flat in makeshift ways. We found an artisan who installed an ugly wood-burning terra-cotta stove in the living room and with kerosene burners and electric heaters managed to take the chill off the rest of the apartment, but not well enough to protect us from our first dose of chilblains, painful red swellings of the tips of the nose, toes, and fingers.

The city gasworks, too, ran short of coal. The fuel was rare and expensive that winter because of strikes in Pennsylvania, a hint of how closely bound together the West was becoming. Gas was cut back to three hours' supply a day. My wife cooked one meal for guests on five different heaters, not just on the kitchen stove, but also on a sooty charcoal burner, a bedroom kerosene heater, the parlor woodstove, and at the neighborhood public oven. The latter charged five cents for roasting a turkey. There was a small flat rate for all items. Prices were only slowly adjusting to inflation, so that some, like those for the use of the public oven, were next to nothing. But it was wise, we learned, to sweeten the payment to the public cook with another fifteen or twenty cents to be sure that a good eye was kept on a crucial item like a roast. A charred entrée could be the fruit of routine attention.

Whoever did the day's shopping had to make a second trip if she forgot to bring a bag for purchases. The market had no wrapping paper. Our maid took one of my newspaper's enormous Sunday editions and traded it for two pounds of fruit. Sparingly dealt out, the one day's paper wrapped sales for a week.

Nothing seemed to go right. Water ran out. The head of one American news agency in Italy, our good friend, boiled up a bath and, fifteen minutes before a dinner appointment, found there was no cold water to cool it down. He took his tub with ice cubes around him.

I learned two more Italian words, *pazienza* ("patience") and *coraggio* ("courage"). They were on everyone's lips. Usually they were spoken with a laugh, but they signified virtues which were real and ever-present. With hope and faith the huge work of restoration was starting. Everything needed redoing.

"Do you think war helps religion?" an eminent member of the Catholic hierarchy asked me. "Well, it doesn't. Wars break homes and cause promiscuity. Fewer go to mass now in Italy than before."

Fascism had been overthrown and everyone was enthusiastically anti-Fascist, but few seemed to know what that implied. Some apparently reasoned: "Fascism was order, therefore we should now have disorder." My chauffeur, really my car watcher, who drove in order to have something else to do, gave me an example of this one day as he shot through a line of people who were getting off a streetcar. Tram users leaped clear like spray from a ship's prow.

"You know," the driver said, "we wouldn't have been allowed to do that under Fascism!"

"Anti-Fascism" to the contrary, we imposed our own rules after that. We stopped voluntarily for discharging trolley cars.

Police scarcely dared intervene in the face of the most outrageous conduct. An arrested black marketeer needed only to raise the cry of "Fascist" against the officer and bystanders would free the captive.

Thievery and riots became everyday events. That was the reason for car watchers. Most of the American newspaper correspondents, who in turn were the bulk of the nondiplomatic United States civilian colony, bought jeeps from the departing army. German prisoners courteously soldered chains to the dashboard, with which the steering wheel could be immobilized, since the vehicles had no locks, but neither that nor any other scheme could protect the cars from Italy's postwar army of hungry looters. Each of us, at the usual low wages, hired a car guardian. Even that was not enough. The watcher for one of my colleagues provoked his employer's wrath by walking into the reporter's office.

"What are you doing here?" the correspondent cried. "I told you never to leave that jeep."

"That's just the point," the man said miserably. "I was right next to it. I was standing with my head on my hand and my elbow on the top—when it drove away."

My own disappeared one midnight. I had discharged the car watcher for the night and was telephoning my day's story to New York from the long-distance exchange, one of the few places in Italy at the time from which a transoceanic call could be made. Police said thieves had snipped the German-installed chain with specially adapted hedge clippers.

Naples had the worst reputation. Its misery was so deep that even the most sympathetic Americans tended to lose touch with it. It was so far removed from anything an American knew that it seemed unrelated, somehow inhuman. Yet there was something more than human, something divine, in the smile of one twelve-year-old girl I watched selling cigarettes. She was chanting the black marketeer's cigarette call, "America! America!" It meant "I sell American cigarettes illegally, smuggled cigarettes on which no tax has been paid." It also implied "I sell 'America'! I sell happiness!" The little girl waited twenty minutes for a buyer and then sold only a single cigarette. At that her face lit with an angel's joy.

There was a story in the Naples of the immediate postwar period that some of the city's ingenious people had even managed to man a ship and sail away with it and its cargo. Certainly no truckload was safe unless a man sat in back with the goods. Even then there was danger. One night I drove from Allied headquarters at the royal palace of Caserta, near Naples, to Rome, riding the army mail truck. A soldier with a tommy gun sat beside the speeding driver in front. I was with the mail guard in back. We were inside a closely meshed wire cage with a tarpaulin pulled tight around the outside. A light burned within. Even with those precautions the young soldiers sat armed and on the alert during the whole of the ride.

The variations on the thievery story never ceased to intrigue me. A boy of ten hopped on the running board of my jeep in Naples and asked if I wanted to buy black-market gasoline. I told him I did not but that I wanted him to get off the car.

"Then do you want to sell some black-market gas?" the child persisted.

"No, thanks! Get down!"

A policeman with drawn gun interrupted the exchange. The little boy's confederate, another child the same age, was making use of the distraction to perch on our spare tire on back and to unstrap the five-gallon reserve can. With gasoline going for one dollar or two dollars a gallon, the can would have made a good haul.

Storekeepers not only were rolling iron curtains down in front of their windows at night, but they were locking the grilles to the sidewalk. On one such shield I counted thirteen padlocks. I went to the Naples police station to do a "story" on the situation, but native pride interfered.

"There's no special thievery to report," the police official said stiffly.

"Well, could I put it this way?" I tried. "Would you say that you could leave an automobile at the curb and expect to find it in the morning?"

"That," the Neapolitan answered, "is something you couldn't do anywhere in the world!"

The thought of many young car owners in fortunate America who had never paid a night's garaging ended the conversation. It did not, however, finish my interest in the problem of Naples.

"It's true that they tried to steal your five-gallon can," a former rabbi, a convert who had become a Catholic priest and monsignor, told me years later as we discussed the Italian character. "They did steal cans, but so far as I know not one of them turned in any of your hundreds of escaping pilots for the reward." A "redistribution" of petty wealth, with the desperately poor profiting at the expense of the affluent, was one thing. Trading on grave human distress was another.

I visited Gennaro Fermariello, who had been the Allied-appointed mayor of Naples. He shivered inside an overcoat in his unheated office as I asked him how much damage had to be repaired. The factory zone had been so pulverized, I learned, that the Neapolitans joked about it as the "new Pompeii." It was even worse than the volcano-buried, ancient Roman city, for a great deal remained of the chariot-rutted streets and frescoed walls of the first century after Christ, but bombs had left little but dust where the job-giving industries of Naples had stood.

"It's better not to estimate," Mr. Fermariello replied with a Latin reaction. "It's better just to work at repairs. Anyway, the main thing is that in ten years Naples will be better than ever."

The prediction proved correct. A decade later Neapolitan artisans were still working in the streets outside their offices to save electricity. There seemed to be more casket makers among them than practitioners of any other single trade, but the city bustled with life and the worst of the war's ruin was gone. The Italian Navy was no longer using the hulk of a partly-capsized ship as a sailors' dormitory, and ridges at the ankles showing where the leg of one stocking had been sewn to the foot of another no longer were the feminine style.

But in 1945 and 1946 thievery in Naples had been such a scandal to the British Army that His Majesty's forces had erected a prim sign at the entrance to the city:

New to Naples?
Watch your kit!

The sign was good advice to anyone anxious to hold on to his toothbrush, his wallet, and the rest of his possessions, but of course it could not plumb the economic and sociological phenomena behind the appalling performances of the Neapolitan looters.

My wife and I began to understand some of the background as we started trips into the southern Italian interior, including the forsaken mountains about which the north Italian

Carlo Levi had written in his postwar best seller *Christ Stopped at Eboli*. Levi was an anti-Fascist who had been punished by being confined to an interior village in southern Italy, behind Eboli. The latter was the last modern city on the plains below Naples. As the Socialist Levi had said in his bitter book, the modern European world, the world of twenty centuries of Christianity, remained largely unknown in the superstitious, ignorant, hideously poor, and often pagan world of the hill land beyond Eboli in the arch of the Italian boot. Northern Italy, close to Austria, France, and Switzerland, was educated and prosperous. Southern Italy—and one could add the islands of Sicily and Sardinia as regions Christ had stopped without reaching—was the land which had produced the waves of Italian emigration to the United States. The swarthy, short, stocky southern Italian was the man Americans knew as "the Italian." The often tall, angular, and blond men of the North, much like Austrians or French, were Italians most Americans had not encountered, even though many among them, like De Gasperi, ran Italy. Southern Italy was the land of the criminal Mafia, that Sicilian regional phenomenon which had helped shatter the reputation of all Italy in America.

One of our first southern Italian trips was completed within sight of Rome. Mary and I put on hiking shoes and set out for Guadagnolo, a village on a skyscraper-shaped hill on the horizon east of the Eternal City. We could see the hamlet's narrow plateau from our Rome apartment, and its 1,200 residents could make out the domes of Rome's churches, but centuries separated the two communities. Rome had traffic, parking trouble, neon lights, and most of the conveniences and annoyances of the mid-twentieth century, but Guadagnolo lacked even a *strada rotabile*, a wheel-bearing road. It was five miles to the village over a path of ruts and boulders, passable only for men and mules. The wheelless road led across a hot landscape to the foot of a perpendicular rise which reminded me of the sheer wall of New York's Empire State Building. Women were washing clothes in a brook at the foot of the cliff. There was no water in Guadagnolo, except for a stagnant pool. The ladies of the community had to climb up and down the vertiginous cliff to do their laundry.

"Why are you here?" a woman ill-temperedly challenged us. "Out to enjoy the walk? Well, we take the walk not because we like to, but because we have to!" But hostility faded as we talked.

"You know we have no idea where the next lire for salt are coming from," the woman said.

I had always heard complaints about privations, about the lack of an automobile or, later, the need for a new automobile, but it was the first time I had ever listened to anyone lamenting the lack of salt.

The parish priest bore out the woman's picture of the community. His black cassock was dusty and soiled at the collar. He excused himself to make a weather observation and to radio a report of it; he eked out his sparse living as a part-time meteorologist. In a country where the government subsidy to the Catholic clergy was only a few dollars a month and where worshipers sometimes dropped as little as two lire (one third of an American cent) into the collection basket at mass, it was easy to understand the priest's need for other sources of income in Guadagnolo.

Among all its other privations the village had no electricity and no telephone. "The only time anyone goes out at night is when there's a storm," the priest said, smiling. "It's a case of taking one step every time there's a lightning bolt."

The people of Guadagnolo studied us curiously during our visit, but the momentary unfriendliness at the foot of the hill was not repeated. I began to learn what was expected of us in meetings like that.

"Don't you think our village is ugly?" someone would ask us.

"Your village has wonderful air."

"The air? Well, you know, you're right! We do have good air."

Perhaps this point of view was inherited from generations earlier when malaria killed farmers on the plains and spared only those who retreated for the nights to cold hilltops. Certainly wherever we went we found joy and pride in the mountain air.

A village without a "wheel-bearing road" was hard for an American mind to conceive, but Italy had hundreds of them. We climbed to another at Pogerola on the Amalfi coast, south of Naples. The people of Pogerola had had a front seat from which to watch the American landings at Salerno, on the eve of the Allied capture of Naples in World War II, but they might just as well have been living back in Italy's medieval past. A staircase of a thousand steps led up to the village. It was the only way in. The community's industry was timber cutting. All the wood was carried out on the backs of the people. A woman could manage to tote one hundred and forty pounds on her shoulders down the steps, a man two hundred and twenty pounds.

Some minutes before Mary and I finished the forty-five-minute climb upstairs to Pogerola we made out the black figure of an old man waiting at the top. There may have been something in our angular movements, our weariness, or our bright clothes which marked us for Americans, for the old man soon had got out of us that we were from the United States.

Two goats nosed Salvatore Amendola's knee as he talked. He was an American, too, he said proudly, an American in the sense that he had lived for a while in the States. He had packed bullets in a Remington factory in Connecticut. The pay was not much by New England standards, but the old man had been carried away by his dreams as he calculated what his small hoard of dollars, translated into lire, would mean in penniless Pogerola. He would be a village leader! He had returned, but wars and inflation had taken everything. Watching two goats was now his full occupation.

"Tell me," Mr. Amendola said, "when I went to America in 1905 the fare was thirteen dollars. What is it now? I'd still like to go back."

His face fell at hearing that the current charge was twenty times as great. In his seventies he had no real thought of returning to Connecticut, but in Pogerola idle talk about doing such a thing was a consolation of a sort.

Mr. Amendola took us to the mayor, Don Pasquale Rocco. Father Rocco was also the village priest. If it were not for the United States, Pogerola would not get by, the youthful clergyman said smilingly as he welcomed us into his combined bedroom and office. Many southern Italians such as Mr. Amendola had answered the siren call to return to the old country, sometimes because their wives or sweethearts at home were too timid to take a chance on a sea crossing, but fortunately enough of the emigrants had stayed in America so that a stream of parcels came at the rate of ten a week.

"Look," the priest said, pulling out the drawer of the small chest beside his bed. "My new American socks."

Clothes were what the Pogerolans hoped for most in the packages from America.

"They have a saying here," the priest said, "that you can go without eating but that you can't do without clothing."

Father Le Klerk's parishioners on Guadalcanal might have disputed the point, but, in truth, the Pogerolans were proving that you could do without just about everything. Some load carriers went by with one shoe on and one shoe off like characters in a nightmarish nursery rhyme. Others used rags tied on with thongs.

Pogerola had no telephone, no stores excepting two run by the government to sell the tax-raising national monopoly items of tobacco and salt, no hospital, no doctor, no midwife, no school beyond the first four grades, and not only no automobiles but also no horses, no mules, and no donkeys. The usual breakfast was a piece of bread, a slice of onion, and a small glass of wine. Most people ate no lunch. Supper customarily consisted of corn-meal mush, another glass of wine, and whatever fruits were in season, such as grapes and oranges. The latter grew on the sunny, south-exposed cliffside of Pogerola.

"But they rarely die here," Father Rocco said cheerfully. "I've had twenty baptisms during the past year and only three funerals."

Pogerola had got up on its hill in the eleventh century, when iron was found there and a long-since-defunct nail industry had started. I did not ask the Pogerolans why they stayed on such a site, but I did put that question to the people of another community just behind Pogerola. This was San Sebastiano al Vesuvio, "St. Sebastian at (Mount) Vesuvius," a volunteer Pompeii of the twentieth century. San Sebastiano was perched high on the flank of Vesuvius in a spot which not only could be devastated by the notorious volcano but which actually had been hit four times in a century and almost certainly would be struck again within a generation. In 1944 the town had been crushed under an outpouring of lava fifteen feet deep. The American and British armies were so impressed by the disaster that they had left off chasing the retreating Fascists and Nazis for a moment in order to help the San Sebastianese. For a while San Sebastiano stole the news play. War correspondents wrote for days just about the village. American Army trucks carried in food and carted out refugees.

A decade later I found San Sebastiano rebuilt on the same spot. The only difference was that the altitude of the village was one and one-half stories higher. By a freak of the laval flow the bell tower of the church had been left standing. Using that as their landmark, the people of the village had calculated where their property boundaries had been and had whitewashed the outlines on the black volcanic refuse. They had carted in earth to cover the rock and had rebuilt their homes. In some ways the village was better than before, for many Neapolitans had been encouraged to exchange the high rents of their city, twenty miles distant by a good road, for the relatively low ones of San Sebastiano. With the extra money to spare some of them had put up pleasant villas.

San Sebastiano's perilous site was at the bottom of a natural chute leading down from the lip of Vesuvius. Every twenty-five years, on the average, the volcano's 600-foot-deep crater had filled and the infernal mess from the bowels of the earth, sometimes sterile mud, sometimes molten rock, had spewed down over the village. Seventy-year-old Father Raffaelle Simeoli, the dean of village priests, well remembered the 1906 disaster. It was mud that time. For three or four years it had been impossible to work the poisoned fields.

Why did the village rebuild on the same spot? Father Francesco Scarpato answered with another question. "Where else can the people go?"

Part of it was a touching love for native, even though volcanic, soil. "We live with fire under our feet," Father Simeoli said. "The volcano is an enemy but he is not treacherous. He sends out warnings. It's better than earthquakes." It reminded me of the Pacific where every soldier knew another whose assignment he considered more awesome than his own.

Primarily, however, what kept the people of San Sebastiano from settling elsewhere was the general overcrowding of southern Italy, the critical new overpopulation problem now reaching out of Asia into Europe and the West.

Even San Sebastiano, however, was not in the blighted area Carlo Levi had described. Occasional banditry made the Levi region of Lucania, southeast of Naples and just above the arch of the Italian boot, insecure in the first postwar years, but with cans of gasoline piled in the back of the jeep, Mary and I tried it.

We knew we had arrived when the proprietor of the best hotel in the tiny Lucanian village of Sant' Angelo smiled as we checked in. "You're a traveling man," the hotel manager said. "Tell me, what is going on?" Here the villagers rarely saw a newspaper. Even radios were few. Travelers, as a half a thousand years earlier, were relied on to bring news.

The hotel man showed us to a dingy gray room more alarming than depressing, with four beds.

"Don't worry," the proprietor said, mistaking our expressions and grabbing bedding from two of the beds. "You are to have the entire room to yourselves." Only later did we realize what a concession privacy was in a southern Italy ac-

customed to public dormitories where a dozen travelers sometimes shared the same chamber.

The Sant' Angelo–Rotondella–Policoro area summed up the
plight of southern Italy. The remains of Greek temples on the
nearby shore of the Ionian Sea recalled the prosperity of
twenty centuries earlier, but pirates, brigands, malaria, and a
scarcity of social justice had ravaged the region. Rotondella
was so poor that Mayor Giovanni Scaiello had ordered classes
in one of the first-grade rooms suspended for the six worst
winter weeks. The room was on the very edge of a crumbling
cliff. Other buildings along the precipice had been condemned
and pushed over the brink, but so much of the indigent village was threatened by erosion that the town fathers had decided they could not afford to go further with the razing.
Cracks ran up the classroom walls. If the building went over
the edge, it would surely be when the rains were heaviest or
when snow was on the roof, so a midwinter suspension, the
mayor reasoned, would probably catch the building at the fatal
moment. The dire six-week period had not yet arrived. Some
children were in class, but the parents of others had refused
to take a chance. Their six-year-olds stayed at home or had
already started their lifework as shepherds.

Below the hill of Rotondella was Policoro, a township of
good farm land centering on a castle. Much of it was one
estate, one of Italy's many large private properties. The estate
covered twenty-five square miles. It was one of several broad
holdings owned by the same man in various parts of Italy. Six
square miles of the precious Policoro property were kept in
brush as a preserve for the hunting of wild boars. The rest
was divided and subdivided among a hierarchy of tenants,
subtenants, wage hands, and day laborers. The day workers,
with a daily pay of $1.50 and often eight months of jobless-
ness every year, were the most miserable, but even the salaried
hands did poorly. One, who had to fold up shop as a Rotondella electrician, listed his earnings as follows: as base pay,
the equivalent of $195 a year or not quite $4.00 a week; a
grant of 1,014 pounds of wheat a year (worth the equivalent

of $60.00 and far from too much when one realized that the average southern Italian ate nearly two pounds of cheap, filling bread and spaghetti a day); 13 quarters of olive oil a year (worth $10.50 locally); 26 pounds of salt (worth eighteen cents a pound); ten pounds of cheese, as much wood from the boar run as needed for heating and cooking; the use of a free medical dispensary; the loan of a cart once a year to take wood and other gifts to relatives in Rotondella; and time off on Sundays and twenty-two other days a year.

Somehow, out of these rewards, nothing was ever saved.

At the castle I talked to the representative of the owner. He admitted that pressure from the poor and the land-hungry of Rotondella and of dozens of other towns like it was severe.

"It's like a crowded streetcar," he said. "Everybody's uncomfortable—even those who are sitting down."

The remark, I thought, could be applied to all of still relatively prosperous mid-twentieth century Europe and to America and to the rest of the West. Whether it was the well to do inside Italy, or Europe in its relations with the awakening ex-colonial nations, or the United States in the face of the no longer very remote needs of the Asiatics, Africans, and even South Americans, it was a case of the "seated" being "uncomfortable" on the "streetcar" of the globe.

IV

ITALY REVIVING:
WATER FOR SUMMONTE

Italy belonged under the Western "umbrella" as a valued member of the family, but that did not mean that she had no grave weaknesses and no important disagreements with the United States. Like the rest of Europe, she was calling on Washington for leadership, but there was nothing uncritical in the way she was following. The White House and Congress were challenged to show wisdom. Implied was the warning that the alliance of free nations could collapse to the common ruin.

My jeep was surrounded hostilely several times in the early 1946 days by semi-Fascist mobs demonstrating against the Allied decision to strip Italy of her colonies. By expelling them from the dependent areas, Italians argued, the British and others in the West were paving the way for their own eviction. Gradually another idea evolved, that Italy could exploit her colony-free position to establish trading ties with the new free countries, especially in the Arab world of the Mediterranean from Morocco through Egypt into the Middle East.

It was a tricky theory, for it risked a clash with the French, who were being buffeted by Bourguiba in Tunis, by Mohammed V in Morocco, and by other North African enemies far more unreasonable than those two relatively moderate men. It involved the danger of conflicts with the United States and Britain in the Middle East. Frustration marked much of Italy's policy in the mid-fifties as the result of an effort to reconcile a pro-Arab and a pro-Western policy.

Also weakening Italy was the illusory attraction of the Red East. Communism fronted on the country at Trieste. For years, I was to learn later as a correspondent in Moscow, in 1958, the Kremlin coveted the hope that Italy, with its one third pro-communist electorate, would fall to Soviet communism. In 1958 the hope was still bright in Moscow.

Even militarily I wondered about Italy when I talked one day to an officer on maneuvers opposite the Yugoslav border. It was a half decade after the war, Italy was now a member of the North Atlantic Treaty Organization (NATO), and the revolt of the nationalistic Communists of Yugoslavia against Kremlin control had somewhat reassured the West. The Italians had invited me to watch the maneuvers of one of their new NATO-assigned divisions.

"What do you think?" the public-relations officer asked me after the maneuvers.

"Well, of course there are still shortages in communications and in quite a few other items," I answered.

"Ah, yes," the officer astonished me. "But you must judge us by what we are up against. We are quite able to face the Yugoslavs!"

The officer was thinking in terms of a scrap with NATO's American-aided half-ally, Yugoslavia. The fact that Italy's NATO units would be called on in the event of a war with Russia to plug the gap below Switzerland and to prevent the invasion of southern France seemed to miss his mind. It was one of several signs making it impossible not to wonder whether Europe still had a "soft underbelly," as anti-Axis strategists put it during World War II. It was also a sign that the old European habit of thinking in small national terms, forgetting more vital common continental and Western interests, unfortunately was still alive.

My first realization of how much less than complete approval Italians had for the American liberator was on a visit in 1946 to the ruins of Marino, in the Alban Hills east of Rome. Marino had been a German observation point during the Battle of Anzio, when Allied troops leapfrogged from Naples to the outskirts of the capital. It was known locally as the village where wine flowed like water: once a year wine was pumped into the local fountain and all Rome was welcome to come with paper cups to catch some. The festival often ended with celebrants punching slashed fists through the windows of streetcars, but it was always gay.

"Ah, yes, you Americans!" the ragged town philosopher told me with a malicious twinkle in his eye. "You liberated us and everyone appreciates it. But it does remind us just a bit about the poor man who had a devil! Two monks tried to help him. They beat him with rocks until the imp finally left him, but the poor man by that time was nearly dead. He lay on the ground without making a sound. The monks were indignant. 'Aren't you going to thank us?' they demanded. The beaten man finally managed to answer: 'Yes, thank you! But I only wish you could have picked an easier way!' "

The storyteller had been a Fascist or at least a collaborator. The saying then in Rome was that Italy, with her population of nearly fifty million, was really a country of 100,000,000—50,000,000 who were Fascists and 50,000,000 who *never* were Fascists. Certainly few proclaimed openly that they had been Black Shirts, just as few had fought Mussolini during the latter's late years in power. The Marino philosopher admitted that fascism had been a "devil"; but he thought it proper that non-Italians perform the exorcism gently! In addition to the ironic attitude toward the United States, there was either not a very strong anti-fascism or a disturbingly weak willingness to let others do freedom's common chore. Probably there was a bit of both.

A printer in Bari, in southern Italy, indicated a similarly tolerant attitude toward fascism. He told me he had never known that the Black Shirt regime was much of a dictatorship until he heard it after it was over. "If it was, it was a sort of attar-of-roses dictatorship," he said. He was not one of the 10 per cent of Italians voting for the neo-Fascists and their allies. He backed Alcide De Gasperi's Christian Democrats, a Catholic moderate reform group and the main force opposing communism in Italy. What the printer hoped was that all "parties of order," including the neo-Fascists, would cooperate against the Communist threat. With the printer's softness to fascism, De Gasperi, however, disagreed. De Gasperi, as premier during most of Italy's first postwar decade, fought both Communists and Fascists, thus stripping the Communists of their best implicit argument: "All anti-Communists are Fascists."

The trace of acidity in a great deal of Italian thinking about the United States was also evident in comments by two of the octogenarians who were prominent in Rome's political life just after the war. Both had been premiers before fascism. With a whole generation of political leaders outside the pale in democratic postwar Italy, the two had been called back in advanced old age as members of Parliament and potential premiers. One was Francesco Xaverio Nitti, and the other Vittorio Emanuele Orlando.

"Do you want to know the two Italians who did the most to hurt their country?" Nitti asked his fellow deputies one day. "Machiavelli and Columbus! Machiavelli because he gave us the reputation of men who couldn't be trusted; Columbus because he shifted the economic center of gravity from where we are in the Mediterranean to somewhere out in the Atlantic!"

There was more than a grain of resentment in the jest, but however much fellow Italians may have sometimes agreed with Nitti, Columbus remained a great hero in Italy, a man in whom all Italians gloried.

I called one day on the short, stocky Nitti in his middle-class Rome apartment. Face to face with an American he was amiable enough. The flat was up several flights; it was cluttered and unpretentious. The politicians of democratic Italy, on whom the West depended for so much, were not rich men.

Orlando, too, received me at his small villa in central Rome for an interview on his ninetieth birthday. As Italy's premier he had negotiated the Versailles Treaty with Woodrow Wilson of the United States; Georges Clemenceau, "the Tiger of France"; and Lloyd George of Britain, all of them part of that already seemingly distant history to which so much of both the good and the bad of the past third of a century could be traced. In the shaping of the post-World War I peace treaty, Orlando had taken a nationalistic stand. He had clashed with the idealistic American president's defense of the self-determination of peoples and opposition to remaking the map of Europe to pay off winners and to punish losers. Orlando had demanded and obtained sizeable chunks of Austria. The years had not modified his view. "I still think your president was wrong; I think I was right," the old Italian told me.

The Italian attitude toward post-World War II American leadership was expressed also by an aide of one of the Italian premiers of the fifties. We were talking about the repeated illnesses of President Eisenhower, who was then campaigning for re-election. Before the war Italian newspapers had never published anything about American presidential campaigns until the final two or three weeks, but in 1956 every newspaper started early to run many columns on the coming election. It was plain that by now the Italians conceded that the President of the United States was head of the West.

"We feel like people on a train," the Italian official told me. "We know almost everything depends on the good health of the man in the locomotive. We just hope he *is* well!"

The attitude toward the United States was more reserved than I liked, but the essential thing was that Italy was finding within herself the force to recover. Slowly a democratic republic with a strengthening economy took form. Italy turned her back on the fascism minimized by the Bari printer and even on the monarchy of the thousand-year-old Savoy dynasty, the oldest reigning family in Europe.

During my first weeks in Italy I had seen the gradual disappearance of the last symbols of Mussolini's totalitarianism.

One of my first trips in 1946 was to see Mussolini's widow. I found her in her exile in a bomb-shattered building on the island of Ischia in the Bay of Naples. She was feeding chickens. I agreed not to quote her on politics and ended by not quoting her at all. It seemed to me that almost anything the dictator's widow had to say in those weeks of feverish political struggle in newly-liberated Italy was "political." I came away convinced that the scantily educated peasant wife of the inventor of fascism never had been sure what her husband's strange new theory was. I left also with the impression that Signora Mussolini took the loyal and wifely view, even after fascism's lost war, that the fact that newspapers didn't seem able to publish without writing about her husband and his ideology showed that, after all, the "Duce," the "Leader," had had something in that head of his! It was humbly little to say, but in postwar Italy little better ever was said for repudiated fascism.

On another assignment as part of closing the door on Italy's Black Shirt past, I visited the dictator's looted grave on the first anniversary of his death. Presumably Fascists had taken the body to assure it greater honor than it was getting in an unmarked plot in a Milan cemetery. The piercing odor of death, which I remembered from the Pacific, clung to the shallow pit. The dictator had been buried only two feet deep. His coffin lid lay at one side. Only six nails and two screws had fastened the cheap wooden box. A last point struck me as I turned away. The grave was short. Fascism's dictator had been a tiny man.

For the grim anniversary I went also to Dongo, the town where Mussolini had been captured. I had expected festivities, but found the village almost in mourning. The only observance, the mayor said, had been a mass of thanksgiving that no one in the town had been killed as the villagers stopped the fleeing Mussolini and his companions. The people of Dongo had captured the dictator by accident. They were incensed against the Fascists for pushing live coals into the feet and twisting chains on the wrists of local youths accused, sometimes incorrectly, of anti-Fascism. (By the account of the pious villagers, many of them had been neither Fascist nor anti-fascist.) They had decided in retaliation to stop "a column of Fascists" about which they had been telephoned from farther south on Lake Como. They had been startled but satisfied to catch the Duce himself—it was a pure accident. All agreed that the arch-Fascist should have a fair trial, but it had not gone that way. Tough communist underground fighters had come into the town five hours after the capture of the Duce and had taken him, assuring the Dongo people that the government leader was in authoritative and trustworthy hands. Mussolini's prompt assassination had offended Dongo's sense of justice as much as the Black Shirt tortures had.

A few miles down the lake two black painted crosses, one slightly larger than the other, on newly-named "Liberty and Justice Street," marked where the dictator and Claretta Petacci were slain. There were no names, no explanatory tablet. The Italian conscience was not exulting over the end of the number-one Fascist.

I saw the second stage in the creation of the Italian democratic republic from closer at hand. Within four months of my arrival I covered one of postwar Europe's first big choices: whether to preserve or discard the Italian monarchy.

The royalists had one main argument. To try a republic would be a "jump in the dark." It was not a very progressive or inspiring slogan, but in an exhausted, frightened country it had an effect.

A month before the June 1946 referendum on the question of monarchical versus republican government, short, unpopular King Vittorio Emanuele abdicated in favor of his taller, handsomer son, Umberto. It was a shrewd move. The Communists, as the main backers of the republic, had concentrated their attack on the old monarch. But the Reds proved equal to the shift. Umberto, they jeered, would be merely "king of the May."

They proved right.

It was largely a battle of slogans and the Communists proved clever at it. Every time the Monarchists wrote on the walls *Evviva il re* ("long live the king") the Communists added an "o" to make it *reo* ("the renegade") or a few more letters to change it to *repubblica* ("republic").

The best rallying cry, though, was the simplest: *pane*

("bread"). The Communists said simply that they were in favor of "pane" and against the "re." For many, amid Italy's wreckage, that was enough.

Umberto, in an appeal to his troubled people's higher loyalties, invited half of the College of Cardinals of the Catholic Church to a reception at the vast Quirinal Palace, several blocks square. Publicity was essential, and so a few of us of the press were asked, too. The American Air Force party paled into insignificance as the red-robed cardinals swept past six-and-a-half foot Royal Guards, the latter in horsetail helmets and shiny boots, and then past tapestried walls and under ornately carved ceilings into mirrored halls in which dinner was served. Soviet Ambassador Mikhail Kostylev was seated beside the American envoy, Alexander Kirk, and the Portuguese patriarch Emannuel Cerejeira. It was all a mute appeal to the people of Italy to believe that their new king was accepted by all: by the Church from which the royal family of Savoy had captured the Quirinal Palace (it had been a papal summer residence before the overthrow of the independent Papal States in 1870, and the pope's crown and keys still looked down from ceiling decorations), by the Soviets, by the Americans.

If fancy parties had been enough to settle affairs of state in the Europe of a century or two earlier, it was soon apparent that they were no longer adequate in post-World War II, Italy. This was the last party the Savoy family was ever to give in Rome.

An aide of the king invited a few American correspondents to a private supper. If the American press said the king was winning it might swing a few votes.

"You know how it is in Italy," the aide explained frankly. "People like to be with the winner. After it's over, even if the king just barely gets through, everybody will say after a few days that he was always with the monarchy!"

The aide had lived in America.

"I keep telling the king," he said, "that he needs a Jim

Farley, drum majorettes, and people with placards shouting
'On to the Quirinal!' But the king keeps saying that I've been
in the States too long."

No campaign manager of the sort Franklin D. Roosevelt
had had in James A. Farley was ever appointed, and no bare-
kneed, teen-aged girl band leaders showed up, but trumped-
up demonstrations for the king soon were organized. I watched
the demonstrations from both outside and inside Umberto's
palace. Outside ragged youths waved royal flags from a lamp-
post.

"I was offered the same job for a few hundred lire," a tat-
tered young man beside me said, "but I was afraid I'd get hit
by rocks."

Inside the palace I watched as a line of men greeted their
king. Every second or third one followed the handshake by
appealing to Umberto for a handout. With dignity the bald
young monarch of May asked a properly courtly assistant to
take the petitioner's name and other details. At a window
stood the blond eleven-year-old *Principino,* the "Little Prince,"
who was next in line for the throne and in whose favor Umberto reportedly would abdicate if that seemed useful. No one
could say that the Principino had been mixed up with Mussolini. The little boy's eyes opened wide as a royalist soldier
kissed his more-or-less clean hand. The soldier wandered off
and the Principino climbed on a radiator to stare down at the
pro-royal demonstrators. I noticed that the radiator needed
paint. Even the king could not keep up all things.

For every Royalist demonstration the Communists rounded
up another twice as large and, even subtler and worse, kept
the huge throngs of Rome's most wretched citizens in such
submissive, quiet lines that the terrified friends of "order,"
the frightened middle class, began to believe that there would
be more calm and discipline under communism, or at least
less violence than they had dreaded. A new slogan circulated.
If communism came it would be of a gentle Mediterranean
kind, nothing like the fierce, atheistic Marxism of Russia.

The surprise was that the monarchy lost by so little. It was eased out by a margin of a few percentage points.

An institution had vanished. For a while it was a question whether the Communist-sought death of the monarchy meant progress or retrogression. Perhaps it was a good step forward toward equality and self-rule, but, on the other hand, in the first critical postwar months it meant that a prop had been removed from under the tired continental structure. Riots started. I watched a mob one day break sewer plates into murderous missiles, and defeat successive waves of police, first patrolmen on foot, then police on horseback, next police in tanks, and finally rifle-armed officers in trucks. The crowd fled before each attack and then drifted back, taking advantage of the fact that the ill-equipped post-liberation police had no tear gas or fire hoses and were far more reluctant to shoot into crowds than the Europeans of Morocco would be. Fifty were injured, many of them policemen, before the throng sacked a large part of Prime Minister De Gasperi's building and then went home for lunch. Nothing but mealtime had been able to stop them. That afternoon rolls of barbed wire and trucks parked sidewise as barricades ensured that the rioters could not return.

Italy seemed as much on a catastrophic brink as the cracked schoolroom of Rotondella, but the country at least did not go over the edge. The fact that the old nation could survive so close a call in 1946 gave me hope that it would be able to resist again if a new crisis beset the West.

Meanwhile the building of a republic got under way. As a reporter I watched that, too.

I was present for the impromptu ceremony in which Italy's first full-term president was notified officially of his election. As in France, the election was by the two houses of Parliament rather than by universal suffrage. A few of us dashed from the voting in Parliament to the designee's villa on the edge of Rome. Police sealed the entrance as security proper for a chief of state was organized, but by then a half-dozen of us of the press had slipped inside. The new president, Luigi Einaudi, a university economics professor, welcomed us into his book-lined home. He had already heard the news by radio.

"I've always been a man of few words," he told us. "I'll be one of even fewer now!" The president of Italy, as in France, had few powers. The premier and Parliament held most of them.

The delegation from the legislature arrived. They were all smiles until the president-designate told them there was a difficulty. He pointed to his informally cut black suit.

"All I've got is this! The rest of my clothes are up at my place in the north."

It seemed for a moment that the lack of the right suit might change presidential history, but the republic's agents were equal to it.

"It's all right," the deputies said. "It's in keeping with the times."

The new chief of state was sworn in next day in his dark, informal, everyday suit.

Two groups especially fascinated me as I tried to foresee the future of Italy. They were the strangely contradictory "Catholic Communists" and the Italo-American emigrants. The first particularly interested me because of what they suggested about the philosophical competition between East and West going on inside so many minds; the latter because of what they revealed about national capabilities frustrated inside Italy's cramped borders.

One of the first Catholic Communists I met was a share cropper in the valley of Chianti, between Siena and Florence, the home of Italy's best-known red wine. The Communists had succeeded in the valley. The Reds had much to work on: not only such poverty as made it impossible for a young man to treat a girl even to a soft drink or a movie, but also an old anti-clerical tradition going back to the papal rule of the early 1800's. In the Papal States prior to 1870 taxes had been collected and wrongdoers jailed in the name of the Pope, so that there were many who were on the one hand believers and Catholics, but on the other hand were opposed to the Church in politics.

The share cropper of Chianti kept his cattle in a stable in the first floor of his house, while a throng of parents, siblings, and in-laws lived on the second floor. The women were kept busy carrying water from a spring one hundred and fifty feet away. With shoes at a prohibitive $14.00 a pair, the farmer worked barefoot. The family went to bed with the sun except on rare occasions when they stayed up by the light of olive-oil lamps. The farmer's ambition was to get a bicycle. He was active in civic affairs, managing the local communist cell and carrying the statue of the Madonna in parish processions.

"Don't you know the Pope has said you can't be both a Catholic and a Communist?" I asked.

"Ah, yes," the farmer answered, "but that's where the Pope is wrong."

The ideological "iron curtain" ran through the peasant's mind.

Which side was winning? To the extent that the farmer was religious, and I was convinced that he was so, the Italian bulwark was holding against the tide running from Moscow. But there was no ground for complacency, as the Pope in his role as patriarch of Italy was first to realize. Unquestioning acceptance of the Pope's leadership had been broken.

I saw the Catholic Communists again in three other areas: in Grassina, near Florence, and in Sezze Romano, south of Rome, in both of which towns large communist casts presented elaborate Passion plays; and in Genzano, also near Rome, where the heavily communist village decorated its streets with ingenious pictures made of flower petals to be trod by the priest in the annual procession of the Eucharist.

At Grassina, I had heard, the townspeople donned their costumes as ancient Roman soldiers and biblical figures in the schoolhouse. I asked a youth the way to it. I was obviously a foreigner; perhaps that explained his answer.

"The schoolhouse? You mean the Party school? It's in there to the left."

It was for a Russian rather than an American that the boy had evidently taken me. The Grassina "Party" school was the latest in a chain of instruction centers the Communist party had just opened throughout Italy.

At the other schoolhouse, the one for general instruction, hundreds of villagers milled about as they buckled on facsimiles of ancient uniforms, wrapped themselves in sheetlike togas, or prepared Italian Army anti-aircraft searchlights which would illumine the hillside stage. Twenty-four-year-old Novello Righi, a delicatessen operator, would be suspended for thirty minutes half-nude on a cross in a renewal of the Crucifixion scene.

The enactment of the drama had been a tradition in Grassina for three centuries, but it had been suspended during the recent postwar period until Vasco Petrioli, the carpenter who was Grassina's communist mayor, revived it.

"If we Communists hadn't taken the initiative someone else would have," Mr. Petrioli told me with the disarming frankness characteristic of many of the lower echelon workers in the army of Italian Reds. "It's a grave error to be against what the people so deeply feel."

Similar was Sezze Romano. The Passion play there was an ambitious one, taking in many scenes from the Old Testament as well as many from the New. Sezze was so poor that the milkmaid brought her goat to the customers and drew as many cupfuls as they wanted on the spot. A large share of the 8,000 actors were Communists. Notable was Moses, a patriarchal share cropper, so well known in his Passion-play role that he had little use for his real name, Carlo Vaiardi. "Moses" was got up to look like the long-haired, strong-muscled statue of the prophet which Michelangelo had carved for the Church of St. Peter in Chains in Rome.

"We're not in the Party for ideological reasons; we're Communists for motives of social welfare," "Moses" explained as we chatted on his cliff-edge doorstep. Below us lay a fine view of the Pontine Marshes, the draining of which was one of

Mussolini's most constructive works. Beyond them stretched the sea. The reclaiming of the marshes had given Italy additional farming areas, but not enough to help the many such as Vaiardi who were still starved for land. In other towns the panoramic view that Vaiardi enjoyed might have been prized, but here, with an unfenced narrow walk as the only protection against the abyss, and with the underpinnings uncertain, it was a site for a poor man's home.

"We're Catholics," "Moses" added. "If you Americans do well by us, we'll be for you."

Mayor Italo Ficacci, of Sezze, also a Communist, agreed with his opposite number in Grassina. The people, he said, "felt" the Passion play and so it had to be tolerated.

At the old town of Genzano on the Via Appia the ceremony of the *Infiorata*—literally "enflowering"—had been traditional since the late eighteenth century. Its beginnings were contemporary with those of the American Republic. Each year on the occasion of the Feast of Corpus Domini (the Body of the Lord) it was village tradition to scour the hillsides for tons of daisies, roses, poppies, carnations, grape mash, and pine scrapings with which to make mounds of pure color: whites, pinks, reds, blacks, and a dozen others. With these, kept fresh overnight in the deep, cool wine cellars, young men holding Party cards would create startlingly precise replicas of great masterpieces of art. Over these floral designs, rather than over the usual manure-littered cobbles, the priest walked with the Eucharist for an open-air ceremony of Benediction.

In the first postwar years I noticed that Genzano's Catholic Communists picked equivocal biblical scenes: Judas with the noose of his hanging, St. Paul with a sword, violent episodes easily adapted to the ferocious communist view of the world. A decade later the Red capitulation was complete. Only the gentlest Christian scenes were portrayed: Correggio's "Holy Night" (depicting the birth of Christ); Beato Angelico's "Annunciation to Mary," and the centuries-old reputed miracle worker of the Eternal City, "Mary, Salvation of Rome."

I questioned Umberto Baldazzi, chairman of the Infiorata

and special representative of Genzano's communist mayor Er-
cole De Santis. "Aren't you afraid—" I began.

"I fear nothing!" interrupted Signor Baldazzi. "I was a
Partisan!"[1]

I rephrased the question.

"Isn't there a contradiction here—between Catholicism and
communism?"

If he had needed it, Baldazzi by now had had time to think.

"We are all of the Catholic faith," he said. "The mayor, too!
We rise above certain things. We don't mix politics with the
Infiorata!"

From both the American and the Vatican points of view it
was deplorable that so many religious people should support
communism, but it was encouraging, at least, that the hardships in postwar Italy and the anti-clerical traditions of the
former Papal States had failed to push the Catholic Communists all the way. Ancient civil traditions had erected a
barrier against the full acceptance of the violent Moscow
creed. Even more heartening was the fact that most of the
poor peasants who were confronted with the same Catholic-
Communist dilemma did not attempt the Genzano, Grassina,
or Sezze compromise but renounced communism altogether.

While the Catholic Communists were intriguing me for
what they revealed about the things going on in Italian minds,
the Italo-Americans impressed me for what their stories had to
tell about the old country's human potentialities.

In the United States, that land of opportunity, many Italo-
Americans had made good. Their success was so great that
when I arrived in Italy in early 1946 an odd problem beset the
Allied Military Government. The army found that it was often
better to assign a non-Italo-American to rule Italians, even if
he spoke only a few broken words of their tongue, rather than
a man of Italian origin who could rattle off the language
fluently. The reason was that the great majority of Italo-
American officers had come from such miserably poor southern
Italian families that the dialect they spoke horrified the cul-

---

[1] A World War II underground fighter.

tured Romans, Florentines, or Neapolitans they were assigned
to govern. At least a non-Italo-American with a newly learned
vocabulary spoke a broken Italian of good accent. It was a
source of humiliation for many of the Italo-Americans, but
at the same time it indicated how far they had come in one
generation: from serfs of princely families to command over
their old masters.

Correct Italian was "the tongue of the Tuscans in the
mouth of the Romans," the language as it was spoken in Florence and Siena, in the Chianti Valley area, with a few correc-
tions applied by the people of the Italian capital. It was not
the all-but-unintelligible dialects of Sicily, Lucania, or a dozen
other areas. The language traced back to Dante in the Middle
Ages but the country had stayed fractured into so many separate principalities until the mid-1800's that the schools never
had succeeded in putting "good Italian" on everyone's tongue.

To my humiliation Mary, my wife, who had good French
from two years' study in Paris, learned Italian in six weeks,
studying a book and later practicing on good-natured table
companions on the liner coming to Italy. I had no chance to
show off the vocabulary of sixteen words I had acquired in my
first two months before Mary started a conversation with our
moving-van driver that lasted the four hours to Rome. It was
two years before I could do as well.

But there was comfort for me in an episode in Sardinia.
There snatches of pure Latin, such as *est bonus* for "he is
good," instead of the Italian *è buono,* are still spoken. A Sar-
dinian girl of eighteen broke off a conversation with us because, she confessed, "You'll laugh at me: I really don't know
how to speak Italian; we studied it at school but my mother
doesn't know any and we've never used it at home." It was a
rare experience to tell a young Italian lady to speak freely,
that her command of her country's language was good enough!

All through Italy, especially in the south, Mary and I met
self-styled "Americans," men such as Pogerola's Mr. Amendola,
who had made the mistake of returning to their impoverished
though beautiful homeland. All showed the same pride in

having been residents of the rich and powerful States. The most spectacular was an old man Mary met on a trip to Sulmona, birthplace of the Latin author Ovid, on the Apennine ridge east of Rome. He insisted that she visit his family for a few moments to see his Sunday suit. The buttons were American nickels and dimes from 1910 or earlier, some of them coins Mary had never seen before. The traveler had brought them back a half-century earlier.

The humble and often pitiful former Americans were in contrast to those who had become citizens of the United States and who returned merely for short visits. Scores of them could tell tales of spectacular achievement. Perhaps the most striking single illustration of the capacities not only of Italians, but specifically of the southern Italians, was provided by the 1951 mayoralty election in New York City. Of the four candidates running for mayor of New York, three were natives of southern Italy: Angelo Corsi, American federal immigration commissioner and a close aide of Governor Thomas E. Dewey of New York; Justice Ferdinand Pecora, who had won a reputation for rooting out and prosecuting civic scandal; and Vincent Impelliteri—"Impy" for short to the New York tabloids—a lawyer who had captured the popular imagination by rebelling against the New York Democratic machine of Tammany Hall. (The fourth candidate, incidentally, was also born in Europe; he was Paul Moss, a native of Russia.)

As the correspondent of a New York newspaper, I decided during the election campaign to visit the native towns of each of the three Italian-American candidates. All of them proved to be reasonable facsimiles of Abraham Lincoln's log-cabin community in the sense that each bolstered the old American democratic belief that society's humblest stratum could produce her great leaders.

Mr. Corsi's home town was Capestrano in the Apennines, not far from where Mary had met the man who wore nickels and dimes as buttons. When I visited it in 1951 Capestrano still remained much as it had when the child emigrant Angelo Corsi had left it. A controversy over whether to pave the main street had just been won by the donkey-owning opposition. They wanted the old cobblestones retained so that their animals would not slip on the steeply slanted village street.

A plaque on the walls of the local castle showed where Angelo had got his flair for politics. It proclaimed the virtues of "Liberty, Justice, Democracy." It had been put there by Angelo's father, a newspaper editor who had fought fifty years ahead of his time for an Italian republic, and had had to flee into political exile in Switzerland where he raised his dramatically named children, Angelo (the angel), Liberta (Liberty), Elvezia (Switzerland), and Garibaldi, named for the heroic soldier who united and helped modernize nineteenth-century Italy. The elder Mr. Corsi's story had ended when at thirty-three he dropped dead of a heart attack after election to Parliament had permitted him to return to Capestrano. His fatherless children had emigrated to America.

Justice Pecora's birthplace was in Nicosia, Sicily, a town still dominated by the cathedral which had been six centuries old when the candidate's shoemaker father had emigrated to the States. The village editor reminded me that the judge was not the only famous son of emigrants from Nicosia. He pointed to a third-floor balcony where laundry hung over a rail. That, he said, was the birthplace of Vincent Riggio, the president of the fabulous American Tobacco Company.

A young man of the village well to do showed me around. The tragedy of his kind, he said, was that his parents and grandparents had owned enough land in Nicosia so that they had not joined the indigent in their desperate flight westward. In a half-century the roles had been reversed: the "rich" of Nicosia were the poor now when emigrants returned to visit.

It was the native of the third southern Italian village who won the election in New York: "Impy" Impelliteri. I accompanied him on his triumphal trip back to the little village of Isnello a year later, on the fiftieth anniversary of his departure. He had been carried out of the village at the age of one and never had been back.

Isnello gave the mayor of New York a reception worthy of

a Roman conqueror. A sign in what the village hoped was English stretched from side to side across the main road: "Welcome to your nice country!" In Italian the word *paese* means both "home town" and "nation." Whoever had figured out the sign from a dictionary had picked the wrong word.

The mayor was shown the stone ring in which his mother had cooked on the floor of a soot-stained room. The apartment was rented now to a share cropper for $5.00 a year. The number-one New Yorker heard mass in the church, built in 1490, where he had been baptized. At the city hall he saw the register in which it was recorded that two illiterates, Isodoro Curcio and Tomaso Cicero, had dropped by on January 4, 1900, to report his birth as the first Isnello baby of the new century. He wept as village orphans sang for him. His bodyguard, Lieutenant Mauro Contrastano, well trained in the importance of "firsts" to newspapermen, turned to us.

"It's the first time I've seen the boss cry," he said.

The mayor struggled through a speech in Italian which engineers of the sophisticated Italian national radio network recorded and preserved as a collector's item. There were many words philologists had thought had long since vanished from the Italian memory, old phrases which had clung to the isolated Isnello valley of a half-century earlier. The mayor, not a rich man by American standards, made a gift of $2,400 for "a major public work" and $800 for the cloistered convent in which lived his sole relative, a cheery nun in her sixties. Isnello's young mayor, Giuseppe Monteleone, chose the most desirable "work"—a public shower. Not more than a dozen in town had regular bathtubs.

As the mayor of New York left Isnello, conversation centered on what he would have accomplished if he had lived on in the town. Some thought he would have been a shoemaker, as the father of the Sicilian-born candidate had been. Thirty-five-year-old Mayor Monteleone thought his New York opposite number might by then have been a retired *carabiniere* sergeant, with an income of sixty cents a week. None thought he could have done better than that had he stayed in his native country.

Another who received a triumphal welcome in Italy was Mr. Impelliteri's nemesis at Tammany Hall, Carmine G. De Sapio. He had been born in New York, but in 1958, as boss of Tammany, he journeyed to Monteforte Irpino, his father's place of birth.

The village did not understand quite who Mr. De Sapio was, and even the relatively well-informed newspapermen listened attentively as I explained that he was a "kingmaker," a man who had a major say in picking candidates for mayor of New York City, governor of New York State, and even president of the United States. One Italian reporter painfully scribbled down the word "kingmaker" in English, deciding that it was best to describe the Tammany boss that way, without even translating the word into Italian.

The villagers bombarded Mr. De Sapio with flower petals and let their imaginations run wild as to the possible civic improvements he might bestow. The uninstructed, said the village priest, would probably want Mr. De Sapio to pave the square in front of the church or perhaps to tack up the seventeenth-century ceiling painting which was dangling limply from the church vault. He, instead, the priest said, wanted a sawmill so that the scantily employed townspeople could process the local furniture-grade chestnut logs before shipping them out.

"Wrong," another town leader, the sergeant of carabinieri, objected. Mr. De Sapio, he said, should put in sewers now that the national government had promised the first adequate water supply.

The Tammany man, another who was not rich by American standards, gave $1,000 to the orphanage, school, and hospital.

One of the emigrants of whom I saw the most in the course of his repeated trips back to Italy was Tony Cucolo, who had left Summonte, behind Vesuvius, when he was not yet in his teens. He had started in Connecticut as a builder of curbstones, had talked himself into bank credit, and had managed, after some twenty years, to secure one of the biggest road-building contracts New York State had ever awarded, the construction of the cutoff for the Storm King Highway on the sheer cliffs above the United States Military Academy at West Point.

Tony Cucolo's energy and imagination were without limit. He had stared down at the Military Academy, had dreamed that his sons should study there, and had managed to put both of them through it. Each had become an American Army officer, a member of the Academy-trained elite. In Suffern, New York, a handsome residential area north of New York City, Tony had assisted in organizing a community self-help project.

Then Tony thought of Summonte. To go back in style he hired a Cadillac. His wife, another Summonte native, came back with him. Neither could wait as they drove toward the village. Mrs. Cucolo especially remembered the great flight of stairs leading up to the village church. Tony knew he would be welcome. He had been sending back packages of spaghetti for every family in town for several Christmases.

In Summonte the Cucolos were stunned. The "great flight of stairs" before the church was only three steps high. It was all Tony could do to find a space to park his enormous automobile. Mrs. Cucolo washed up. Then she was pink with embarrassment. She had used up days of rations of water for all purposes, drinking and cooking included. Summonte had only three quarts of water per person per day, and to get even that much, women went out in the middle of the night to stand at the village's one trickle. All of the laundry for the entire community was washed in the same three tubs, the first for rinsing, the last for scrubbing. The end tub, as one drained into the other, was as opaque as mud. Even the rinse tub would soil anything it touched.

Tony, who had helped Suffern, resolved to aid Summonte.

"Why don't you run a pipe through the mountain to the brook on the other side of the hill?" he asked.

It would be too expensive, he was told.

"Well, why not a pump?"

The answer was the same.

"Well, then, why not get the Marshall Plan to do it?"

The American aid plan was just beginning. The villagers smiled at Tony's innocence. No one in Summonte could get in to see a Cabinet minister in Rome. No one could even see a regional engineer in nearby Avellino, the first step on the road to the capital.

Among those in Rome at the moment whom Tony knew was J. P. McEvoy, a writer for *Reader's Digest*. McEvoy was acquainted with George Washington Baker, head of the Marshall Plan. Mr. Baker, of course, had easy access to the right Cabinet minister. The minister could not resist Tony's sales talk: "All we need is $100,000. You give me your contracts and I'll trim all we need out of other projects: there's always $100,000 worth of fat on anything this big."

The minister's pride and his sense of sportsmanship were touched. Summonte got a pump.

I was there with Tony when the first spout of water from the new pump drenched half-a-dozen villagers who stood too close to it. The water leaped twenty feet into the air, falling back on the dry ground as if water were something so common it could be flung away. Villagers watched, blank-faced, from the terrace of the $10,000, six-bed hospital Tony and his friends in Suffern had built as their own contribution to the village. A bust of Tony was unveiled near where he had struggled to park the Cadillac. It was a new chapter both in the story of Summonte and in that of open-armed America, Tony told the poorly comprehending crowd as emotion carried him away. It was a chapter, too, Tony said, in his own life, in that of a "Summonte boy who—think of it!—had risen to break bread with President Eisenhower."

The people of Summonte still did not seem to grasp it all, but they applauded for the water.

There was a reason why they could not understand. It was because the American dream had faded from village aspirations since the time, after World War I, when the United States had closed its doors against most Italian emigrants. It was estimated in 1946 that 10,000,000 Italians, a fifth of the population, needed to leave the country, but the Italian quota for immigration into America was only 5,200 a year. At this rate, for the United States to take all the Italians who need to emigrate, would require two thousand years, the equivalent of the length of the Christian era. Summonte may well have had a few other potential Tonys but it was no longer likely that they would ever get to America.

What they could do was to turn the same talents to Italy's service. It would not be easy in a land of such scant opportunity, but my trust in Italy rested on the knowledge that great human potentialities were there.

The Italy with which I was by then acquainted was many things. It was the home of the people of Summonte who were almost without water until the experienced returned emigrant told them how to get it.

It was the nation of the De Sapios' Monteforte Irpino, with dream castles in air built above the shoulders of a shrewd and successful son of an emigrant whose role overseas no one in the village could understand.

It was the land of Pogerola and Guadagnolo; of the Catholic Communists who thought they knew "where the Pope was wrong"; of postwar thieves; of economy-ravaging monopolies and socialization measures; of persisting military weakness; and of lurking, communist-encouraged neutralism.

But it was also the country of *pazienza* and *coraggio;* of brave reformers such as the ascetic Premier De Gasperi; of those who managed to hold back the cynical and despairing communist tide despite their own misery; of those whose sons had proved their talent when opportunity offered.

When in 1952 I was transferred to France for three years as my paper's bureau chief there, I knew that I left behind me an Italy where twenty centuries of Christian civilization had created a hearth of Western values, an ally whose defense might be difficult but whose preservation was of high concern to America. Italy would need aid, but she would help the helper and would assist herself.

V

FRANCE: WHITE NIGHTS
AND WEARY PREMIERS

We were a family of five as we boarded the train in the re-built Rome railway station in December 1952 to transfer to Paris. Andrew, Rome-born, was not quite three; blond Betsy, five. Bill, the only one with vague memories of life in any country but Italy, was just under ten.

We climbed aboard the train with excitement at the thought of living in Paris, the capital of modern Europe, but we left Italy with regrets.

Italy by then was symbolized for us by the former monastery in which we had just passed our final summer. Though it was only forty miles from the capital, it was in another uni-verse. The monastery was one hour by foot uphill from the nearest road, and was served, if that was the name for it, by a village another hour deeper into the roadless interior.

The memory of our gentle neighbors, so far removed from the twentieth century, stayed with us as we pulled out of the station Paris-bound. We thought of fourteen-year-old Franca who had come to the monastery-villa each morning to carry us fifteen pails of water from the spring. We remembered her mother, Graziu, who used to yearn for winter, when the long nights made much field work impossible and forced her little family to stay together. We recalled many others: the man who brought vegetables on muleback and said that the one thing he would like most was a raincoat; the man with the certificate as an Allied war hero who explained that he had helped escaping American pilots not because of disloyalty to Italy or even because of anti-fascism, but only because he could not bear to turn down young men in need; the priest

who feared that if a road were built to the village it would
"bring in Communists on wheels"; and the ragged shepherd
philosopher who conceded that he possessed a great treasure:
the silence of the mountaintops!

It was into another existence that we stepped in Paris, one
undoubtedly closer to the sad, grim realities of the century.
Italy's peak of greatness had been touched two millenia before, and again four centuries ago, at the time of the Renaissance; but France's moment of greatest brilliance was far
more recent, as we could see through the windows of the taxicab that carried us along the Seine toward a temporary home
at a bend of the Marne in the suburb of Varenne-St. Hilaire.
Along the Marne, with its shimmering lights and colors despite a December overcast, we recognized the mood of the Im-
pressionist paintings of the late nineteenth century.

The little house at Varenne-St. Hilaire was a source at once
of charm and of disillusionment. We had rented it sight unseen in Rome because of the housing shortage of which we
had heard in an Italian joke: one Italian, proud of his country's postwar reconstruction, asked a friend whether he had
noticed building going on in Paris.

"Oh, yes," the other replied. "You mean as you come in on
the train—the two houses on the left side of the track?"

The quip was not quite fair. France had done some rebuilding, but a Maginot-line psychology, the spirit of defense and
security carried into the realm of economics and social welfare, had frozen rents at so low a level that there was little incentive to build any more. Owners were letting houses collapse around the ears of tenants, satisfied that the land at
least would remain to them as an asset.

We squeezed into the snug house with its two bedrooms for
our family of five—the living room provided an extra sleeping
corner—and then set about learning our neighborhood.

The garden inside its six-foot walls was a joy. We understood when we learned that our neighbor was a Sunday
painter. In that tranquil river bend it was easier to think of
tints and forms than to ponder on the Marne's other associa-

tion, the murderous battles fought along it, farther east, in disastrous World War I.

Soap, water, and paint seemed to be needed everywhere and the owner amicably agreed to American ideas for a refurbishing, but the problem of a telephone was insuperable until the café next door agreed to let us use theirs even for incoming calls. Immobility, it seemed, extended not only to World War II frontier defense concepts and frozen rents, but to the installation of telephones as well. Those who had them kept them and those who did not learned that new lines would be needed before new outlets could be added. There were no immediate plans for additions.

The café had a certain hominess but it was never idle. The loyal clientele presented itself for wine on empty stomachs at sunrise and never thinned until the doors were locked late at night. Wine-induced liverishness may have accounted for what we noticed: although our neighbors were far better off than their counterparts in Italy, they were also far more morose. Few smiled. But perhaps the relative rarity of blue skies and sunshine was a factor too. The sun did not come out for our first one hundred days in France, so that I thought Paris was a city of pearl rather than the triumph of pinks, roses, light greens, and infant blues it is when the sun shines from the west across the Seine in the spring.

My wife, Mary, chose on arrival to be loyal to Italian cooking, but a single trip to the stalls of the local open-air market discouraged that. The makings for spaghetti—Parmesan cheese and tomato paste—were not to be had. Men at the market wore berets and inclined toward flaring mustaches. Oysters and Brie cheeses rather than Parmesan were what they wanted to sell. Unwrapped two-foot-long sticks of French bread soon started moving into our little house and our diet went French.

The children, too, adapted. Ten-year-old Bill discovered that boys of his age and younger expected to shake hands on meeting, and presently Bill solemnly was reaching for other unwashed outstretched fists. The children went to local French schools with nothing but English and Italian to help them.

We learned something more about acquiring languages. Bill gave it three days and then reported that he had had enough: "It's impossible, I don't understand a word." He agreed to try a fourth day and then never mentioned the matter again. He was on his way. Five-year-old Betsy made no comment and, for six weeks in class, said not a word. "But," her teacher told us after two months, "fortunately for her she had quite a naughty child beside her. The other child would not keep quiet for an instant. She just talked into your daughter's ear for six weeks." At the end of the one-and-one-half months, Betsy replied to her neighbor; Betsy's French was fluent. Three-year-old Andrew was interpreting for our Breton maid and English-speaking callers within a year.

By the time eighteen months had passed, with Papa last of all, we were freely conversant with French, and the great charms of the French world unfolded more rapidly. It was another universe from Italy but the joys were many: the grandeur of central Paris with the nobility of the former royal palace of the Louvre (a visiting American looked at the stains of generations and asked in a scolding tone: "Why don't they clean it; why don't they sandblast it?"); the thrilling sweep of the broad Champs Elysées culminating with the symbol of French military achievements, the Arc de Triomphe; the museums, the shops, the splendor of regal châteaux now open to the gawking of the armies of citizens who went every week-end to stare at the creations of their native brilliance. Best of all, though sometimes bewildering and frustrating, was the fascination of the French brain, revealed to me as an American journalist in evenings with the topmost leaders of French policy. Premiers of the past and present, cabinet members, agents of the diplomatic service, and key figures in the bureaucracy, all of them anxious to tell their story to "American public opinion," a critical factor because of its influence on cash grants and Washington policy in general. For all their memories of eighteenth- and nineteenth-century glory symbolized by the shrine to Napoleon at the Invalides in central Paris, the French of the mid-twentieth century knew that the friendship of the United States was essential if their country was not to step down to playing a smaller world role than in centuries.

The first days in Paris led me into the pleasant mysteries of cuisine, wines, and speech. In the latter sphere I found a war under way against things American, despite all the rest of French dependence on Washington. Snobs were dragging Americanisms into the language much as some in the United States had sprinkled their vocabularies with Gallicisms a generation earlier. The purists were in revolt, but it was clear from signs along streets, from conversation, and especially in newspapers, that English had come to the French language and was there to stay.

Not all the snatches of English were being used correctly, nor were all of them flattering. *Le striptease* was an addition to Paris's uninhibited night life for which the French accepted no responsibility even in the name. A man seized for ransom was *un kidnappé;* robbers engaged now and then in *un holdup* and *les gangstaires* and *les pickpockets* plied their un-French-sounding trades.

Some expressions, however, were take-overs the English-speaking could consider friendly. *Le fair play* was an Anglo-Saxon concept with which the French were careful not to tamper by attempting to put it into their own admirably delicate language. *Les trade-unions, self-service, le wedding cake;* such personal hygiene techniques as *le shampoing* (spelled with one "o" and pronounced *sham-pwang*); the concept of *les gentlemen;* the attractive diplomatic custom of *le garden party;* the American Republican idea of the political contribution which can be made by *les businessmen;* and the concept of *l'underdog* (translated in one Paris paper as *le pauvre type,* the "poor sort") were all cheerfully snatched up as a change from the French of the classics but also as transmission belts for attitudes from a world which was just as remote as Italy, the world of the Anglo-Saxons.

The problem of English and American concepts in French was having political repercussions, too. Pierre Mendès-France,

who was prominent on the French political stage in the first
half of the fifties, knew the words in English to describe the
political movement he was creating, but he could never find a
translation. The nationalistic M. Mendès-France would not
call his group by the English phrase he actually had in mind:
le New Deal. Two obstacles were in the way: the phrase was
non-French and had been used before by one whom Mendès-
France admired but could not so blatantly copy, the late
American President Roosevelt.

An American introduced me to some of France's food mysteries. He was Joe Hyde, of Palisades, New York, then twenty-
six, who went through Trinity College in Hartford, Connecticut, worked for a while as a cook in Washington, became an
army chef in Japan and Korea, and then decided to study
eating at its world capital. Joe arranged to exchange jobs with
a Frenchman who wanted to learn American restaurant cost
accounting. (The Frenchman admired that but had no respect
for the kitchen of the Washington, D.C., restaurant to which
Hyde directed him. "They make soup in a pot big enough to
swim in," he wrote Joe in astonishment.) Joe in return was
given a one-year French job at $57.00 a month plus meals in
the kitchen of Joannes Nandron's restaurant in Lyon.

Three rivers run through Lyon, according to a French saying: the Seine, the Rhône, and a torrent of the full-bodied
local red burgundy. Too much alcohol desensitizes the taste
buds, Joe was told, but the exacting Lyonnais, the premier
gourmands of France, managed somehow to put away both the
river of wine and also a hundred exquisite food specialties
from M. Nandron's incredibly varied menu each day. If he
were to realize his dream of starting a restaurant of his own,
Joe soon decided, he would have to limit himself to not more
than three of Nandron's hundred choices.

Unbelievably hard work, long hours, and low pay were the
secret of the unequaled French cooking, Joe concluded. American unions never would put up with the Lyon kitchen, the
American was sure.

"Many days we've worked fifteen hours. There are eight

chefs in the small old windowless kitchen where I work, and more upstairs in the pastry bakery. Some of the apprentices get half my pay." But the results were masterpieces of ingenuity. "It seemed to me when I started that there were ten thousand steps to preparing some of the birds!"

By "birds" were meant both poultry and songbirds. There was no prejudice against eating the sweet, tiny carcasses of the latter.

M. Nandron for the occasion of the interview invited Joe and me to choose a dinner. We ate without music. "M. Nandron," Joe explained, "is against music because it distracts attention from the eating." Joe did the ordering, steering away from such simple delicacies as oysters and weaving his way through sauces and pastries instead. "You can't imagine the work that went into this," he whispered with reverent ecstasy, the Paris political world of communism, rearmament, neutralism, and the colonial wars being lost happily out of our minds.

There were comfort and elegance in the France of the debates over how to translate "New Deal," and the France of M. Nandron's crowded Lyon kitchens. A little even crept over into the France of politics which was my daily concern for three years as a Paris reporter.

One Cabinet member invited a few of us to lunch at his ministry to give us a report on a crisis calling for urgent American aid. Footmen in knee breeches served us beneath high ceilings in eighteenth-century luxury as we jotted down notes on the minister's appalling tale. The food and wine again would have had Joe's approval. There was a gulf as wide as the distance from the Louvre to the Bastille, the old royal palace and the site of the French Revolution's beginnings, between what the minister planted "for use but not for attribution" and the splendors of the scene and menu.

A premier met a few of us at a dinner in a gem of a small room in a former royal palace, now used as a ministry. The room, green-brown, Directoire style, had survived many tumultuous generations.

By then, even without hearing the story from the lips of the

men who were dealing with the critical national situation, I
had begun to learn the other side of a France which was not
all good foods and language debates.

I had seen some of it on a trip to Britanny, the peninsula of
relatively devout peasants stretching toward the channel separating France and England.

Our Paris maid was on her way home for vacation and we
agreed to drop her at her parents' Breton farm. "But don't
drive me to the house," she urged as we reached her village.
"My mother might die. The only time a car came to our place
was when my sister fell dead in town. They drove her out. My
mother would be afraid the same had happened to me."

We did as requested, driving up a few minutes behind the
returning daughter. The mother soon got used to our car. We
asked her if there was anything we could do for her.

"Yes," she said. "All my life I have wanted to arrive at
church in an automobile."

It was three miles to the chapel, but Madame always had
walked it. She sat stiffly in the back seat, her grown son beside
her. He, too, was rigid, as if balancing on a bicycle. Each time
we passed someone he twisted awkwardly to show his face in
the back window. Everyone should know that our friends had
gone that day by car.

Religion was an issue in the town's quarrel between the generations. The elders and those who stayed behind in town
went, in large part, to the thousand-year-old church. With
those who set out for factories in Paris the story was apt to be
different. It had taken one village girl only a few months, with
the help of fellow mill hands on the Paris outskirts, to decide
that "the priest is just another man in business." She doffed
her religion just as she tried to forget the fieldstone houses and
the ski-jump roofs of her Breton home country.

"You think they're beautiful?" she asked with astonishment
as visitors marveled at their grace. To her there was such an
ugly side to Breton life—the side of hard drinking, penny-
pinching, and poverty—that nothing was pretty.

As paying guests of one Breton farm woman we saw some

of this dark side. Our hostess put on weight as she shared the regular meals we asked her to prepare. Like everyone else she had so much hard cider, some of it fizzy like champagne and held in similarly with wired corks, and so much Calvados applejack, that it seemed pleasanter a good part of the time to take a drink or two and to skip eating. This was especially true when Madame's "fool," her gentleman friend, came to dine, as he regularly did. He was a silent, morose man, who ate with his hat on.

Alcohol was the center of attention. New apples were coming in and barrels were awash with last year's cider. Even the most notorious skinflints were inviting casual acquaintances to share a glass. The barrels had to be emptied in time. The Calvados distiller would soon be around. With his little traveling still he would run off seventeen bottles for $1.50. The first two or three were fine ones, seventy proof. As water carried over toward the end there were bottles of merely twenty proof, poor shakes by Breton standards, but the average was a sturdy fifty. Even at the wheat harvest the alcohol kept a central place. The *frèrie* (brotherhood) converged for a day's toil to be repaid in kind on the plots of the brother farmers. A quarter-of-a-century-old harvester chewed a pile of wheat sheaves fifteen feet tall into 150-pound sacks of grain and a ten-foot-high mound of straw and five-foot-tall heap of chaff, the latter destined to be pig food. As men atop one pile slowly descended and others on the slippery straw gradually rose, frèrie brothers dropped off the hot, dusty job in turns to duck into a cool cave, the cider cellar. They sat solemnly opposite one another in a narrow, medievally dark, Gothic-roofed tunnel, one man tapping the barrel at the back and two glasses moving constantly between spigot and lips. The glass shortage helped limit consumption, but still brooks of cider ran.

Lunch was served at a table under the trees: veal and a kid roasted over the open fireplace of the farmhouse, and all the cider the brothers chose to absorb. Forks were set out but no knives; it was assumed that every man carried his own jackknife for such purposes. Bottles of Calvados appeared at the meal's end.

Our host was still limping from a year-old break of a knee-cap suffered in slipping off the top of the straw stack during the previous harvest. This time, plentiful fluid notwithstanding, there were no accidents. "Thank God," Madame said at the end. "No one got hurt." A few, however, needed pick-me-ups. One man downed an egg-sized serving of salt in a cup of coffee. It was a rough but instantaneous antidote. One gulp and a man might be momentarily nauseous but he was no longer tipsy.

For cash the farm leaned heavily on butter, eggs—and babies. A girl of the family had married and in short order had a houseful of tots; twins and two others. Eighty dollars a month in state help came for them. It was the new household's sole cash revenue, but it was enough. Family weaving was going out, but until recently each family had been self-sufficient, growing and making everything it needed.

One Breton farm was not all of France nor even of French agriculture; but when Colonel Gribius had talked of his soldiers in the mop-up in the Tunisian hills he had spoken of "my good Bretons" and the young man of the farm where the harvesting had been done was just getting ready for military service as one of the soldiers on whom France was leaning as she defended her shrinking empire. One thing was sure for the young man: he would not go to Indo-China. If the Foreign Legion, troops from the colonies, and the few volunteers could not save that Asiatic possession, it would have to go. Whether or not they were typical, the members of the frèrie surely would never object to such a national policy. Nowhere was one more conscious than in that Breton village that Indo-China was the other side of the earth.

No, the Breton farm was not France, but it told much about the national problems of alcoholism, of economic backwardness, of the people's inverted concentration on family and lack of interest in the world holdings which had made France a great power. Among facts not reflected were the regional differences that helped produce Frenchmen of such contradictory political ideas that there was permanent paralysis in a Parliament of proportional representation, of self-seeking, and of scant apparent concern for overriding national interests.

Many of my daytime hours and many "white nights," as the French Parliament members called their all-night sessions, were passed in the Seine-bank Grecian temple which served as the Chamber of Deputies. There I was introduced to the turmoil of super-democratic French politics which was to bring the threat of civil war in early 1958, when the weary French Army in Algeria, exhausted by two decades of nearly steady fighting, insisted that France adopt a new constitution giving more power to the premier. The army's demand succeeded in putting General Charles De Gaulle back in power after a dozen years' absence. With De Gaulle at the helm, France started once again down an oft-traveled road in quest of stability without dictatorship, a problem both England and the United States had solved by avoiding the pitfall of proportional representation and by giving real power for sufficiently long periods to either of the two main social groups, the conservatives or the reformers.

The Parliament I got to know was where all the interests of France met and fought: my Breton farm friends who, like the rest of the politically powerful farmers, had managed so far to protect themselves against paying any but token direct taxes; the drinkers who wanted the cider, the Calvados, and the wine to flow freely and cheaply; the students of the glorious national history, such as former Premier Georges Bidault, who wanted France to continue as a great power and to hang on to every possible inch of earth in Indo-China, North Africa, and Black Africa; the poverty-strapped southerners who were caught in a net of many taxes and had neither the factories nor farm land to support them; the Socialists of the northern coal mines who felt that every other group selfishly was looking after itself and that they deserved raises as a price for not going Communist; the Catholics of Alsace-Lorraine who wanted state aid for religious schools; the Communists of the factories who looked for leadership to Moscow; the Nationalists of General De Gaulle.

There were other groups, too, in the Parliament of the early fifties: manufacturers who wanted to live behind protective barriers with small production, scanty progress, lofty prices, good profits, and little public service; the philosophical children of the eighteenth century watching the Catholics of Britanny and of Alsace-Lorraine as an ideological threat to laic ideas of church-state separation; and a dozen further splinterings.

For three years I watched the Parliament roll like the chance-churned barrel at a lottery. Chaos reigned. Every six months on the average, as it had since the start of the modern republic in 1871, the Parliament ousted a premier and the president of the Republic was compelled to hunt for another. Repetition was not making the machinery work more smoothly. On the contrary, it grew harder to agree on the deputy who should stand before the world as government head of one of the Western Big Three. Within a week of my arrival the provincial-mannered, typical "Mr. Frenchman," Antoine Pinay, a tax foe, was tumbled from the premiership and I saw my first cabinet "crisis," as the politicians term the government breakdowns. Within another half-year I was to see the all-time record breaker. For thirty-six days deputies turned down the president's proposals for the government leadership, at the rate of one a week, until the chief of state, Vincent Auriol, was alarmed. Joseph Laniel, a conservative linen manufacturer, finally turned the trick and gave France its nineteenth postwar cabinet. Helping him was his obscurity. Nobody knew much about him—and thus little was held against him.

The difficulty in patching together a fraction more than 50 per cent of the Parliament as a platform on which to base a government was blamed in part on the Communists, who had had an important share in rewriting the constitution after World War II. Another reason for it was the perpetual dread of a dictator. Liberty was more than revered; it was treated with an idolatry that tended to transmute it into social collapse. Laniel went to power with the help of some who thought little of him.

"Not the brightest?" repeated one of the new premier's main backers. "So much the better! It will make him easier to lead."

Laniel, to his credit, proved less easy to steer than some had expected. To the shock of various men near him he proved to have his own opinion in favor of the six-country pooled army which was the diplomatic topic of the moment. It was a plan to revive German military power inside an inter-European armed force, in order to use the Germans for defense against the Russians but to pen in the risks of renewed German aggression. It was a French suggestion and had delayed German rearmament two years, but now, with the kinks ironed out, France was hesitating to go through with the plan.

"What the French really want," one diplomat said impatiently, "is a German army bigger than the 175 divisions the Russians have but smaller than the 14 the French have."

France was divided, torn between fear of the Germans and dread of the Russians; but as one observer noted, "the dividing line between those who are for and against runs through the brain of every Frenchman." It was like the East-West split in the minds of Italy's Catholic Communists. Two conflicting ideas were entertained, with no ability to make a choice between them.

At least for his part Laniel pushed the German rearmament dilemma toward a decision. Months later, under another premier, when the French ended by killing the pooled army idea they themselves had originated, they agreed quickly and in some panic to another plan—the virtually uncontrolled restitution of German armed force.

The fiasco of the German rearmament debate served the good purpose of provoking studies of France's critical weaknesses. Some of the country's many brilliant brains laid ills bare. Remedies were not yet as clear but the diagnoses included these points:

The collapse of cabinets had become so frequent that a decade after World War II one fourth of the non-communist deputies could boast having had cabinet rank or its equivalent. The situation was so bad, one parliamentary leader reported, that a legislator who had not been a minister was ashamed, and some often named ministers had begun to feel the same way about being premier. There were about a score of living former premiers compared with two living American former presidents. When premiers began to tumble, a deputy's own personal ambitions tempted him to vote thumbs down to get another chance on the ministerial and premiership lottery.

Furthermore, the merry-go-round of two cabinets a year with many of the same men rotating at the heads of different ministries had several harmful effects: a good deal of the real work of decision slipped down to unelected permanent functionaries who might make their own uncontrolled policy or let their sections wallow in inactivity; and ministers were tempted in successive cabinets to pursue their own political goals, not their premier's.

Time and again one month's minister came back as the next month's premier. Premiers, too, came back as ministers, but generally not immediately.

With his ministers veering off about their own premiership-conscious business, government heads were inclined to do more and more themselves. Premiers became so tired that deputies reportedly felt that they were doing the government chief a favor when in the end they voted him down.

To get necessary legislation through a Parliament which wanted to lower taxes and increase expenditures, premiers used their ultimate weapon on an average of once a month: they threatened to resign.

Witty and rather cynical young Edgar Faure, still in his mid-forties, the boy wonder of the postwar premierships, see-sawed between opposite theories about such threats of resignation.

One theory of Faure's was that the menace should be used

freely to drive through a coherent and sufficiently radical program. During his first period as premier, in 1952, at the age of forty-two, the original M. Faure divided a long bill on tax and economic reform into twenty parts and announced that he covered each part with a threat of resignation. It made him, he said later, the "record man" of such threats. Nevertheless, the Parliament decapitated the Faure cabinet on the bill's second section.

In his second period as premier, in 1955, while I covered his activities, M. Faure used reverse tactics. This time he felt that resignation threats were like aces in a game: a player never knew how many he would draw, but could be sure he would never have many.

The eminently adaptable, nimble-witted but rarely firm M. Faure was a professional lawyer and, by hobby, a detective-story writer. He had authored three police mysteries, using the pen name "Edgar Sanday" (*"Edgard sans 'd' "*—Edgar without a "d," a reference to his oft-repeated explanation to his fellow French in earlier years: "I spell my name the English way, without a 'd' ").

Even more remarkable than the feat of writing a trio of police mysteries was the government leader's capacity for reading those that others wrote. He devoured one an hour. Before every trip as premier he sent an aide out to buy the latest two or three on the newsstands.

"Why do you read them?" I asked the premier. "Because they puzzle over the same problems of human behavior which crop up in the decisions of government?"

"No," the never-predictable leader retorted. "Because they're soporific!" They were the easiest way to sleep awake, a brief and undrugged release from the problems of the future of France and of the world.

On his second round as premier, M. Faure lasted longer than the forty days of his first try, but even though he let the Parliament steer its way rather blindly through secondary economic and foreign policy problems, the premier foundered as the customary half-year period ended.

That was M. Faure, France's representative among the Big Four at the 1955 Summit Conference, the meeting I missed as I covered Oued Zem and North Africa. Even in a Paris political world of facile minds his was unique, that of a man so fast, as one diplomat put it, that "He's behind you before you know it." There was something dazzling about him, but he, like most of the rest in Paris that summer, could find no answer to the slow decline of France.

M. Faure's humble taste for who-done-its was typical of the modest characteristics of many of the men at the top of France's political pyramid.

René Mayer, who took office as premier just as I began my Paris assignment, went to the glories of the government leadership from a cramped middle-class apartment on the Left Bank of the Seine. Half a year later the former premier was back in his book-piled flat, out of office. Georges Bidault, architect of much of France's postwar foreign policy, and another in the parade of premiers, lived in a small house, not far from that of Grandval of Morocco, in Saint Cloud just outside Paris. His, too, was a book-filled home. A visit one day caught the Bidault family as they were finishing moving out of the Foreign Office back to private quarters. Books were not only stacked to the ceiling on shelves but also heaped everywhere, on tables, on chairs, and on the floor.

"Pas mal de desordre ici!—Some mess! No shortage of disorder here!" a servant urbanely apologized.

Robert Schuman, the "Father of Europe," a pious Catholic premier and foreign minister who tried in vain to lead France swiftly into a brotherly alliance with Germany and a beginning of a United States of Europe, lived so humbly that one guest was sure he had mistaken the address. The visitor, an ambassador, was preparing a report on European trends which was sure to have an effect on highest Western policy. He had chosen Schuman as a key advisor. The modesty of the homes of such influential men was little surprise, considering their salaries: Parliament members received only $7,288 a year, Cabinet ministers $9,000, and premiers $11,717.

With necessary guarantees that confidences would be protected the deputies, ministers, and premiers aired ideas which often came as a shock:

"The only hope in Algeria is for the people to Brazilianize —for the 1,000,000 Europeans to marry into the 9,000,000 Arabs and Berbers. But they won't!"

"There is real danger that the 1,000,000 Europeans in Algeria will secede, forming a new country allied with South Africa against the Moslem natives. There could be a terrible slaughter, but the Europeans would win."

"The Russians and Chinese are sure to split, but it may take twenty years. Then we may have an alliance of the West and Russia against China, and, maybe, against the other colored races. An alliance with Russia is a necessity of geography, regardless of Moscow's political regime of the moment."

"American anti-colonialism! Watch out—we may have a situation where every American will be against every Frenchman, and vice versa."

"The real people are the North African settlers from France. They are true defenders of your American bases. You journalists don't understand that, but you are shallow! And you have a responsibility to be profound!"

The typical American hesitancy about being controversial, about expressing disturbing political views, was not reflected among the articulate French legislature. Many of the French ideas canceled one another out. A recurring thought in many minds was that France should come to some terms with the communist bloc. American insistence on refusing recognition to Red China was, in many French parliamentary minds, absurd. "Chou En-lai is no low-level person," one top French figure decided.

Some views, rather than neutralizing others, clashed so violently that men who succeeded one another at the helm of key ministries or even in the premiership sometimes so detested their successors that they hesitated to pass on certain secrets of office. Relations between the Catholic conservative leader Bidault and the anti-clerical, semi-Socialist Pierre Mendès-France were an example. Bidault as foreign minister had fought to save every inch of Indo-China and North Africa; Mendès-France, in the name of realism and on the grounds that France was overextended, agreed to an Indo-China partition and set the machinery of Tunisian and Moroccan independence in motion.

"Anybody could get an Indo-China peace that way, by a partial surrender," one conservative former premier protested against the man who was one of his successors, Mendès-France.

"He's treating the world holdings of France like white elephants at an auction," lamented another of Mendès-France's predecessors in the premiership.

Mendès-France just as furiously struck back at those who would not "choose." To govern, he said, involved selecting among alternatives. France could not do everything its people liked.

The whirlpools of French theories and rival interests, each of them free to struggle for dominance inside the generous limits of French social freedom, often meant exasperation among France's allies.

"That Robert Schuman!" one diplomat objected. "His intentions are noble, but he got us all to agree to something— the European army plan—on which he could not guarantee support from his own parliament."

Idealism should be tempered with a sense of reality, the frustrated ambassador implied.

"White nights" aplenty for reporters covering Paris were the result. There were at least two kinds of Paris night life— that of the uninhibited floor shows, another form of French freedom with few limits, and the night life of the politicians. After the first shock of having to work all night after toiling all day (the five-hour time difference meant that a dawn event or even one at 8 A.M. was still in time for the morning papers in New York, and thus called for through-the-night coverage), I puzzled over the reason.

The deputies liked to argue through the night so that they could get so tired they agreed, one student of Paris politics

gave solemnly as his judgment. René Mayer made his successful effort to form a cabinet by pledging not to take off his
clothes or go to bed until enough of the warring politicians
agreed on a coalition. Forced to stay up with the potential
premier, the wearying faction leaders finally came to terms; by
one o'clock of an afternoon after a "white night" Mayer had
his cabinet. It lasted only a handful of months, but few other
premiers could claim better.

Another theory was that Parliament members liked to decide major matters at 5 A.M. because the streets were sure to
be empty then and the danger of rioting was less. Mobs always
are worst when fresh bad news is handed to them.

There was even one timid theory that the deputies secretly
had the interests of the Parliament ushers in mind: the poorly-
paid employees got overtime during white nights.

The truth, I finally gathered, was that one of the prices of
the overgenerous freedom enjoyed by the France of the mid-
fifties was extreme disunity and the inescapable loss of precious time in seeking compromises. And the French had discovered that there are not eight but twenty-four hours in a
day. By pushing on, in spurts, the length of the costly breakdowns in administration and in foreign relations could be
kept to a minimum.

Another problem was that under the liberty-conscious constitution and laws of the mid-fifties, the Parliament was allowed to propose new expenditures and the often-exhausted
premier had to take charge of the ungrateful work of turning
back the frequently irresponsible demands. The result was
that the French Parliament was passing four times as many
laws as was Britain, a country with a far more disciplined
system. The premiers were managing, by demanding votes of
confidence, to fend off many of the demagogic proposals, but
never enough of them; the country gradually was bowing
beneath a weight of foreign loans, the humiliating need to ask
American aid, and a system of social welfare and industrial
protection which was boosting prices to one of the highest
average levels in the world.

The demagogy of politicians who asked that France spend what it was not producing was only one of the currents setting through the vitally important legislature. Another was "Poujadism," an expression of lower-middle-class psychology. It was anti-communist but it was also hostile to the generous ideas of Robert Schuman or to nationalistic appeals to a spirit of responsibility such as those from M. Bidault.

I talked for an hour one day with the father of "Poujadism" —Pierre Poujade. His story would have been incredible if every detail had not been checked.

M. Poujade, a beefy man in his middle thirties, given to rough talk bordering on gutter language, was proprietor of a small-town stationery store in a poor section of central France. He was unknown in the early fifties, but in a year or two became acknowledged master of nearly a tenth of the Parliament, a band of more than fifty deputies.

The leap to notoriety was faster than Mussolini's. Admiring female relatives must have pondered uncertainly, as Signora Mussolini did, what was "in that head of his."

M. Poujade was a former sergeant and former captain of a soccer team. Other than that he had no qualifications for a role as one of the great political leaders of France. But M. Poujade had a point of view and the daring to act on it. He detested the tax collectors who combed the books of his fellow small merchants, hunting for the tax violations which were many a shopkeeper's sole source of revenue. When a tax inspector visited one of Poujade's neighbors, the burly youth and some of his friends threw the investigator out bodily.

It was estimated that the hideously complicated French tax system included some two thousand different scales of payment, with certain advantages going legally to large enterprises. It was common knowledge that many professional men were evading their taxes wholesale, and that even though a third of the French national income was going in tariffs (a higher rate than in the United States), a good share of it was in the form of inequitable sales taxes. (Cigarettes, for example, cost the equivalent of sixty cents a pack, three quarters of the price representing taxes.) Such taxes hit the poor and missed the rich. A good fifth of assessed taxes, nearly two billion dollars a year, was being dodged.

It was the classic vicious circle. Tax dodging by men such as the small shopkeepers encouraged it in others and, in reaction, the store owners insisted on surrendering even less.

Government officials knew the bitter feelings of the storekeepers, so they winked an eye at M. Poujade's misdeed. He, in turn, would not forgive a Parliament which kept the taxes on the books and a government which tried, however halfheartedly, to enforce them. M. Poujade took part in other tariff revolts and then organized a shopkeepers' protection service. A man threatened with a visit from the collector needed only telephone for a Poujade flying squad. M. Poujade soon boasted 800,000 followers.

Men reached out to grab the triumphant M. Poujade's hand as he and I entered a crowded, antiquated café for a drink and a talk. M. Poujade's collar was turned up fighter fashion. He waved his admirers aside with a grin. In the back alcove he asked his trailers for privacy and got it at once. He took a beer.

"There's no civic sense here," the astonishing M. Poujade said of his country. "If there were, as there is in Anglo-Saxon countries, people wouldn't follow me!

"It's a forced labor offense here to encourage people not to pay taxes. In England it would be a violation of the Queen's regulations and I'd be in jail. But here they don't do anything!

"The fact is, everybody here ignores the law. Even the cabinet members!"

It was not the time to argue the justice of the young man's scorn for his national leaders. I asked a question instead: what had triggered off M. Poujade's own flight down the road of lack of civic conscience and lawbreaking?

There was no hesitation in M. Poujade's reply. When a man had met what he could of his expenses out of the small income from a scantily patronized shop, he pointed out, there was nothing left for the probing, avid tax collector. "You can't take more than a man has," he said. "Something has to give." Was his "direct-action" movement Fascist?

"Is it Fascist to be for 'fraternity, liberty, and equality,' on which the Republic stands? We're for equality, not for crushing the little fellow. . . . I tell these Parliament deputies: give us what we want or others may come up behind us to make use of our movement for Fascist reasons. Democracy is deputies doing the will of their voters! Not crushing them.

"And you Americans give France a lot of money. The people who go to you cheat us and you both! If Premier Faure resists me he will fall!"

The marvel was that M. Faure very nearly did. By pleading until three o'clock one morning, he squeaked through. His argument was reasonable: a "great power" could not meet obligations without taxes. Election-minded deputies conceded the logic but dreaded to defy the former sergeant.

With my young companion's "Poujadism" sloshing around the foundations of the French social structure on the one side, communism sluiced in from another.

I asked the Communists whether I could attend one of their quadrennial national conventions. They agreed. It was a strange experience. There was a certain odd comfort in its physical setting, but there was also an ocean of intellectual mediocrity. There was prisonlike regimentation and merciless severity.

A problem of this convention was to endorse the expulsion of Auguste Lecoeur, until then one of the top five of the Party. The short, fat, Humpty-Dumpty-shaped acting head of French communism, Jacques Duclos, a former pastry cook, pronounced the exclusion and the thousand delegates rose to applaud. Not many weeks earlier they had sung Lecoeur's praises as one of the best sons of the French working class; in an instant, on orders, they had switched.

The external beauty was in the womblike cloths of gold and cream which covered the walls and, overhead, hid the steel rafters of the factory-district auditorium. The cloths wrapped us in gay, restful colors, subtly promising physical well-being. Only later did they cloy and smother.

The intellectually primitive quality of the convention and the prisonlike atmosphere that hung over it arose from both the speeches and the comportment of the crowd. Duclos spoke for five hours, calling for applause whenever he wanted it by switching his drone to a rising crescendo and then stopping. The dull-faced delegates brightened as the tone of his voice changed and never failed to fill the void as Duclos paused. Sometimes they clapped Russian-style, all beating their palms in unison, at first a slow drumming, then a mounting rhythm with, finally, a little jig of quick blows at the end. Duclos set the beat for that, too. Like a concert master he spread his hands wide and slowly brought them closer together until the final rattle ended the applause.

It was dull and sometimes distasteful even for the delegates. When an Algerian Moslem native stood up to suggest that, in line with Moscow's wishes, Algeria should be cut off from France, the audience dissolved into chatter. None raised a voice of protest, but it was clear that the Frenchmen who were delegates could think of pleasanter things than listening to a call for their nation's truncation.

The delegates were plainly a third-rate group socially and apparently also intellectually. Much the same could be said of the party's parliamentary representatives. Communist parliamentary speeches sounded so much alike that it was a common opinion that only Duclos wrote his own. The party organization which took all parliamentary pay from each communist deputy except for a shade more than $100 a month, reportedly wrote the deputies' speeches, gave them use of a car pool and a secretarial service, the latter obviously adaptable to counterintelligence activities, and in general tied them in. A few top leaders visited Russia but the mass of the communist deputies, according to research by their political opponents, never got an opportunity to see the Red promised land and thus to weigh claims against realities for themselves.

The real core of French communist support, I became convinced, was not in an intellectual appraisal of the four-decades-old Soviet experiment, but in frustration against the same economic breakdown that had provoked former Sergeant Poujade to open war on the taxes. One survey gave these statistics:

Only 4 per cent of the French population had water, gas, electricity, a private toilet, a bathroom, or a shower bath. Even fewer had running hot water, central heating, or modern kitchen conveniences. In the light of these figures our frustrations with our rundown temporary home at the bend of the Marne became more understandable.

There were other figures; 47 per cent of the apartments in Paris had no private toilet, and only 18 per cent had bathrooms. There were no sewers for 96 per cent of the homes in Versailles, the town of the still preserved, magnificent royal palace and one of the starting places of the Revolution. In towns with populations of from 10,000 to 50,000, 47 per cent of the homes were without running water.

Beside Poujadism and communism ran another powerful current of opinion, merging sometimes with the others—neutralism. Two youths expressed it to me one day at Caen, the town which was chewed to the ground by the Allied assault when America and Britain opened the "second front" in World War II.

"There is only one thought we have—to live in peace," thirty-four-year-old newspaper reporter Louis Bigorgine said.

France was a small country now, caught between "two imperialisms," agreed Guy de la Brosse, twenty-four, one of Bigorgine's fellow reporters.

The best solution, both of them declared, would be for Russia and America to settle things between them, even without the presence of France.

It was alarming, though by then not unfamiliar, to hear the United States matched with Russia as just another imperialist power. It was disturbing, too, to be told that the United States should settle with Moscow alone. Western strategy needed France as an ally in the defense of common democratic concepts. The European defense system centered on scores of American airfields in France. To agree that there was little to choose between the imperialism of Moscow and that of Washington was to prepare a collapse of Western strategy in the resistance against communism.

Not so much neutralism as hedonism was implied in another comment made to me during a visit near the old Normandy beachhead I made there a decade after the war.

"Don't use my name, but I'll tell you how my wife and I reacted," said the town secretary of one of the battered villages in the landing area. "Before the war we always saved and saved, like almost everyone else. We put money aside to furnish our home. Then, when the war was over, what do you think we did? Our home was ruined and we were sleeping on a mattress on the floor. We bought a car, the first we had ever had, and went on a trip to Belgium! We decided to get some fun out of life!"

Millions like him spent what they had on the day's pleasures and left the future to take care of itself.

Yet it was not that there were no generous and dedicated spirits. There were many in a country where the ideals of Jeanne d'Arc still excited so many imaginations.

There were the brave young officers who lived alone as "native affairs" officials in a sea of Moslems, Arabs, and Berbers in the remote corners of North Africa.

There were the officers of the Foreign Legion, a handful of Frenchmen leading adventurous and sometimes desperate foreigners forward into constant combat for France, a France the officers saw not as one power alone but also as a symbol of human freedom and culture. When national egotism clashed with the generous ideal of universal liberty, many French people suffered.

The austere General De Gaulle, a man of noble instinct and no self-seeker despite his authoritarian manner, was one of the many dedicated French.

So were another group with whom I was especially intrigued, the "worker-priests." They were a band of a hundred Catholic clergymen. They had been appalled at the way a century of Marxism had de-Christianized the factory workers. In reply they had "taken out citizenship papers in the working class," doffing the ankle-length cassocks the French clergy usually wear and taking eight-hour-a-day jobs as common hands in factories. They proved thus that they were not parasites cynically "avoiding work."

The collapse of the worker-priest experiment was one of my saddest French experiences. To be real "citizens of the working class" the priests agreed that they had to join "the workers' organizations," which meant the communist unions and front societies, such as "peace" groups. To avoid the impression that they were spies of the bourgeoisie they shunned contact with local parishes and Catholic Action organizations. When rioters demonstrated against American General Matthew Ridgeway, the then newly-appointed head of the West European defense organization, club-swinging police discovered that the two leaders of the manifestation were worker-priests.

I visited one of the priests in his humble lodging in the slums of a large seaport. A rickety wooden staircase led up to his tiny room, about the size of a monk's cell. There was a crucifix on the wall, but also a communist dove of "peace." A file of *Humanité,* the Paris communist paper, was on his table beside the cup he used as a chalice for mass in the bedroom-living room. A hard-eyed, unfriendly young man sat awaiting the young clergyman's return. I had heard that the Communist party had surrounded each of the priests, giving them "friends." I assumed that this fierce young fellow was so assigned. The priest, an attractive youth, smiled pleasantly as he climbed off his bicycle at his return, but he refused to speak. The Pope had decided to disband the worker-priest corps as an experiment that had failed. A dozen or so of the priests, alone among their new acquaintances, had progressed from concession to concession until they had broken their vows

of celibacy and had married. Most of them later gave up the
mission, but a large minority chose the "worker" side of what
had proved to be an attempt to join incompatibles.

France was in trouble, as the French leaders themselves
never ceased proclaiming.

"We are on the eve of another 1789," political orators
often repeated.

Was liberty destroying itself? Was there no will to do what
brilliant French minds outlined as essential (quadrupling the
use of fertilizer on the farms was only one of a hundred
ideas)? Would Frenchmen always answer, as I heard from the
lips of one old fellow when he was told to drink milk for his
bad liver: "I'll drink milk when cows eat grapes!" Were industrial protectionism, economic stagnation, Poujadism, communism, neutralism, and hedonism bound to demolish the
homeland of so much literary, philosophical, and artistic
genius, the land of "liberty, equality, fraternity"?

Part of the answer lay in the De Gaulle experiment of 1958,
an effort which faced difficulty from selfish groups from the
first.

It was easy to be discouraged, but I agreed, nevertheless,
with the military attaché of an Asiatic embassy in Paris who
had told me, years before the De Gaulle reform experiment:
"It is only in a real crisis that France unites and shows her
best, but she can be counted on to do it then."

Perhaps it was merely an act of faith, but despite communism within and anti-colonialism pressing down on North
Africa and Black Africa from without, I believed in the future
of a France of ingenuity, humanity, and bravery.

It might be a smaller France. As one Italian journalist
shrewdly told a high French official, "We Italians know we are
Number Three on the Continent; what we don't know is
whether you or the Germans are to be Number One."

It might not be a France of a Western Big Three, excluding
Western Germany and Italy from the topmost councils, but it
would be no France of mere self-indulgence, cynicism, and
the meanly narrow.

VI

THE VATICAN:
FAITH IN THE CONTINENT

Part of the reason for my faith in Europe, despite the ills within and the attack from without, lay in the Vatican. I was a child of the Irish-Catholic immigration of the mid-nineteenth century and of the German-Catholic wave of immigration of the 1870's, and it was to Rome and the Holy See especially that my mind had turned when as a boy at Brooklyn's Narrows I yearned to sail out over the gray horizon.

The Vatican I first saw on my six-week assignment to cover the election of Pius XII in 1939 was not what I expected, but in the decade thereafter during which I was to cover the Holy See my confidence in the nobility of very much that is European was strengthened nonetheless.

Just as poverty was what struck me most in postwar Italy, so did the modesty of the accommodations for the electors of the new Pope impress me in 1939. Fresh from an America where physical prosperity was so important, I was astonished by the preparations for the sixty-two Cardinals who would choose the new Pontiff. According to tradition the Cardinals were to be locked into a suite of rooms around the Sistine Chapel, decorated by Michelangelo, in the Vatican. Cut off from civil governments and all other outside influences, they would vote twice a day until the balloting was successful. For sleeping they were assigned makeshift bedchambers in the drafty halls of the surrounding art galleries.

Typical were the facilities that had been prepared for the Jesuit Cardinal Pietro Boetto of Genoa. On his plain bedstead were a single homespun sheet, a blanket, a thin bedspread, and a pillow. There were three face towels, two armless wooden chairs, a table with a wooden dip pen of the simplest type, a small electric heater to stab a ray of warmth into the chill of the thick-walled old building, and a red-cushioned kneeling bench set before a small wall crucifix.

The facilities for Cardinal Boetto were better than those for some of his colleagues. A few of them were even quartered in hallways, with nothing but red screens to afford a bit of privacy.

There were also a few proper bedrooms, and all three of the American Cardinals, William O'Connell of Boston, George Mundelein of Chicago, and Dennis Dougherty of Philadelphia, were assigned to them. The reason, we understood, was the length of the sudden trips of many thousands of miles which the aged American prelates had had to take. Transoceanic plane travel was not yet a commonplace, and each of the American clergymen had managed the sea voyage only by packing and leaving instantly.

Most of the sleeping places for the Cardinals, we gathered, had been assigned by lot. An exception was cell thirteen. The Cardinal-Chamberlain, acting head of the Roman Catholic Church during the papal interregnum, had taken the popularly ill-omened number for himself. He was Eugenio Cardinal Pacelli, the Secretary of State, or foreign minister, for Pius XI. It was from cell thirteen that the new head of the Catholic Church, the world's largest single religious denomination and the faith of one fifth of humanity, was to come.

The Sistine Chapel with its masterpieces of Michelangelo, the "Creation of Adam" and "Last Judgment," was a spectacular sight on any occasion, but it was even more moving then. There was drama in the sixty-two equal thrones and in the slip-knotted cords behind each which could drop the overhanging baldachin at a tug. The first act of the remaining sixty-one Cardinals on the election of the new Pope would be to lower their canopies. The new Pope's alone would remain raised. It would be to the single covered chair that each Cardinal would make his way to honor one of whom he was no longer the peer, the latest in a succession which claimed an uninterrupted sequence from Peter, as the first Pope, and thus from the immediate company of Christ.

In the corner farthest from the "Last Judgment" was a tall, slim, aluminum-painted stove. In it each round of ballots would be set afire, thus destroying the evidence of how each Cardinal had voted. In keeping with another of the myriad customs of Rome, brush would be burned with the unsuccessful papers. That would be a sign to hundreds of thousands outside that the Church was still leaderless. The black smoke of the brush would be unmistakable. The *fumo bianco* ("white smoke") of the final ballot would mean that Rome had a new "man in white."

Even as the smoke arose the message would be literally true, for in keeping with one more tradition three cassocks of papal white were ready, one for a large man, one for a small, and one for a man of average size. The chosen Cardinal would don the one which fitted best, and within a half-hour would appear on the central balcony high on St. Peter's Basilica to give his blessing *urbi et orbi* ("to the city and to the world," to Rome and to all the earth).

One hundred bundles of brush were stacked beside the stove, enough for more than a month of ballots.

A few score of us were permitted into the Sala Regia—or Royal Hall, for the final ceremony before the sealing of the quarters for the conclave. The Cardinals filed past into the Pauline Chapel for the chanting of *Veni Creator* ("Come, O Creator!"), a prayer to the Holy Spirit for inspiration in the choice of the new Pope, and then, four minutes later, walked out again, past us in the Sala Regia, into the Sistine Chapel, where the last of the lead seals on doors and windows were fastened.

Cardinal Pacelli was the second to arrive at the Pauline Chapel, twenty-five minutes ahead of time, exactly at 3:45 P.M. Domenico Cardinal Jorio, the prefect, or head, of the Sacred Congregation for the Discipline of the Sacraments, had been first. Jorio had smiled and chatted for two minutes at the doorway with officers of the 100-man detachment of the

Holy See's Noble Guards. We had passed time by staring at the uniforms of the honorary soldiers, shiny Grecian helmets with a bar curving forward over the crown, thick gold epaulets on the shoulders of black tunics, pale blue trousers with wide gold stripes, and long swords carried at the shoulder. The outfits were splendid rivals to the richly colored Renaissance murals that covered the walls of the Sala Regia, to the lustrous red garments of the Cardinals, and to the costumes of the Swiss guards who were also on duty in the broad hall. The Swiss stood soberly alert in uniforms of orange, blue, and red and yellow stripes, the points of their halberds rising above the crimson plumes atop their metal helmets.

Unlike Archbishop Jorio, the Cardinal-Chamberlain had no smile. He talked gravely for a moment to an official at the door of the Pauline Chapel, touched his finger to a holy-water sprinkler held by an acolyte, crossed himself, and went into the room of prayer.

I watched the future Pope again as he walked in procession into the conclave rooms in which he would take up the world's heaviest spiritual burden. His face was rested and relaxed but solemn. His hands were clasped as if in prayer, his head down, and his eyes fixed on the crucifix cord on the back of the Cardinal before him. His air was self-conscious. I was convinced that he was certain of election and had decided to accept, although awed by the responsibility. As the closest collaborator of the dead Pope, the Cardinal could have had no illusions about the burden. The story was told later of how he replied as Pope to a boy who called out during an audience: "Holy Father, when I grow up, I'm going to be Pope!"

"Oh," was the answer, "poor boy!"

"Isn't it good to be Pope?" the boy asked innocently.

"It's not how you think!"

"Then I don't want to be Pope, either!" declared the child.

The balloting, judging by other elections, might take several days, so I did not go again to St. Peter's Plaza until the second round of balloting, the next afternoon. The laundry someone had been drying from a window of the cinnamon-colored

Vatican Palace had meantime been taken in. It was a soft, late
winter afternoon under a cloudless sky, another of the perfect
days of the old capital of the Caesars.

There was already a crowd. German theological students in
scarlet cassocks which are the most striking sight of Rome; Fran-
ciscans with beards, brown robes, and sandals; young priests
in low-crowned, broad-brimmed "shovel hats," laughing and
chattering. Four small boys played puss in the corner with the
pillars of Bernini's three-hundred-year-old colonnades as their
bases. A woman, unashamed, breast-fed an infant a few weeks
old. Sunken-lipped, white-haired old ladies took the sun
around the obelisk of the infamous Emperor Caligula, now
engraved *Christus Vincit, Christus Regnat, Christus Imperat,
Christus ab Omni Malo Plebem Suam Defendat* ("Christ con-
quers, Christ reigns, Christ rules, Christ defends His people
against all harm"). All Rome was there. To the Anglo-Saxon
eye it was chaotic, undignified, irreverent. The "color" was
too much. But at least no one was indifferent. I was to hear
it said that "there is only one person in Rome—the Pope; you
either are for him or against him, but never unconcerned."
There were skepticism and hostility, rooted in part in the history of the Papal States, but there was also a deep religious
faith, with very many seeing the Pope as God's agent on earth.

I circled around a man renting rickety canvas seats for two
and one-half lire (thirteen cents) and talked to an American
news-agency reporter. He was still troubled by a story he had
sent about the mood of the crowds in St. Peter's while the late
Pontiff had lain in state. Pius XI was the Pope of *Quad-
ragesimo Anno* ("In the fortieth year"), the influential encyclical on the rights of working men, and of the powerful
letters against "Atheistic Communism" and National Socialism, but no one had wept at his wake in the vast Basilica, and
some in the crowd even had laughed.

"I faked my story," the reporter said. "I wrote that there
were 'mournful throngs.'"

The reporter was not a Catholic, but he had been scandal-
ized. He wrote his dispatch the way it "should have been."

What had been the complicated truth? I was still aboard ship at sea with two of the American Cardinals when the Pope's wake had taken place, but it seemed to me that the complex fact had been this: many believed simply that the dead Pope had gone to a reward and needed no mourning; others never had felt close to the *Santo Padre,* "Holy Father," to one whose words and studies were helping form Western thought and history; still others felt that the death of one Padre meant the coming of another, the man going, the institution never changing.

I glanced at the stovepipe eight stories up on the wall of the Vatican Palace. A smoke puff hung in a fragile balance at the lip of the pipe. It angled off capriciously and more followed. It was gray but, instants later, it blanched.

"Bianco" (white)! a woman cried beside me.

"Bianco! Bianco!" others called out.

The twelve-year-old girl who had been sitting with up-drawn knees, her back to a Bernini column, sewing a doll's dress, jumped up to join the rush to the ramp to St. Peter's. The score of rowdy boys who had been playing a finger-guessing game, clouting the unfortunate who was "it," gave up the rough pastime. Hansom-cab drivers, half asleep in the sun, woke up.

I was among the first up the ramp, but before many others could follow four lines of troops, 3,000 strong, cut off the approaches from the plaza. The soldiers were in full Fascist war kit, with metal helmets, knapsacks on their backs, rifles, and daggers at their belts. One of the first sights the new Pope would see would suggest the military power of the Axis. The man of peace would see the challenge of the men of war.

In the fading sun the smoke seemed to darken again. Was it from the successful ballots, or had brush, after all, been burned in a confession of failure? A new mood took possession of the crowd, quiet uncertainty. But far to the rear thousands streamed in through an arch in the medieval wall linking the Vatican to the Pontiff's old fortress of Castel Sant' Angelo (the Castle of the Holy Angel). Others poured up the

Via della Conciliazione (Conciliation Street), the highway to St. Peter's which Mussolini had built in celebration of the pact of 1929 which ended the estrangement between the Italian government and the church of most Italians. The newcomers knew what many of us had not yet heard. The radio had announced: "Holy Church has a new Pope!"

The insecurity ended as the doors on the balcony of St. Peter's were pushed open. An acolyte came out carrying a crucifix. It was a moment choked with emotion. Pius XI, the doughty, blunt-spoken mountain climber, was gone, but he had a successor. The aged Cardinal Dean stepped to the balustrade.

"*Habemus Papam*," he said in Latin. "We have a Pope!"

Shouts from tens of thousands of throats filled the night air. The new Pope, said the Cardinal, was "Eugenium . . ." There was another roar. There were two Eugenes among the Cardinals but the choice could have been only that of the Cardinal of cell thirteen. "Pacelli" was an anticlimax.

The new Pope, gaunt and tall, surely in one of the two larger cassocks, stepped forward. His hand rose in a benediction and after the sibilant "s-s-s-s" with which Italian crowds impose silence, the multitude went to its knees. Soundlessly the crowd made the sign of the cross.

The coronation, a few days later, completed the process. I arrived at St. Peter's at 6 A.M. There was an hour or two to spare but, even with tickets, it was prudent to find places early. I took a quick coffee at a café on Via della Conciliazione and hurried into the great church. Thousands already were there. A sweltering crush of 40,000 were inside two hours later as the new Pope arrived, borne on the shoulders of a dozen footmen. It was my first sight of the *sedia gestatoria* (the "carried throne"). It was strange to the eyes of an American democrat, though old in the traditions of once-imperial Rome, where much of the pomp of the Caesars had been baptized and spiritualized in the service of religion. Only years later was I to hear from those close to the Pope that the swaying ride on the high-held throne was a sickening experience and that it called for an act of the aging Pontiff's strong will each time he mounted it.

Hemp fluff soaked in olive oil was burned three times before the new Pope between the rear of the long nave and the altar over what had long been considered Peter's tomb. The intensely inflammable material flared up for twenty seconds each time and then vanished, consumed.

"Holy Father, thus does the glory of the world pass away," the liturgist told the new head of the Church each time, in the traditional warning against letting the honors of the sacred position corrupt the very man chosen to lead others away from temptation.

Between the burnings the Pope's right hand moved ceaselessly in a blessing, first over the throng on one side of the nave, then over that on the other. The new Pontiff's expression was changed from that I remembered in the Sala Regia. The serenity was gone. The pale cheeks were sunken, the half-open lips were tight, the unblinking eyes were apprehensive, almost terrified.

The Cardinals came forward for the ceremony of obeisance. Before the man who had been their brother and their choice the Cardinals prostrated themselves in turn, each kissing the new Pontiff's slippered foot, his ring, his cheek. The twentieth-century congregation looked on with the tangled emotions of its era, with the eyes of faith beholding the unseeable divinity honored through the elected leader, with the eyes of a republican new world in which no other man received such homage.

I followed a few drifters into the sacristy of St. Peter's and was astonished to find a bar. There were coffee, soft drinks, and a wide variety of cognacs and other liqueurs. It was another Vatican surprise. We were still inside the ticket-control lines for the Basilica, although outside the crucifix-shaped outline of St. Peter's itself, to which the sacristy, a separate building, was linked by a covered bridge. To one fresh from an America where total abstinence from alcohol often is identified with religiosity, the sight of the bar practically in the church was at first amazing. As I thought it over, however, it

made sense. The scores of attendants at the four-hour coronation ceremony and the others who served the Basilica full
time on other days throughout the year needed sustenance
and, on subsequent visits, I never saw intemperance there.

The coronation ceremony was nearly over. At the Pope's
direction the triple crown, the six-century-old sign of papal
authority, was imposed not inside the church but back on the
balcony so that more in the immense Roman throng outside
could see. An estimated quarter of a million looked on as the
first of the Cardinal-Deacons placed the crown encrusted with
its 146 gems on the new Pontiff's head with the ritual words:
"Accipe tiaram!" "Accept the tiara!" A new Roman pontificate, with all its influence in a world of shaken values and
philosophical searching, had been launched.

It was a pontificate I was to watch at close hand for a decade
as a resident of Rome and one I was to see at its close nineteen years later. Again in 1958 the ancient ceremonies unrolled, and that time I was not to come in "in the middle,"
after the end of the unparalleled nine-day funeral service for
the dead Pontiff, but was to see it all from the grim beginning
to the end.

It was noon on Monday, October 6, when I returned from
a two-day trip to the American advanced atomic base in Avi-
ano, Italy, near the Alps.

"The Pope is sick," a friend telephoned. "He is better now,
but it is very serious."

The Pontiff, who had worked sixteen or more hours a day
for the whole two decades since the dramatic balcony coronation, was ill indeed. He had suffered a stroke. That night and
for the next three nights I joined the rest of the press corps of
Rome sleeping in my car at the entrance of the papal residence in Castelgandolfo, near Rome, the Pontiff's summer and
autumn home, or beside a periodically ringing telephone at
home in Rome. At 3:52 A.M., Thursday morning, as we waited
beside an Italian news agency ticker in the Foreign Press Club,
in Rome, the news came. The Pope of World War II and of
the atomic cold war was dead.

Popes live and die in ceremony. The sweet privilege of privacy is not theirs. We were allowed in to see the rigid, waxen-white remains of the great Church leader at six o'clock that night. Men of the papal Noble and Swiss guards stood stiffly at his side. Dozens fainted in the crush.

Nine days of the most elaborate rituals followed, but the climax was far before the end. A Pope belongs to all. All, certainly, in the chaotic Middle Ages when Popes were central Italy's temporal rulers, had a right to be sure that the Pope lay at rest where he was said to lie. In obedience to old tradition three groups were admitted into St. Peter's Basilica to see Pius descend to his tomb. There were Cardinals and bishops to represent the hierarchy, Roman princes to serve as formal witnesses for the people of the Italian capital, diplomats to the Holy See to look on in behalf of the "people of the Catholic world." By dint of insistence we journalists were admitted too. Amid the pomp of a magnificent Church ceremony, I looked on then at a scene I never had beheld before: a man, the dead Pius, lifted into his triple coffin of cedar, lead, and elm, fastened inside with blows against the lead which boomed like the warnings of the death which awaited us all, and then lowered on a crude gallows-like block and tackle to the spot near Peter's believed grave, where Pius was laid away. Even in death the pitiless publicity was "not how you think"!

Within days the old ceremonies I had witnessed in 1939 unrolled again. The elderly Cardinals went into conclave on the same poor seminarian beds in dangerously drafty halls, dined on the butterless and tasteless food prepared for them by Vatican nuns, and chose another Italian Cardinal to ascend Peter's throne. He was Angelo Roncalli, Patriarch of Venice, the new Pope John XXIII, a veteran of twenty-eight years in the Vatican diplomatic service in Bulgaria, Turkey, and France. Son of a northern Italian share cropper, Pope John XXIII was an affable, easily approachable Churchman who treasured the memory of the humility of his origins, but one who had shown rare diplomatic skill in reconciling the former German collaborators and the pro-Allied underground fighters of the

French Catholic Church after World War II. Following the patrician-mannered Pius XII, a new-type clergyman was on Peter's throne, but in self-sacrificing devotion to the cause of the Church and civilization there was sure to be no change. This was my first impression of John XXIII in the late months of 1958, but Pius XII remained, of course, the Pontiff I knew best.

My first assignment on my return to Rome in 1946 had been a key event in Pius's reign, the creation of thirty-two new Cardinals, nearly half of the Sacred College's maximum membership of seventy. The mass appointment of Cardinals was unprecedentedly large. It was Pius XII's first naming of Cardinals, and for the first time in centuries the ruling Pontiff had made selections guaranteeing that the majority would pass to the non-Italians. Only four of the thirty-two new princes of the Church were Italian. All five continents were represented. That, too, was for the first time. It was the new Pope's will that it be clear that the Church was for all nations, not just for the West and certainly not just for Italy, though the latter had given Catholicism all its Popes for four centuries and very many of the others who had ruled in Rome in the thousand years previously.

Archbishop Francis J. Spellman of New York, very Catholic and very American, very devout and very practical, had listened to the argument I and others had given him, to the effect that the American press would want to accompany him to Rome. Two planes had been chartered, one for the prelate and other American Catholic churchmen, the other hired jointly by three dozen reporters and photographers.

It was in his role as an American that the democratic prelate of New York gave each of us a souvenir, a one-dollar bill signed "F. J. Spellman." It was a "short snorter." As the well-traveled chaplain of Catholics in the American armed forces the future Cardinal well knew that it was the custom of the time to commemorate ocean crossings by getting the names of fellow passengers signed to bits of paper currency. Presumably one of the Archbishop's several lay attendants had contributed the $50.00 or $60.00 worth of bills, for two laymen of the party came down the line scribbling their names on our dollars without asking whether we wanted their signatures beside that of the well-publicized New York church leader.

The American and practical side of the New York Archbishop was not new to me. I had covered his arrival in New York as the appointee of Pius XII soon after the coronation ceremony of 1939. The relatively obscure Monsignor Spellman, son of an Irish-origin Massachusetts grocer, had served in Rome in his early years as a priest and had made the acquaintance of Cardinal Pacelli in the Vatican's Secretariate of State. One of the new Pontiff's first acts was to name his old acquaintance to the vacant New York see, one of world Catholicism's most important.

"I will pray as if everything depended on God and I will work as if everything depended on me," the new head of the New York see had told us.

Later, during the Holy Year of 1950, the New York Cardinal's Americanism was to show itself again. When he arrived with a pilgrimage his group walked into St. Peter's behind both a cross and a shiny new American flag, the latter carried by a retired New York policeman. It was one of the few times a flag of any nation appeared in the Basilica that year, for orders soon went out that no more national banners were to go in.

On our arrival in Rome for the ceremonies of the coronation of the new Cardinals, Archbishop Spellman was met at plane side by a nephew of the Pope. It was one of the many signs of the special affection the Pontiff and his family had for the head of the Catholic Church in New York, and also of the importance which the relatively young American branch of the Church had assumed.

The New York Archbishop's American side was emphasized a few hours later when he agreed to daily press conferences in a city where no Cardinal ever before had mass meetings with newspapermen. The New Yorker promised also to use his influence and that of the three other American Cardinals-designate, Samuel Stritch of Chicago, Edward Mooney of Detroit, and John Glennon of St. Louis, to get better facilities in general for the newsmen. The Holy See's system of press contacts was so poor that a news-centered American mind could not comprehend it. Partly this arose from the fact that we from the split-second United States had come to a city of "eternity" in which centuries, past and future, counted for everything; partly it was the fruit of the religious wars, generations of liberalism and anti-clericalism, lifetimes of separation between the old Christian headquarters and the modern Western mind; and, finally, it resulted from simple poverty. The Vatican, it became evident, was not able to replace the threadbare cloths on the walls of the Faith-guarding Holy Office or on the armchairs of the dignified Secretariate of State. It could not repair the cracks in the ceiling of the gilded Hall of the Benedictions inside the rear walls of St. Peter's, the hall whose balcony was the platform for the blessings *urbi et orbi*. The Holy See clearly felt that it could not afford an efficient modern public-relations staff such as, for one, Cardinal Spellman had. There was also the essential fact that no one could speak for the Catholic religion unless it was the Pope himself and that even he, in Catholic belief, was infallible only in matters of faith and morals and only when speaking formally *ex cathedra* ("from the chair" of Peter). Rarely in the century since the Catholic promulgation of the dogma of infallibility had Popes so spoken. The most casual words of an official press spokesman would be interpreted as binding in faith on Catholics around the earth. No press officer in the American White House sense was likely to appear at the Vatican very soon, if ever, but the New York prelate promised to do what he could.

"But remember," he told us, "we are only four!"

One victory was prompt. We had been told that "equal" treatment would be given to the "Catholic and non-Catholic press." Twenty representatives of the former and twenty of the latter would be admitted to the ceremony in St. Peter's in which the new Cardinals were received into the College. The ruling had staggered the American newsmen. There was speechless frustration in the thought of comparing a correspondent for a single religious paper with a circulation of a few thousand with a reporter from a news agency whose following might well include one paper for the other man's every reader. There were a hundred journalists in the American "non-Catholic press" group alone.

"Four" were enough. The New York Cardinal-designate took the responsibility for "no bustle" among the transoceanic newsmen; we accepted the restriction; and the ceremony for the creation of the new Cardinals had the greatest coverage ever given to such a religious event in all history.

The end of the war through which Pius XII had steered the ship of the Church, with its dozens of millions of faithful on both sides of the line, and, in his evident view, with some good and bad inevitably involved in both camps, was now confronting the papacy with the new era of reconstruction. The appointment of the new Cardinals began it. It was a time both of profound reasons for being disheartened and also of the liveliest occasions for hope. The advance of atheistic Kremlin influence into Catholic Eastern Europe rated, in the judgment of some of the most responsible Catholics, with the worst disasters that had befallen the Church in four centuries, the most grievous since the Turks and Tartars had poured in from the East and Catholic-Protestant religious wars rent the heart of Europe.

On the other hand, it had not been since the time of the Roman Empire that the world had been so completely one, so closely bound together by the still ill-understood press, by the radio, by the airplane, and by a consciousness of common character reflected in the United Nations. Those near the Roman Pontiff felt assured that the possibility of a single church, perhaps beginning with a reunion of Catholicism and the Orthodox religion of Greece and of Russia, was stronger than in centuries.

Neither the fight against communism nor the cause of church reunion showed great gains by a dozen years later, but I had seen by then many evidences of the self-sacrificing flame of religious devotion and idealism which still burned on the Roman soil of tired Europe.

Part of the story was, of course, in the biography of Pius XII. I had seen something of the exceptional prelate in 1936 when he had visited the United States. Those were the days of the Detroit radio priest, Father Charles Coughlin, whose attacks on President Roosevelt had made him a controversial figure of importance far overshadowing that of many prudent and withdrawn members of the American Catholic hierarchy. None of us who went down New York Harbor in a Coast Guard cutter to interview the slim, dark-skinned Vatican Secretary of State had known the prelate by reputation until then, and few of us had any but one idea in mind, a "follow on the Coughlin story," a comment one way or the other on the Detroit priest and, ideally, on any mission the Pope's closest collaborator might have with regard to a limitation of the Michigan clergyman's activities.

With Cardinal Pacelli as we greeted him was the then unknown Monsignor Spellman.

His mission, the Vatican Cardinal told us in a prepared statement, was to study the great United States.

"And about Father Coughlin?" several blurted.

The purpose of the trip, the prelate repeated, was to learn firsthand about remarkable America.

Usually we would have persisted, but the rebuff had been so serenely firm that we gave up without another try. So determined a personality was an unusual experience. Later, but far too far behind time for that day's story, we were to notice that the Detroit church orator had vanished quietly from the headlines.

A few days afterward, at the Waldorf-Astoria, as my paper's "expert" for Catholic news, I marveled at another of the Roman Cardinal's performances. A text of a twenty-minute banquet address was handed to us at the press table and, for the first time in my career as a reporter, I had not a word to change on my copy of his talk as I followed his memorized delivery. Every other speaker had always changed a phrase or two, sometimes paragraphs or pages. The Cardinal from the papal court altered not a syllable. It was one of the first American encounters with the photographic memory which helped the Pope master nearly a dozen languages as tools in what he clearly considered the mission of his pontificate, to serve as a messenger of spirituality to a shrinking but divided, materially successful but psychologically tormented modern world.

A good share of my European assignment in nearly a decade in Rome was devoted to study of Pius XII. A twenty-minute talk with His Holiness which, like almost every conversation with newspapermen, was sealed in secrecy; attendance at many special and general audiences; and dozens of talks with Vatican officials and Catholic churchmen in Rome convinced me that the ideals and virtues of earlier Christian centuries in Europe were still fresh on the Continent.

In my talk with him I was impressed with the intensity of the attention the Pope accorded. A world of interests and concerns surely fought for his mind, but in those minutes he gave the impression that he was wholly absorbed in our tête-à-tête. He spoke English rapidly, with a fair accent, and understood even the subtlest nuances as I talked quickly, sounding his views on a dozen subjects. Only once did I switch to the Pope's native Italian to clarify a point he seemed to miss. He replied in English. The Pope by then was eighty, but he switched swiftly from topic to topic, touching the affairs of several continents, as I asked his views on each. To every point his answer was prompt, clear, and unequivocal, sometimes touched with emotion.

My family joined me in another audience. I remembered it mostly for five-year-old Betsy's achievement. When the official photographer took the picture of the score of us in the "special" audience, camera-conscious Betsy managed to slip exactly in front of the Pontiff's tall white figure. No one going through the file and seeing that picture would fail to notice that Betsy had been there.

By then His Holiness was known around the world for certain of his accomplishments. His place already was assured in the rank of Catholicism's remarkable Pontiffs. He was known not only as a linguist, but as the Pope of the Audiences who had received more millions in his receptions than had any other in the chain of more than two hundred Pontiffs, and perhaps more than all the others combined. He was recognized as a phenomenally prolific preacher; as a daring ecclesiastical archaeologist who had permitted diggers to explore the spot reputed to be Peter's tomb; and as an internationalist who saw no reason why black Africans should not be Catholic bishops, why Chinese should not be in the College of Cardinals, and why non-Italians should not resume a place on Peter's throne after an interruption since the Renaissance.

An extraordinary dedication added to innate talents had made the Pontiff's myriad achievements possible. His were eighteen-hour days even at eighty, days divided with an un-Latin, rather Teutonic precision between morning calisthenics, light meals, an hour or so each day given to pro-communist as well as conservative newspapers, three or four hours assigned to audiences, and one afternoon hour, from 4 P.M on the dot to five turned over to a brisk reading-walk alone in the Vatican garden. For relaxation of sorts there were late evening readings of Cicero, Dante, Fénelon, Goethe, and other classics in a half-dozen languages; occasional music (Bach, Wagner, and Verdi were especially enjoyed); and listening to the radio, with the British Broadcasting Corporation a favorite.

There were few close associates. The Roman Pope was a lonely man. Even Cardinals saw him so seldom and one another so infrequently that one of the most prominent admitted that he did not know what his fellow members of the Papal "Senate" were thinking. The Cardinal did know, however, that whenever he carried a problem of his congregation to Pius XII the latter seemed already well informed upon it. His information was derived perhaps from the reports from the forty Papal Nuncios, or ambassadors. He read the Nuncios' reports attentively. Audiences, too, added to the Pontiff's extraordinary founts of information.

The diggings under St. Peter's, in which hundreds of truckloads of earth had been removed, revealed an ancient Roman cemetery thirty feet beneath the Basilica floor. It disclosed also that Constantine, the first Christian emperor, had constructed the first St. Peter's on the side of the Vatican hill. The broad church rested half on a ledge cut out of the slope and half on fill. It was an awkward spot. Surely, Vatican archaeologists reasoned, there must have been a special reason for its selection; something must have "tied" Constantine to the place. That something, they affirmed, was the point exactly under the three now ancient superimposed altars which stand beneath the center of Michelangelo's dome. For many centuries it had been considered the site of Peter's burial and thus the earliest vestige of Christian leadership. The excavators found a crude altar of the first two Christian centuries over what might have been an earthen grave. From the earliest Christian decades the corner of the old cemetery under the later altars and under the dome had been a place of devotion.

Cardinal Spellman arranged for a few of us to go down into the ancient graveyard in the subbasement. We walked through streets which had been buried for fifteen hundred years; entered old mausoleums; saw statues, wall carvings, niches for the ashes of cremated pagans, floor graves for Christians, and funerary inscriptions of days when Rome still had imperial grandeur. All the scores of thousands who were to visit Rome during the 1950 Holy Year should be allowed to circle through the ancient cemetery, Cardinal Spellman urged, but his Vatican guides would not agree. The space was too damp with drainage from the buried Vatican hill and too cramped ever to be opened to many travelers, they said. Scholars could come, but few others.

The excavations permitted by Pius XII had revealed no sarcophagus inscribed "Peter, Prince of the Apostles, First of the Popes." The spot had yielded few remains. There were traces of bone at what might have been the edge of an earthen grave. But the rediscovery of the old cemetery, certainly the logical place for the earliest Christian burials, had been a major archaeological contribution, had produced some new evidence to support ancient Christian traditions, and had affirmed the Pontiff's determination that science and religion should move closer to one another, helping close a gulf that had split the Western intellectual world for centuries. If the dilemma "science versus religion" could be resolved surely some of the weakness in the beleaguered West would be removed.

The issue of science ran as a thread through the speeches the Pope of the immediate post-World War II period never tired of giving. There was no conflict between science and religion, the Pontiff repeated. Slowly Pius's key ideas emerged. In questions of sex, he emphasized "natural law," right and wrong deduced from human reason and from a consideration of the natural effects of sexual relations. Christian Revelation, sex ideas drawn from the Bible as the given word of God, was the basis merely for insistence on the permanence of the marriage bond. Pius's fight against contraceptives as a frustration of the natural effect of intercourse, against sterilization as a device for avoiding conception, against artificial insemination in the majority of its forms, was all based on appeals to reason. The same was the case in other scientific and intellectual fields. The Pope's aim, I was told, was to give believers the widest intellectual latitude inside the Pontiff's interpretation of the limits set by Christian traditions. The story of the creation of man and of the world in Genesis was interpreted to mean that the evolution of the human body was possible so long as the direct, instantaneous, divine creation of the human soul was not denied. Pius accepted scientific evidence that the world probably began five billion years ago, infinitely long before the start of the comparatively minute Christian era.

It was manifestly painful labor to reconcile the old faith of nearly half the Europeans (231,000,000 of Europe's 550,-

000,000 people were Catholic) with the puzzling mass of new facts turned out by the atomic researchers, but the never-resting Pius and his hundreds of little-known assistants toiled steadily at this essential intellectual and spiritual task.

The Pope was alone but he was "many persons," as I heard it said. Dozens of priests and some nuns, even many hundreds of them, contributed anonymously as Pius called for help of many sorts, including assistance with speeches and encyclical letters on almost every phase of human activity, from the virtues of sport to the social responsibilities of bankers and the proper limitations of trade-union activity. On the latter, Pius warned that unions should not reply to employer greed with a similar ruinous thirst for what an enterprise could not yield.

In a chat with an American priest in Pius's immediate entourage I had an indication of how the Pontiff was "many persons." Pope Pius was writing a speech on the occasion of an English Catholic centennial.

"How do you pronounce 'centenary'?" he asked an American associated with his household.

"Sén-ten-erry," the American answered. He put the accent on the first syllable.

"But don't the English say 's'n-teen'erry'?" The Pope's emphasis was on the second syllable.

"Yes, Your Holiness, but four fifths of the English-speaking world speak American!"

"But it's the English language! They started it! It's for them to say how it should be used!"

"S'n-teen'eery" with the hard second syllable was the way it was pronounced in the papal allocution, but days later, when an English bishop came to call, the Pontiff, meticulous in his lifelong hunt for precision in all the main European languages, was still seeking opinions on the word. English nuns helped by sending a book on how to pronounce place names of the British Isles. It became one of the Pope's prized possessions. I was to think of it later in Moscow when my Russian tutor pointed out how vowels in Russian, as in Italian, always have the same sound, so that if you could read you could pronounce correctly. "What a difference from English!" the Russian woman exclaimed. "We have a saying: 'English is very easy—if it reads "Manchester," it's pronounced "Liverpool." ' "

Pius's struggle with English reflected both the limitless pains he took even with unessentials and also the way in which countless men and women of religion collaborated selflessly to help the Rome-born prelate present to the world the spectacle of broad knowledge and wisdom which astonished the newspaper readers of many countries.

Slowly my mental portrait formed. Pius XII was a man more of persistence than of the quick brilliance of French politicians I had known. He was a priest dedicated to the uniquely twentieth-century apostolate of being seen by the seekers who came to Rome (he appeared at the window of his small apartment above St. Peter's Plaza even when horns were blown in a most informal and unconventional appeal that he let himself be seen). He was a man of an optimism rooted not so much in the often frightening facts which reached him as in a faith as simple and confident as that of the Roman school child he had once been.

In its fruits the Papacy and its policies also were to be known. They, too, took shape in my years as a Vatican reporter. One affected anti-colonialism, the phenomenon I had seen ravaging North Africa. In a single move the Vatican under Pius created more than fifty self-governing dioceses in Africa. Since the days when Arab invaders had wiped out the prospering North African Christian community of which St. Augustine was an eminent member, Africa had been considered a "mission" land, a predominantly pagan region where envoys from Europe or the Americas had to guide the destinies of the tiny Christian congregations. There had been no black African bishops on the day the triple crown was placed on Pius's head; there were thirteen by a dozen years after the war, and there was reason to believe that there would soon be a Negro Cardinal. Negroes had been among the first Popes.

There was evidently no reason in Pius's mind why his successors should not include blacks again.

A Chinese, Thomas Tien, was among the thirty-two I had seen receive the "red hat" of Cardinal in 1946. He was the first of the yellow race to sit in Catholicism's highest college.

The four hundred years during which Italy had given the Church all her Popes had established a firm tradition, but by spreading his first appointments of new Cardinals among nineteen countries on all continents, the Pope reduced the Italian membership of the College to one third. A second naming of Cardinals in 1952, with eleven Italians and twelve non-Italians, tipped the balance somewhat back in the Italians' direction, but the eventual choice of a non-Italian and even of a non-European remained virtually certain. Was it a sign of weakness in the continent which had given the world twenty-five centuries of leadership? I did not think so. I thought it rather an indication of the courage to renounce dead traditions and to grapple with world issues in the common interest, regardless of immediate setbacks to Europeans themselves.

How soon it would be before a non-Italian returned to the Papacy remained a question as the Italian John XXIII succeeded Pius in 1958. At least for one more time, the foreign majority in the College had decided to abide by the old tradition. An argument for another Italian was that such a choice tended to avoid injecting the dangerously divisive issue of nationality into the Church leadership election. Even so, many in the diplomatic corps to the Holy See were convinced that the time was nearing when the 90 per cent of Catholics outside Italy would again contribute a Pope.

The strengthening position of non-Italians at the Vatican during Pius's reign implied a rise in status of the United States, and that, too, occurred. Eire, Yugoslavia, Romania, West Germany, and Ethiopia soon had American citizens as envoys from the papal court. They remained Americans, for the representatives of the Holy See were diplomats of a church, not of the 108-acre "City of the Vatican State." For several days in 1946 five of the Cardinals were Americans (7 per cent), the largest single national group except for Italy and, by a shade, France. The death of the former Archbishop of St. Louis, Cardinal Glennon, on his native Irish soil during a brief visit there after receiving the red hat, lowered American representation quickly again to four. Even so, the affluence and generosity of American Catholics who sometimes contributed half of the total of certain Vatican funds, and the emphasis Pius XII placed on the exceptionally well-educated and pioneer-spirited American Catholics as a fount of missioners for work in Africa, Asia, Oceania, and nominally Catholic South America, made it clear that the once-frail United States offshoot of continental Catholicism was now one of spiritual Rome's main hopes.

As I fenced verbally one night with Myron Taylor, the Episcopalian steel millionaire who was "special representative" of two American presidents in a mission to Pope Pius, I realized the importance of our conversation to the Holy See. I tried to get the discreet Mr. Taylor to confirm or deny that his "mission" was ending. As in the case of Cardinal Pacelli in New York, almost anything would have been a "story," but the American, too, evaded any hint. Soon there was no secret. The Taylor mission was over, and the United States Congress, no doubt worried about American Protestant objections to a special position accorded to the Pope, refused to allow the opening of a legation or embassy to the Vatican such as Britain, France, and nearly fifty other nations maintained. There was sharp disappointment at the Holy See. Years later regrets were still keen. No doubt there was a difference from 1862 when Abraham Lincoln sent "Alexander W. Randall, Esq., as Minister Resident to His Holiness Pope Pius IX" (the Vatican Radio broadcast the text of the Lincoln letter on its ninetieth anniversary, in 1952). At the time of the appointment by Lincoln the Pope ruled the 16,000 square-mile Papal States with its population of 3,000,000. Even so, the Holy See had a claim to special consideration, as Mr. Truman's attempted appointment had implied, for a fifth of the world's population, 90 per cent of South America's, nearly half of Europe's, and more than half the world's Christians looked to the Roman Pontiff as their spiritual leader. The diplomacy-minded Pius XII, a lifelong servant of the Vatican diplomatic section, wanted diplomatic ties with Washington so that he could discuss matters of "peace and religion." No satisfactory intermediary in the absence of direct contact was worked out after the departure of Mr. Taylor. In a determination that its 1929-sanctioned independence from Italy should not be placed in doubt, the Holy See refused to permit the Italian-accredited embassies of the United States or any other country to serve as a channel for negotiations.

Although the issue of the omitted Vatican embassy was a source of grief to the Holy See, the Papacy's dominant view of the United States was one of trust and expectation. There was worry about American Protestant missions in Latin America, for fear both that poorly educated, poverty-ravaged South Americans would give up their Catholic faith brought from Iberia, and also that the spectacle of discord among Christians might hasten the inroads of communism. Latin America, like Africa, was, in Vatican minds, a prime new target of Moscow. There was concern, too, about American "materialism," a fear that good fortune and the quest for even greater prosperity might smother spiritual values. To that extent the Vatican was "neutral" between Washington and Moscow, but it was an impartiality in words only, for there was no doubt in the Vatican that Soviet communism was the greatest threat to Christian and Western ideals in many generations.

Dramatic speeches of Pius from the balcony of St. Peter's to crowds estimated at half a million were among the visible measures with which the post-World War II Pontiff fought back against a Red tide which put the Communists in control of even the Rome provincial council. Letters to the religious behind communist lines, including even the largely Orthodox believers of Russia, were other instruments in the papal struggle. Some Catholic clergy went over to the anti-Vatican and ultimately atheistic "patriotic" religious movements which the Communists organized behind the Curtain, but Pius had the consolation of seeing the Catholics of East Europe, in good part, standing firm. The Church in China, on the other hand, was all but razed. All told, communism had dealt a severe blow.

Vatican prestige, despite communism, or perhaps partly because of it, was at its highest level in generations. Catholics, who had had secondary positions for decades after the liberal revolution in France, assumed some of the top posts in the former Axis nations and elsewhere in Europe: Konrad Adenauer as chancellor in the Federal Republic of Germany; Georges Bidault and Robert Schuman as foreign ministers and premiers in France; Alcide De Gasperi and a score of others in Italy. President René Coty of France called on Pius XII for the first friendly visit from a French chief of state since a Pope had crowned Charlemagne more than a thousand years earlier. Eminent non-Catholics, including all three Trumans from the United States and hundreds of the topmost officials of the free world, took part in the endless audiences.

Yet the goal of a reunion of the religious, the perennially cherished objective of the Holy See, moved nearer very slowly if at all. An effort was made to get a Greek diplomatic mission to the Holy See as the first step toward a reunion of Catholicism and of the Greek Orthodox Church, but clerical objections in Greece stopped it. A Cardinal told me that there were virtually no doctrinal reasons why Catholicism and the Russian Orthodox Church should not merge, but obvious political barriers, the Kremlin's virtual imprisonment of the Orthodox leadership, blocked that. The hope, however, was not abandoned. A revolt of Russia's religious against the Kremlin atheists could still provoke a move of the two peoples— Roman Catholics and Russian Orthodox—toward one another, it was believed in the Vatican. It would have to come from the laity in mass, not from the Cardinals and Archbishops negotiating at the top, the Vatican felt.

Father Charles Boyer, a black-clad French Jesuit and one of Rome's experts on church reunion, told me some of the concessions the Catholic Church could make to achieve the coveted merger of the believers or at least of the Christians of the world. The use by the clergy of the reversed *Roman* collar, mark of the Catholic clergyman in many countries, was a "nonessential" which Catholics could waive. Even the question of papal infallibility, an enormous hurdle for the liberal mind, was less so than most people thought, the priest argued. Fewer than a dozen papal statements in the century since the promulgation of the infallibility dogma, exception made for the proclamation of saints and "blesseds," had been classed as infallible. It would be "imprudent" to say that papal encyclicals were wrong, but the possibility of error existed just the same, the Church expert said.

Catholics would insist on acceptance of papal primacy, however, and prospects for a reunion of Catholicism and Protestantism remained slim. The proclamation of a new dogma, that Mary was bodily in heaven, seemed to widen rather than to narrow the Catholic-Protestant gulf. The Roman attitude was that although new sources of discord were regretted, Church tradition was a "living" thing and "clarification" of what had always been "implicit" was a process which could not be arrested. A move of the Anglicans toward reunion with Rome in a common defense of the deepest Western values, with the London *Times* and its letters columns for a while as a rallying post, ended, instead, with deepened bonds between the Anglicans and more completely Protestant groups in India. Moslem countries sent embassies to the Holy See, but talk of a common Moslem-Catholic front against communist atheism produced little that was tangible. The pressure of predominantly Moslem Egypt against even the native Coptic Christians (Protestants and Catholics), who predated the Mahometans in the Nile Valley, raised fear of an Islamic Holy War against non-Moslems.

Reunion of the religious was for the far future, if ever, but the headquarters of Christendom's main church had the ear of free-world governments.

"They speak of the 'listening post,' but if by that is meant up-to-the-second information on what is going on in the world, it just isn't here," a long-time dean of the diplomatic corps of the Holy See told me. "The Nuncios don't have money to spend on cablegrams. But what there is is thought. Governments are so busy with strikes and all the other day-to-day problems that cabinet members do not have time to think."

During the immediate postwar blockade of Berlin one diplomat was told at the Vatican: "War won't come there, but watch Asia!"

It was many months before the headlines spoke of Korea.

It had been a different Vatican from what I had expected. There was no enormous organization, no miniature "Washington" administering the affairs of a church in scores of nations. Many Vatican posts were vacant. Many Cardinals among the little more than a dozen in Rome were too old to take an effective part in the international Church government. Pius's rule was more by encyclical letters than by the toil of a busy clerical bureaucracy. The Pontiff's leadership mainly was exercised through the careful choice of good bishops. Through them the Pope trusted that the unique Catholic Church organization would operate effectively.

The Church was old in many of its Cardinals; poor in the state of physical maintenance of the Vatican, ill-staffed in terms of personnel on the rolls of Rome congregations; and lacking in a dozen other ways; but the selfless dedication of the Pope and of missionaries much like Guadalcanal's Father Le Klerk who streamed in and out of Rome; the devotion of tens of thousands of priests, nuns, and laity; and the visible seeking on the part of thousands of others made plain that the finest human aspirations still found hospitality on Roman soil. America and the world for a long time to come would find inspiration there.

Whatever minor changes John XXIII, with his different background and his more informal personality, would make, it was clear in late 1958 that there would be no alteration in these essentials.

That did not mean, of course, that such gestures as clearing the road to the Papacy to the colored peoples of Africa and Asia would be enough to avert costly setbacks in the ex-colonial areas. It did not mean even that Rome might not, in a new disaster, become part of what Pius XII called "the Church of Silence," the mute Church surviving in a communist state only in its public ritual and not in the preaching Pius insisted was essential. Grievous reversals would come, but regardless of that, the glow of twenty centuries of Christian ideals would remain as a light.

VII

EASTERN THREAT:
EGYPT AND EXPULSION

Just as I had seen the first long waves of an incoming Arab-nationalist sea lapping at European sand castles in North Africa, so did I see a high tide sweeping over old continental positions in the mid-fifties in the Middle East.

One Middle-East assignment was to go with the United Nations' "world army" in the spring of 1957 as it took back the overwhelmingly Arab-inhabited Gaza Strip from the withdrawing troops of Israel. Egypt's forty-year-old dictator, Colonel Gamal Abdul Nasser, had seized economic as well as military control of the Suez Canal. Oddly, he had had the latter without the former. Britain, France, and the Zionist state had attacked Egypt in retaliation.

To end the risk of World War III, a blue-bereted U.N. force of Canadians, Swedes, Danes, Norwegians, Indians, Yugoslavs, Colombians, and men from a half-dozen other secondary powers had been organized to supervise the withdrawal of the three nations' forces.

The excitement of the almost hysterically nationalistic Arab Middle East was in the air as a half-dozen of us journalists waited with the little U.N. Army for Israeli permission to cross into the Strip. The Israelis already had evacuated the much bigger Sinai Peninsula, Egypt's extension east of the Suez Canal. All that remained to put the Zionists back inside their small national limits was to supervise their departure from tiny Gaza.

The Strip was insignificant in size, about six miles wide and fifteen miles long, but it was great in religious and military history and was a dangerous flame near the explosive fumes of mid-twentieth century East-West conflicts. Gaza, with its almost entirely Arab population, was one of the few bits of the old British mandate of Palestine which the Jewish state had failed to acquire. In Gaza were 200,000 destitute Arabs who had been ousted from Palestine. For years Moslems from the Strip had raided Israel for plunder or vengeance and Israel periodically had struck back with murderous military raids. Renewed full-scale Arab-Israeli conflict would risk a world catastrophe.

American diplomatic pressure, inspired in good part by fear of Soviet intervention, had convinced the Israelis that they should abandon even Gaza, the last prize from their lightning autumn, 1956, victory against the Egyptians, but as we stood on the border that stormy spring afternoon the blue-and-white Israeli flag continued to flap at a road block a half-mile ahead of us. The Israelis temporarily had suspended their plans for retreat. There had been a riot a mile or two ahead of us, inside the Strip, and at least one more Gaza Arab had been killed. The Israeli command had decided that it would be too provocative for the U.N. advance party to move in as planned to reconnoiter the camp sites from which the "world army" was to rule Gaza. The U.N. might be permitted in after dark and the Israelis might still leave, as agreed, before dawn, but the international force might have to do everything by dark under the cover of the curfew.

Among the U.N. men there was grumbling against the Israelis, but there was scant sympathy for the Arabs either. The grievance against the modern, highly disciplined men from the Zionist state was that their decision to repudiate the reconnaissance agreement might endanger U.N. troops; the feeling against the Arabs was because of their almost total lack of choice and cohesion of any sort. Nasser, as he had made clear in his autobiography, had ambitions to guide the destinies of the Gaza Arabs and of millions of others in the Middle East and North Africa, but it was not from his organization that the U.N. soldiers felt a menace. Nasser's strength was in his weakness. It was in the capacity of poor and impassioned

Arabs, and especially of mobs, to sweep away any rival order
and, I feared, any order at all.

The problem of the Arabs was around the pup tents of the
U.N. soldiers as they pitched camp against a sandstorm. A
road block had been set up to keep Arabs from Egypt from
entering into the Strip until after the Israelis were out and
until the U.N. had a grip on power in the area. We watched
nervously as a stream of the Moslem natives turned their
camels off the road a half-mile behind us, and riding in full
sight on the horizon, passed our positions and then drifted
back onto the road behind the Jewish troops. There were not
soldiers enough to close the border everywhere.

Not all the Arabs stayed on the horizon. It was others, who
descended like birds on the U.N. garbage pits, who drove
home to us the natives' desperate plight.

The word had passed that a move at nightfall seemed probable. The U.N. "kitchen police" had been told to bury their
garbage and to discard any extra food that could not be loaded
on the crowded trucks. I watched the expressionless, cream-
complexioned, sturdy blond youths of a Swedish unit, all of
them in their late teens or early twenties, as they lifted the
rear flap of a cook tent, stepped over a low barbed-wire fence,
and began dumping garbage and a few usable food items into
a four-foot pit.

Then it started. Fifty Arabs darted down from a ridge, and
as fast as each Nordic relay could drop a new load into the
hole, scurried in, snatched it up, and fled like pigeons. There
was no common language. For all the Arabs knew the Swedes
might consider the scavenging a capital offense. One Arab
gashed his hand on barbed wire in his haste. Two stumbled
and fell half-a-dozen times as they hurried off with a fifty-
pound sack of flour. By that time the Swedes had begun putting out valuable supplies, setting them gently on the ground
at the lip of the pit, realizing that everything they discarded
would go for other humans' consumption.

The youths from the north were dumfounded.

"Is it always like this?" one nineteen-year-old asked.

It was not the first glimpse the northern Europeans had had of the poverty on their continent's southeast doorstep, although it was one of the most immediate and dramatic. Coming across the Sinai Desert in the wake of the retreating Israelis, there had been other examples. Five-year-old nomad children ran beside the international trucks crying *"Mangiaria, mangiaria!"* apparently a corruption of an Italian word learned from World War II, *mangiare, mangiare* ("to eat, to eat").

"I will never forget one little girl," a Canadian told me. "She was not quite six. I gave her one of our oatmeal cakes. You have to soak them, you know, but she crammed it right down her throat and then took a hard-boiled egg on top of it. With nothing to drink!"

In a drive across the Sinai Desert with a member of the Indian delegation I had seen something similar. The Israelis had broken up the one hundred-and-seventy-five-mile highway from the Canal to Gaza, using modern wrecking equipment, and the Egyptians, with hand labor, were only slowly restoring the pavement. Nearly a half-year had gone by and at least another six months' toil by the Egyptians would be needed before the road would be back in service. Most of the traffic had been suspended, but the U.N. movement by itself had been enough to churn holes five feet deep in the loose sand beneath the old surfacing. It was hard to think of anything but hanging on as our truck lurched along for five hours, but the Indian driver had had something else to concern him. He spoke no language I knew so we sat together silently, but no words were needed as we approached the many begging Bedouins along the road. The driver kept up his thirty-mile-an-hour speed; if we were to stop, the desert poor, like locusts, might pick the truck clean. But not pausing did not mean lack of sympathy. The American-packed U.N. rations had been more than any of us could eat in the desert heat. With one hand the Indian scooped up the crackers and other extras he had saved from our roadside lunch and dropped them as carefully as he could over the side.

The Indian's problem, how to help the Arabs without getting his truck raided, was typical of what the U.N. forces faced
as they weighed the problem of how to assist the people of the
Strip without exceeding the limits of others' rights. It was the
question of the whole world's relationship to the Arabs and to
emerging ex-colonial peoples in general.

"I don't like murder," one U.N. platoon commander told
me, "but if the crowds swarm over us I'll shoot into them. I
can't let my men be overrun. I'll shoot first into the air and
then into the ground, and if they issue tear gas I'll use that,
too, but nobody can criticize me if I have to fire into the mob
in self-defense."

His unit already had been harassed as it crossed the Sinai
Desert, the officer said. Bedouins had scored a near miss with
rifle shots at one point, and the U.N. soldiers had fired into
the air in return. Five prisoners had been taken and there had
been no more trouble.

There had been no indication that Nasser, as the main Arab
leader, had been behind the Bedouin attack. On the contrary,
Nasser had been rather understanding and cooperative in talks
with the United Nations' Secretary General Dag Hammar-
skjold. The Bedouin raiders, like all too many in the revolu-
tion-torn Arab world, presumably were on their own. An indication of what was going on in the minds of the Egyptian
nomads had been given in several talks between U.N. officials
and some who were, in international law, Nasser's people.

"Who are you?" one desert chief asked a U.N. detachment.

"We are the world army, here to see that the Israelis get out
and to give back the desert to you Arabs," the commander
answered in effect.

"But why? They won, didn't they?" the Arab answered. The
idea of nations and of national rights might be something
Nasser's sophisticated aides could argue in New York at U.N.
sessions, but it was a concept generations or even centuries
removed from a typical citizen of Nasser's Egypt.

Another U.N. unit gave medical assistance to a Bedouin
tribe. The chief was touched. "I'll tell you something," he con-

fided. "There are Israelis in the area. I will protect you from them." The protected would protect the protectors.

Part of the problem was the lack in the Middle East of modern nations in the form democratic Europe so long had known. Part of it also was the reflection of the strange world of Islam, where victors were reverenced as Allah's chosen with little or no concern for the illegality or brutality which might have paved their road to triumph. The U.N. stories reminded me of one the French had told in Morocco. In the course of the two years in which Mohammed V had been off the Rabat throne, the French one day had brought the gloomy and worried puppet sultan, Ben Arafa, a rare morsel of good news.

"Pleasant information, Your Highness," the French had told the puppet monarch. "The Americans have lent us some helicopters to fight the locust plague."

The sultan had stared moodily for an instant and then had brightened. "Ah, yes, the locusts," he said. "Allah sent them and Allah will take them away."

There was no room in the sultan's formula for thanks to either the French or the Americans, and scarcely any chance for either mentality to meet the other.

If the Arabs were ill-organized there was no question but that they had passion. On the night before the U.N. troops were to move into Gaza a few of us had a soft drink at a table set up in the dust of a street outside a native café in El Arish, the last Egyptian outpost. Three excited youths insisted on buying us a round. They took seats beside us. One or two of them had been schoolteachers in Gaza, and all three said they had had to flee as the Israelis tried to control the hostile Strip. One of the young teachers described in frightening detail how he had escaped through a back window when the Israelis had come hunting for him as an Arab nationalist. The U.N., the young men said, could not govern Gaza. The people of the Strip might have been Palestinians and thus somewhat different from the Egyptians, but Nasser's Egypt had to resume control, the youths said fiercely.

"They are Arabs, and Arabs understand Arabs," the three insisted.

The fact that two thirds of the 300,000 inhabitants of Gaza were penniless refugees who were being fed, housed, educated and, in part, employed by the U.N., and that a breakdown of order might touch off a new round in the Arab-Israeli war, did not concern the youths. The U.N. aliens could nourish Gaza but not administer it.

The night of the long day fell and orders to enter Gaza were passed. It was a strange sort of going "over the top." No declared enemy lay ahead, but there was nervousness just the same.

"Carry on!" U.N. soldiers of various nationalities called to one another. "Good luck!"

A world effort to bring peace and order to a chaotic corner of the vast ex-colonial region was under way. A few minutes' jeep ride brought us abreast of the Jewish Army emplacements. We peered curiously. I had seen the birth of the Jewish state reflected in Rome, where a suitcase of explosives had blown up the British embassy in a warning that Zionist terrorists meant to eliminate English domination in Palestine even at the expense of an underground world war against Britain. I had seen the Israeli national flag hoisted over the Jewish Agency building in Rome, offices which were merely a private organization's headquarters one day but a diplomatic mission the next. The shadow nation had emerged.

All of us in our jeep were struck by the square shoulders, the strong faces, and the calm self-assurance of the smartly-uniformed, khaki-clad Israelis. Perhaps some of them were the same people I had seen in el Glaoui's Marrakesh, in the compressed, centuries-old ghetto there. In Morocco and in other areas in North Africa and Europe the Jews had revealed a certain timidity, the mood of an eternal, often persecuted minority. These were transformed men.

"They look confident and tough," I suggested.

"And ruthless," one of my jeep companions added. He had seen the Israelis in action against the far-more-numerous Egyptians. In the sand by the broken road from Suez to Gaza scores of abandoned shoes were still to be seen. They had been cast off, we were told, so that the broken Egyptian army could flee faster through the sand.

Modern arms in Israeli hands had conquered the Arab forces, but the threat from Russia and the menace from the passions of Arab mobs and from individual Arab terrorists along the strategic Suez Canal and through the rich Middle East oil fields had won the political, diplomatic, and final victory. Our mission that night was to put the seal on the Israeli loss.

We rolled through a storm-blackened night. The Israeli curfew was holding. The streets were empty and there were few lights. Below us on the left passed Rafah, one of Gaza's many points of interest in a fantastically long history. It was where Esarhaddon had rounded up camels for the Assyrian attack on Egypt in 1671 B.C. Whatever it had been then it was only a penurious settlement now. The whole area, centering on El Arish behind us, was the region Napoleon had described as the military key to the Middle East. Ahead in the dark lay the town of Gaza where Samson, by biblical account, had pulled down the temple.

In the community of Gaza, as often happens with newsmen covering history, the minds of several of us in the small U.N. reporter corps were soon absorbed in immediate personal problems. We had been happy at the thought that we had a good "story," but in the main settlement of Gaza our way was blocked by a hundred newsreel cameramen, still photographers, radio commentators, and newspaper reporters. They were with the departing Israelis. They would be back in Tel Aviv or Jerusalem after an hour's drive, with instant communications to the rest of the world. The thought of trying to match that with our own primitive arrangements—relaying copy by jeep twenty miles to El Arish, by truck over the shattered road to the Suez Canal, by a waiting taxicab from there three hours to Cairo, and then through the more-or-less-admitted Egyptian government readers to the telegraph wires to

London, was enough to put profounder problems of the Arab crisis out of our minds.

The story ended cheerfully. We drove through the dimmed-down town to the jail which served as Israeli headquarters. We saw shell holes punched through some buildings and listened to the clattering and groaning of Israeli tanks, with their implicit warning that any further Arab insubordination could expect more such treatment. We glimpsed the buxom women soldiers who were part of the Israeli army. We were shown the way to the villa of Israeli Intelligence, whose occupants no longer would need it. We emptied the pad-filled shelves, lowered chests and other furniture as makeshift beds, and cooked our supper out of U.N. rations.

Then the miracle happened. Reynolds Packard, a veteran of a generation of news coverage in the Fascist invasion of Ethiopia, the Spanish civil war, World War II, and postwar China, picked up the phone in the hastily-abandoned villa and asked for Tel Aviv. Within a half-hour all of us had our stories out—phoned through the correspondents of our papers in Israel. In a Middle East of confusion, inefficiency, and hate-fostered splits it had not occurred to the rest of us that the telephone in our makeshift home for the night could give us almost instant contact with our distant offices. It proved to be a marvel for one evening only, for next day, when I tried again, the wonderful phone was dead. "Normal" Israeli-Arab relationships had been resumed. An impassable wall of enmity once again separated the Jewish State and the Arabs of Gaza.

Within a week Nasser was administrator of Gaza as the young men in the El Arish café had demanded. At dawn the morning after our arrival we were awakened on our beds of chests, tables, and rows of chairs by the sound of hundreds of people running and shouting. Barefooted Arabs in white robes and skullcaps poured through the streets. There was a din across the street from us at the jail. The prisoners of the Israelis were crying out demands to be released and a street mob was supporting them. The crowd already showed bitterness against the U.N. for its delay in opening the cell doors. Most of the demonstrators seemed cheerful but all of them were violating the curfew and I remembered how the Meknes Arabs had switched in a split second from cheering the Paris-appointed Grandval to stoning the French.

Only then did we notice that our jeep, an unhappily exact duplicate of the Israeli army cars, had no U.N. markings like those of the rest of the international force. It seemed wisest to begin our day's reporting by leaving the Israeli Intelligence villa at once and, in our equivocally anonymous jeep, finding a U.N. armed detachment as companions until the drift of events was clearer.

A few of us crowded into the jeep and at the high speeds Westerners found appropriate when cruising streets otherwise occupied only by demonstrating Arabs, we hunted until we discovered a U.N. unit up a side street. It was Gaza town headquarters, set up in a sturdily built modern schoolhouse.

The U.N. command shared our uneasiness. Soldiers, perhaps the same ones who had fed the Arabs at the garbage pit at the edge of the Strip, were rolling out barbed wire. Desks from the schoolrooms were being piled up as a barricade. Patrols were being organized. Bayonets were fixed as psychological deterrents and ax handles were distributed as more practical weapons. If the worst came, the soldiers would beat back the crowds long before they would imitate the quick-triggered police of Morocco.

"There may be a raid on the supply dumps," a U.N. staff officer told us.

The U.N. had huge stores for the feeding of the refugees. They would be logical mob targets.

We followed a patrol by jeep. The crowd pushed up toward the thin U.N. line as I had seen the other mob do a decade earlier in the successful sack of the Italian prime minister's headquarters, but the international officers apparently had had briefing enough on how to cope with throngs. Each time the crowd came too close the officer leading the patrol took out his pistol and fired into the air. The brutal bark was enough each time. The crowd recoiled.

For the moment the U.N. had the upper hand and the supply dump and other key installations, including even the jail, seemed safe for a while. We used the lull to interview some Gaza celebrities. One had given a speech in the jail at midnight at the ceremony of handing over by the Israelis. He told us now about a stream of Zionist misdeeds: there had been some rape cases; the Israelis had bought up onions, sugar, and other items which had been plentiful until then behind Gaza's lines but scarce in Israeli; the invaders had thinned out the Gaza government pay rolls, adding thus to unemployment; and economic conditions had been so bad that it had been impossible to collect the assessed taxes. Worst of all, the Israelis had walked off with the land registers. The books might be used to get refugees behind the Israeli lines, or their representatives, to sell land at the low prices of despair.

Some of the complaints tended to cancel one another out, such as the charge that government income was too small to permit needed public works coupled with the lament that official pay rolls had been slimmed down; but what seemed to matter that morning on Gaza lips, particularly on those of men who had collaborated with the Israelis, was to speak ill of the departed.

One of us had a question in reserve.

"How can you say all this when your speech at the Israeli departure was so different?"

The man blanched. "Were you there?" was all he could reply. He had forgotten the Israeli-U.N. overlap.

He recovered slightly in a moment. Well, it was true, he murmured, that the Israelis had done some good, as he had observed at the evacuation ceremony. "They did bring food which made life much less difficult for the people."

We visited both mayors, the one the Egyptians had named during the period after the first Israeli-Arab war when they administered the Gaza Strip, and another who had served fourteen years at the time of the British mandate and again during the Israeli occupation just ended.

The mayor of the British-Israeli era, Roushdi Shawa, was

a cultured, dignified man who spoke gravely of Gaza's long-term needs. As the mayor of yesterday talked, youths stared insolently in through the barred windows of his office. As we left we received a farewell salute which surely had a second purpose. A friend of our host accompanied us the few feet across the official's small garden and at the gate jerked a pistol up into the air. Six shots went off almost as a single burst. I cringed instinctively at the man's shoulders; the gesture, to say the least, had been unexpected. It was a sort of journalists'-size royal twenty-one-gun salute. As such it was pleasant enough, but the second and true purpose was plain. Wandering mobs who might escape the ax handles of the U.N. were put on notice that sackers at the villa of the British-Israeli mayor would not be received with folded hands.

The mayor of the Egyptian era was Moneir Rais. We met him just after the U.N. troops began a precipitous freeing of the Israelis' prisoners. Ax handles and pistol shots aimed at the sky were working so far, but there were signs of deeper trouble brewing. Releasing the convicts was one way to lower the temperatures.

Rais struggled visibly to control his emotions. He was smart looking in his silver tie and dark blue suit. His hair was cut short in what he said was his first trim in forty-five days. The former mayor received us in his brother's villa, next door to his own. He apologized for not welcoming us in his own home. The Israeli shell hole we had seen in his wall was, he said, the reason.

His clothes, too, were something new, Rais added. They were his first change in a month. The bitterness of being jailed by the Israelis was something our host would not soon forget.

Mr. Rais crooked a finger. A servant brought him a cigarette and match. The Gaza prison had not eliminated the habit of command.

A sweet fruit drink was passed to each of us.

"Not speaking emotionally," as he said, Mr. Rais summed up his views. The Arab-to-Arab relationship had to be restored in the Strip. The Egyptians must return as administrators. The U.N. could not stay as governors. It was just what we had heard at the café. Arab organization had not been sufficient to keep mobs from running amuck, but with the help of the Cairo radio it was adequate to drive home to many a few simple, deeply felt and embittered ideas.

Why there was fury was clear as we visited another of Mayor Rais's recent companions in jail. He was J. A. Filfil, an English-speaking newspaper publisher. He had been released a few weeks earlier, but he invited one or two of us to his home to be present for the return of his thirty-year-old son. The youth, too, was an Arab nationalistic journalist. He had studied at the American University in Cairo.

Mr. Filfil, like former Mayor Rais, made an evident attempt to control himself as he told us in a nearly conversational tone that his son had been beaten until deep slash marks were left in his buttocks. The enraged father only deepened the fury of his story by insisting that we share the family's liberation banquet as we listened to the account. It was with a strange mixture of hunger and revulsion-weakened appetite that I took notes, nibbling at the delicious spread of early March tomatoes, cheese, olives, rich Gaza oranges, and tea. We had cooked our own lunch many hours earlier out of dry U.N. rations. The fresh food was a delight.

Mr. Filfil's words were restrained; they were chosen carefully, but the very limits he set to them heightened the contrast with the sounds of passionate emotion vibrating through the walls beside us. It was a modern, European-type house, but in the next room, as we had seen through an open doorway, the women of the family were crouched on the floor, some of them rising occasionally for the same writhing bosom-and-hip dance I had seen as a guest of the French in nomad tents in the Atlas Mountains of Morocco. The music was the same I had heard in Arab quarters all across North Africa, a thin, eerie wail with a beat set by tomtoms. East and West met under Mr. Filfil's roof. That night, as the music worked on our taut nerves, it seemed as if the Orient was winning.

The gate bell rang and the son returned. The women rushed into the garden to embrace the grim young man. The father, his face tense, walked stiffly to the youth, embraced him, and then led him back to the casual Western guests of the evening. The American-educated young man shook hands unsmilingly and then touched his heart in the gesture of the Arab. In dress, manners, home furnishings, and command of English, it seemed a thoroughly European or even American family, but a new Arab nationalism, with all that implied for a changed future, obviously had captured the family's allegiance.

We drove next day to the Israeli border. It was only two miles from the homes of Mr. Filfil and the mayors. It was across Gaza town, out through the two or three blocks of shanty suburbs where children aged four or five, gleeful at imitating their elders, chanted "Nasser, Nasser," and then across a narrow field. There was no buffer, just the teeming Arab town and then suddenly the Israeli farm land.

Major Singh Backshish, an erect, gracious Sikh from India with a command of Oxford English, was in charge of the U.N. frontier post. His name, he told us patiently, was pronounced the same as the word for a handout, for a tip, even for a small bribe. It was the thousandth time he had given the explanation, we were sure, but his good spirits kept up.

Our friend's cheeriness dwindled as he explained his problem at the border post. Around him was a knot of Arabs in despondence. The old border which was now restored, they had been telling the Sikh, ran to the very edge of their fields. The onions were just coming in. How were they to harvest them?

The major didn't know. All he could say was that the Israelis had informed him that they would shoot anyone who crossed the fields in the direction of their lines. But what guarantee was there that Israeli night raiders would not take the harvest, the Arabs had demanded? The major had no answer for that, either.

A field of onions! That was the true dimension of the

Israeli-Arab struggle for existence. Unless wisdom and charity found a solution in time, the fight over onions could degenerate and expand into a war of atoms.

How Major Backshish was to seal the border was a mystery, he said. He had a searchlight to throw on any who moved in the dark, but his part of the front was long, his troops few, and his orders were to shoot only in self-defense.

Clearly the Arabs had little organization when it came to educating, feeding, and caring for their swarming populations or controlling depredations by savage mobs, but Nasser sympathizers did know how to work underground to undermine any who opposed them. They could rally crowds and unleash them against those who resisted. A new kind of mob now appeared on the streets of Gaza, and within hours the U.N. surrendered administrative control to Cairo. The streets were filled with crowds marching with signs, some of the placards in misspelled English:

"Welcome [to the U.N.] as visitors, not rulers!"

"Welcome for Egyptions." (*Sic.*)

"Down Mole." (French Premier Guy Mollet.)

"Hell to criminals, colonials!" (Meaning: "Damn the criminal colonialists!")

"We do not accept any rule but Egypt!"

"Never forget Palestine!" (Israel's expulsion of the Arab refugees.)

"Long live Arab unity!"

"Peace for the land of peace!"

The latter tied in the soil of the Bible, the country of Christ, with the mid-twentieth-century slogan of revolutionaries who wanted "peace!" even if they had to "fight for it!" as some European Communists ingenuously had expressed it after World War II.

The technique in the Gaza mob was "typically Communist," the U.N. commander, Major General E. L. M. Burns, protested. It was less clear whether Communists were directing the pro-Nasser action or whether Nasser's own revolutionaries were taking a page out of the successful Communist book, but the effect was the same. Shooting broke out at the U.N. head-quarters at the jail, an Arab was killed, the Nasser government protested that the international force was endangering Arab lives, and an Egyptian general within hours crossed the line to take over civil administration.

The U.N. submitted quietly. Legally, as the international officers saw it, they could not object to a restitution of conditions which existed prior to the Nasser seizure of the Canal and to the three-nation attack against the Gaza Strip and Egypt. Local authorities were sovereign. No matter how much logic could be rallied to the support of the views of the U.N. command, there was still no international government and no real world army either.

By jeep, by truck across the disintegrated Sinai Desert road, and by taxicab from the Canal to the Nile, a few of us drove back to Cairo. The U.N. continued to feed the 200,000 Gaza refugees. The Egyptians permitted the world troops to patrol the frontier. The rest of the Gaza administration was taken back by Egypt. Whether such an arrangement made sense in an area where the U.N. contribution was so great and where war danger was so large was something I had no further time to contemplate as I grappled with the much bigger issue of Arab-nationalist Egypt itself. Egypt had been in a hurry to take over the government of the Gaza Arabs but in Cairo I doubted Egypt was ready even to govern itself.

A passion of nationalism was sweeping the key country. What Napoleon had remarked about shabby El Arish as the instrument for control of the Middle East could be said about Egypt with regard to a much bigger area. As its young president, Nasser, had said in his autobiography, a book reminiscent of Hitler's *Mein Kampf*, Egypt was at the center of several circles, an Arab world reaching from Morocco into the oil lands of the Middle East, a Moslem region stretching from central Africa through the whole of the northern half of that continent and out across South Asia to the Pacific, and an ex-colonial neutral zone encompassing almost all of Africa and a good part of Asia. Not only Egypt but the whole area centering on it needed a leader, Nasser had said in his book. The question was who that leader would be, the young man had added with only the thinnest veil drawn over a vaunting ambition.

Egypt was not really the center of such big circles as Nasser conceived, but it was at the heart of a zone critical enough to make it of major importance to the future of Europe and of the West. It embraced the Suez Canal, with all that meant in terms of control over a large part of Western oil supplies coming by tanker from the Middle East. Canal possession also implied power over much of Western trade with Asia, unless the West was to accept the added expense of detouring sea traffic around Africa's southern tip. Egypt, also, with its fiercely Arab-nationalistic and xenophobic radio, had an influence on the Middle Eastern Arab countries which possessed a large share of the West's oil sources.

Egypt's potentiality for causing trouble was immense.

The nationalism of the Egypt of the second half of the 1950's was plain in a single walk through the center of the capital, on the banks of the Nile. Even the silhouettes on traffic lights telling the pedestrians when to cross had been redesigned from Western models to make it plain that the Cairo man in the street was not to be confused with the impersonal man in trousers, woman in skirt, or small child in short pants who march eternally in profile across the pedestrian stop-go signs of the West. Cairo's silhouette was of a paunchy man in a Moslem fez.

I visited ousted King Farouk's palace. A few rooms had been converted contemptuously into a night club. The singer chanted: "I love Cairo in the springtime." The tune was the same as the one about Paris; even the lyrics were identical. But the crooner did not smile as he edited Paris out and Cairo in. The jaded patrons, listening stolidly, were unsurprised.

All signs were in Arabic alone or in English and Arabic, even rooftop billboards advising homebound Americans to "Fly TWA." At the ministry of "Guidance," the propaganda headquarters and the place at which Western correspondents were asked to present themselves on arrival, the ground-floor building directory was exclusively in Arabic. Rare indeed was the Western journalist who knew the Arab language, but the propaganda chiefs were determined that the arriving reporters would have to grope their way. Putting the signs in Arabic alone did not mean that the bulk of the Egyptian population itself could do any better on visits to the "Guidance" ministry. Eighty-two per cent of the Egyptians, according to an American embassy fact sheet, were illiterate in all languages, Arabic, of course, included.

Cairo had been the Westerner's and particularly the Englishman's open doorway to Africa. The door was closed now or at least swinging shut fretfully so frequently as to threaten probing European and American fingers.

Life in August 1956, ten days after Nasser's grab of the Canal, when I made my first trip to Egypt, was going on uncertainly. Business was poor, especially over the chaotic weekends. The government was pressing for Friday, the Moslem holy day, as the weekly day off from work. Businessmen were holding out for Sunday on the ground that it fitted the habits of the continental trading partners. Some shops had switched to Friday, some still stayed with Sunday. The government itself closed on the fifth day of the week, setting an example. Sunday proved a good day to catch officials at their desks. It was all so new that no one else apparently thought of hunting them out at that time. Minor anarchy was the general result.

Anti-Western feeling was high, and yet a good share of the middle and upper classes had been educated in French-Catholic schools scattered through the Nile Valley. I was told of one Nasser diplomat whose children knew no Arabic. One official of a Nasser-seized foreign enterprise confided that his seven-year-old child was only then beginning the study of the Middle-East language. He and his wife, he said, had always talked French at home.

An Egyptian invited me to one of the sports clubs which Europeans had developed on islands in the Nile. There were few other Western faces in the dining hall that day. I was told of another Egyptian member of the club who had taken to deploring, "You never see anyone you know any more." He had been part of the Egyptian minority in the vanished European heyday. Snobbishly he was lamenting the ouster of the Westerners and the arrival of more of his fellows.

There was an evident sense of inferiority. One Middle Easterner put it this way: "We have been dominated by foreigners so long that we yearn to feel really free, at least for a little while. No matter what the price, no matter how dangerous it may be in terms of opening the way to the Russians and the Communists, we crave to have all you Westerners out of our countries."

The emotional anti-Westernism had quick consequences. A picture of a rifle-armed guerrilla, two stories high, stood straddling one downtown Cairo street, a glorification of terrorism.

I visited two Cairo centers of anti-Western violence, the undistinguished business building from which much of the revolution against France in North Africa was being guided, and the home of Abd el Krim, the warrior of the Rif Mountains who had harassed Europeans in Morocco in the early twenties.

An Arab in a garment that looked like nothing so much as a nightshirt napped on the sidewalk in front of the North African revolution headquarters. The contrast was striking. The modern cement sidewalk was typically European; the sleeping Arab, on the other hand, represented a force Europe, in Egypt, could no longer resist.

In the revolution headquarters I was received by Mohammed Kheidar, a gentle-mannered man whose French was as pure as any I had heard in Paris. He had been a French deputy, Mr. Kheidar explained. He still had a French passport, but he did not consider himself a traitor. The passport, he said, had not been granted, it had been imposed. He was an Algerian and, as such, by French law, a Frenchman. To him

France was an invader of North Africa, one he was dedicated to expelling.

The revolution rooms were rundown and unimpressive, but the dark-skinned, intense young men who moved quickly about them were evidently hard at the work of cutting Europe's roots on the Mediterranean's southern shore.

Abd el Krim gave me tea at his villa. I remembered his story from the newspapers of my New York childhood. Krim had come to believe that the Spanish occupant of his corner of Morocco had wronged his people and he had taken to the hills as a rebel at the head of a force which defied combined French-Spanish military efforts for years. The French had finally captured the insurgent and had sent him to exile in the Indian Ocean. Bringing him back as a pacification gesture after World War II, the French had lost their prisoner at the Suez Canal. Arab nationalists had helped Krim escape and Egypt had given him hospitality.

Krim's villa was in a tree-filled compound at the edge of the city. He received me in an airy hall beside a veranda and introduced several sons, erect, quiet young men in their late twenties and early thirties.

I asked how there could be peace between Arabs and the West.

The West had better deal with the Arabs with the utmost prudence, the septuagenarian warned. There was still hope of peace, but the danger line was near. It was all a question of "faith," the old man said. When he had risen against the Spaniards, "I had not more than 400 to 500 men," but "faith" had tipped the balance. As I had read in an encyclopedia, Krim and his little band in 1921 had encircled 30,000 Spanish troops, had cut off their water, and then, for eight days, had worked a massacre.

"The official report," said the old man, as if repeating a many-times-told tale, "said that 23,000 were killed, but there were more than that."

"Faith" did it, and if the West did not beware, "faith," said Abd el Krim, would do it again.

"A woman once asked me: 'Who put you up to it?' No one prompted me! I put myself up to it. And it will be that way anew."

The Russians would not have to joggle Nasser's elbow or that of the slumbering, nightshirt-clad Arab in the street. Instinct would be enough to impel Arabs to cut Western water and to slaughter the men of the inferior "faith."

Krim had been honorary president of the committee for revolution in French North Africa. His status now was that of elder statesman of Arab revolt.

Nasser agreed to see me and for once I went to an interview looking for "good news." It had always seemed to me that affairs that ticked along peacefully like life seen through a ten-year-old's eyes in Bay Ridge, Brooklyn, were not news; that it was when things went badly that headlines were made.

In the case of the Nile's young military dictator I made up my mind to the reverse. So much that was Western was going badly that any ray of good news would be precious. What I avoided as Pollyannaish in an interview with a Westerner I sought with Nasser.

The dictator kept me waiting for two hours. I was to learn later what seemed to be the reason. A group of English and their Arab associates had been arrested as spies, one more move in a tense game that was to bring on the three-nation attack seventy days later. It was a matter requiring the leader's personal attention.

Nasser's headquarters was on the same island as the luxurious sports club. I sipped a soft drink brought by one of the president's polite and silent attendants. The Nile in flood, one of the few rivers to reach high water in midsummer, poured by, black, oily, and silvery under lights from the banks. Upstream glared a rooftop advertisement for an American soft drink. A new bridge being built by the West German gunmakers, Krupp, was a dim outline on the horizon.

I had never before talked to Nasser but I knew a few essentials about him and his country by then. I knew that "Egyptianization" of business firms was forcing unwanted local employees on the foreign companies and gradually was driving non-Egyptian investors out of the country. I had heard often that any man whose first name was George or John instead of Mohammed was having trouble getting work, even if he was a member of the relatively well-educated Coptic Christian community (Catholic and Protestant) which predated the overwhelming Moslem majority in Egypt. I had learned from college examination boards in Cairo that the anti-Christian and pro-Moslem discrimination went so far as to deny university training and degrees to many Christians for none but religious reasons, while opening the door to the Mahometans for the same cause in reverse.

I knew something of the frightful poverty with which the government leader had to deal. I had seen a barber shaving his patron's head as both sat cross-legged facing each other in a roadside ditch outside Port Said, where the Suez Canal enters the Mediterranean. I had seen a barefoot man ironically selling socks on the sidewalk of a Cairo main street. I had watched a child of seven sitting every day in midtown Cairo offering for sale an unwanted lapful of trinkets. Along the Nile I had stared at barelegged men dragging barges upriver, three or four of the haulers leaning into rope nooses seventy-five feet long and heaving ahead the way mules had done along New York's Erie Canal a century earlier.

I understood something of the problem of Israel and at least a bit about the anti-colonist fury in Arab hearts. I had talked with Nasser cabinet members, asking the same question monotonously: How could there be peace with Israel? I had always received the same answer—Israel had done a great wrong against Palestine Arabs, and Israel was expansionist. The implication seemed clear. Israel had to go.

The hatred in Arab hearts had been dramatized for me by an American-educated physician in Morocco. He had refused an offer of $15,000 a year in the United States in order to work for much less among his own North Africans. We had talked over lunch.

"You know," the doctor had said in the easy accents of a

Midwest American, "whenever I look into the eyes of the European nurses who help me, I see scorn. Do you know when I breathed for the first time as a free man? It was when this revolution began."

When native knives began slashing European ears, noses, sexual parts, and throats, the man who was one of the finest products of American schooling had sighed with relief.

There had been no cynicism or hypocrisy in what the physician said. I had met him outside the palace of Sultan Mohammed V sometime later and he urged me to quit the compound at once. The mob was uneasy. Anti-Western violence in the abstract was something my friend could rationalize; cruelty to one he knew was something he could not easily stomach.

I comprehended also some of the importance of the canal Nasser had just taken. A single ride along the waterway was enough to suggest its significance. Ships sailed south so high out of water that they looked from a distance like apartment houses standing on the flat desert sand. They came back north squeezed down in the water to their Plimsoll marks, gliding a few inches off the bottom thirty-three feet below. Oil for the industries of Europe filled the tankers to the limit.

Finally, I knew something of the harshness of Nasser's make-up. I had read his autobiography and especially the story of how he and others, all in their late teens, had decided to "do something" about the bad state of the world and had drawn up a death list. They had picked a victim, had shot him on his doorstep, had listened to the screams of his womenfolk, and then had been glad when he survived because assassinations alone suddenly seemed only "part" of the answer. There was more to it than murder, the strange hard son of the Nile had written, but the killing of a few was something he stood ever ready to repeat. The book was distributed proudly and freely at the "Guidance" ministry, so the words presumably still were official.

My first impression of the strong man of the Middle East was in his favor. A tall two-hundred-and-twenty-pounder, he was handsome and smiled easily. For the first moments he was tense. I was one of the first Westerners to see him since his seizure of the Canal six weeks earlier and he had been denounced in the West with a babel of epithets: as "a Hitler," "a would-be Pharaoh," a "megalomaniac" (the phrase the gentle-mannered French premier, Guy Mollet, used for him), and as the aspirant head of an insanely grandiose Arab-Moslem colored Asiatic-African empire.

Nasser offered me one of his favorite cigarettes (the American L & M brand). He lit up for us, using his thumb-snap lighter. An orderly served sugary lemonade and then, a moment later, thick, sweet Turkish coffee.

A mercy in the room was that no portrait of Nasser looked down. The office was one of the few in Cairo without such a picture. I had not been sure I would not see one. When I had encountered the Moroccan sultan one day in his Rabat palace courtyard I had noticed that the windshield of the American low-priced car he was driving was half-obscured by the monarch's own picture. There may have been a reason other than narcissism, however, even in that case, for nationalist mobs had become so excited in the summer of 1955 that a window picture of the sultan was sometimes the only sure safe-conduct pass for an automobile. The sultan may have feared that if he drove without his own picture a quick-shooting supporter might fire without knowing who he was.

It was a relief, however, to see no picture on Nasser's own wall, because the omnipresent portrait had become oppressive as it stared from every shopwindow. The impression of the leader's Godlike ability to see all and to know all was depressing.

First I asked the Egyptian president the journalistic question of the moment: would he agree to talk to Australia's Prime Minister Menzies and to the committee of Suez Canal users the latter headed? The main national clients of the Canal had met in London and had appointed the Menzies group to speak for them. Nasser had refused to attend the London meeting. His attitude toward the Menzies committee would determine at least short range hopes for peace in his corner of the Mediterranean.

The dictator said he would receive Menzies. "I'll speak to any man except about giving him my jacket."

Nasser's English was good though sometimes awkward. I assumed he meant "giving him the shirt off my back." The dictator meant he would talk but that he would not give up rights and would not even discuss a surrender of them.

Why should Egypt have the Canal?

"Because no one can protect it against us."

The answer startled me. I had expected a banal reply: it is ours because we can give the world better service than the private profit takers from France who have run it until now. The answer sounded like: "Your pane of glass is mine because if you don't hand it over this stone will break it."

It was a naked language of force rarely heard in a West where "rights" and "wrongs" were touchstones of discussion.

The Canal, Nasser went on, was more than one hundred miles long. The best defense system could not keep the teeming Egyptian population of 25,000,000 on the Canal's two banks from breaking through to sabotage the passageway.

Wasn't Egypt unprepared technically for such a job as running the Canal?

"Are you sure of that?"

The answer was quick, and there was an edge of resentment. There was only a trace, but it was evident. President Nasser, like Gaza's Mr. Filfil, like former Mayor Rais and like the North African physician and many other Arabs I had met, was obviously one who knew how to cover anger with civility, but hurt feelings were no less deep for that.

"We have men highly skilled in all fields," the Egyptian president said. "We have men competent in transportation, in cargo movement, in all branches. The only problem is with pilots. And that is because under the old Canal company we were deprived of an opportunity of training them."

The reference was to the Paris-based company which had dug the Canal in the second half of the previous century and had run it since under an odd arrangement in which Egypt handled the policing while the company abroad collected the tolls and supervised the funds.

Nasser pushed up a sleeve to uncover a complicated date watch.

"It's—let's see—the twenty-eighth today. We've been running the Canal a month and there have been no accidents yet."

What about Egypt's internal conditions and the partial Anglo-American boycott?

The young president shrugged.

"It may trouble the upper middle class but it won't touch 80 per cent of the population. They are already on the border of starvation!"

It was another answer I found astonishing. The fact that four fifths were in desperation surely was no reason to risk worse.

The dire plight of his people was used by Nasser a moment later in another direction. I asked about the dreams of empire hinted in his autobiography. Whether out of a sense of tact or for some other reason, he minimized the prospect.

"I think I have to build Egypt before I build an empire," he said. "The average income in my country is $5.60 a month! Eighty per cent eat only bread, milk, and cheese. They eat meat only once a week or once a month."

That was a reason for completing Egypt's control of the international waterway, Nasser went on. Some way had to be found to get money to build the huge Nile dam at Aswan which would increase Egypt's small cultivable space.

"The Canal revenues, that was our money. Our people dug that Canal. We had to use that money for the benefit of the people for whom that Canal was dug.

"And we felt there was a real action directed against the Egyptian people to keep them as poor as they were during the days of their occupation, the days of colonialism."

The ideas poured out. It was impossible to argue them all. Egyptian labor had dug the Suez Canal, it was true, but French capital and engineering knowledge had guided the work. The Canal certainly had not been excavated to damage the Egyptians, but its purpose was no mere elevation of the standards of the country on the Nile; international trade and profits for the capitalists who backed the enterprise were motives, too. The suggestion that a plot against the people of Egypt was at the back of international events was even more extraordinary, and even less adapted to a calm exchange.

"Every year the population increases by half a million," said Nasser, returning to the plight of his people. "In thirty to thirty-five years it will be doubled. It will be 45,000,000. If we don't work hard, the result will be the decline of the standard of living."

How bad that would be needed no comment.

I asked Nasser about American aid.

"What aid?" was the quick answer.

I was taken aback again. I listed the many millions of dollars of assistance in the form of technical advice, and food from the CARE charitable group, about which I had read in an American embassy handout. It was frustrating to tell the government head something which was surely a key factor in his own calculations.

Oh, the packaged cheese from CARE, Nasser shrugged. It cost a goodly penny to distribute all that, and the people preferred fresh cheese anyway. "Give me the money!"

Eyes twinkled at that. Whatever might be done with cash turned over without strings, it was evident that the United States had won no gratitude for the aid in kind it had sent already. I wondered whether it was a case again of Allah using American helicopters to kill Moroccan locusts, with no Moslem thanks due to the Americans.

What about the American-Russian dilemma? What about Israel? What about France in North Africa?

To my renewed surprise and to my appreciation, the Egyptian president patiently took each subject in turn. On Israel he preferred not to speak. He liked to handle one problem at a time and the nationalization of the Canal Company was the issue of that hot summer. Even so, he would say that he had been in the Palestine war against the Israelis, had seen the Arabs of Palestine "transformed into a mass of refugees," and had determined that he would never let that happen to his own country. That had been at the root of years of requests to the Americans for arms, appeals that had received a courteous hearing but had never produced action. One thing had led to another. He had asked the Soviets for arms, had got them, had been struck by the Western boycott, and had begun selling more and more of Egypt's single cash crop, cotton, to the Red bloc.

"They say we've given Russia a port in the Mediterranean. But it was essential to escape the punishment of the boycott. It is not fair to tell me we should have endured that."

France in North Africa? Charges that Egypt was training Algerian rebels?

"Do they need training after all these years? I think France has to put into effect the Atlantic Charter of Mr. Roosevelt —self-determination. You"—with a grin—"were the first people to say that. It was you who declared it."

The answer gave France slim reason for another diplomatic protest, but it supported what one French general had told me in the Algerian hills: "The thing to do is what we would have done in the last century, just send a fleet to bombard Alexandria." Nasser's was an attitude which surely contributed to the French assault which was then only two months distant.

As for America, the president said, what hurt was the way Secretary of State John Foster Dulles had canceled consideration of American financing of the billion-dollar Aswan dam.

"You are a free country. We would have had nothing to say if you had just withdrawn. But to say at the same time that Egypt's economy was too bad and that it was due to the government! To raise trouble like that in Egypt. That was a hostile action."

Egypt was "only a small country," but it had pride, the Middle East leader said several times.

Russia? The "Bagdad Pact" of Egypt, Iraq, and Britain against the Russian threat to the Middle East?

Egypt had been ready to join the Bagdad Alliance, but its warning that neither Britain nor any other former imperialist nation could share membership had been ignored, Nasser said. A potentially anti-Russian Egypt had been converted slowly into a Russian-supported country. With Egypt behind the subversion of the Bagdad Pact in 1958 and Russia profiting month after month in sinking its bear claws deeper into the strategic Middle East, the dictator's version of history had importance. Was it true that an ally too many had spelled the doom of the alliance which had been designed to keep the Soviet Union out of the important area east and south of Turkey? Or was the reverse true, that no pact of weak Middle-Eastern nations could have had any meaning without Britain or the United States to bolster it?

I put the question differently. "I can understand your resentment against your country's colonial past and I can see in a way how you dread that Egypt might slip back again into a position as a European protectorate, but don't you fear that by escaping one colonialism you may fall under another?"

The smile slipped from the young man's face. There was a cold, even fierce, expression for an instant.

"All I can say is that as of tonight the orders are given not in Moscow and not in London and not in Washngton. They're given here."

One night seemed short indeed as the life of a policy. I assumed that Nasser meant again that it was a case of handling one problem at a time, the West now, the East on some tomorrow. Hopefully it meant that Nasser was still not avowedly pro-Muscovite, and even, implicitly, that he was anti-Soviet. Perhaps the Arabs and the Middle East, once convinced of their independence, could still be saved for peaceful cohabitation with Europe and the West. But the reasons to fear worse unfortunately were all too plain.

Was it possible to reverse the anti-Western trend?

"Yes, but we do not have the initiative."

It would be up to the West to convince the Arabs that they were free.

Was I right in detecting deep bitterness?

Nasser nodded. "Arabs in general are bitter. I see it about myself. My own feelings are bitter."

It was a problem of psychology. As one Nasser cabinet member expressed it: "How do you expect me to love you if you do so-and-so?" Nasser and his colleagues consulted their emotions, their likes and their dislikes. Passion, not rationality, ruled. One Western diplomat analyzed it: a fever of nationalism. The feverish are never rational. All the West could do was to work patiently to bring down the fever.

I had a final question about my newspaper colleagues. Why had three British and Canadian reporters been expelled?

Nasser knew the cases. The reason, he said, was that they had written that there were 13,000 in Egyptian concentration camps. The truth, the dictator said, was that some 3,800 had been arrested in four years, some of them Communists, some of them Moslem extremists, some of them members of other political parties. All parties were outlawed. All but 500 who had been tried and convicted "recently" had been released. It was an important point, Nasser said, for in "two, three, four, or five years," when another might have control, he could face jail himself if he had violated the constitutional ban against prolonged arrests without trial in a time when martial law had not been declared.

The remark was interesting for the hint that the Egyptian dictator already was looking toward a time when he would no longer hold power. He felt no security. Even dictators evidently had reason to worry in dictatorships.

"The free press!" Nasser went on, with sudden fury. "Sometimes I think it means lies, lies, lies. It is not a free press but a hostile press. They can lie—but somewhere else."

I was to remember the words when my own copy ran afoul of the dictator's displeasure.

I groped for a phrase with which to make a departure. Nasser had talked for ninety minutes and seemed ready to go on for more, but I knew how much of his country's business depended on him and I did not feel I could take any longer.

"Let me step out of character as a reporter," I said, "to say that as one of the millions concerned I am glad you are going to see the Menzies committee. Critically important rights are involved on both sides."

I thought I was giving Egypt its full due, but Nasser disagreed.

"I understand what you say," he answered with a cold smile. "You would be happy if I were to give them my jacket."

We were back at the beginning. I had found no good news even the time I had hunted hardest for it.

My own expulsion from Egypt came on my second trip to that country the following spring. It was a third of a year after the ill-fated British-French-Israeli attack. For two months I rooted through the facts of economic decay, discrimination against Jews and Christians, and hardships for foreigners of almost every stripe, and slowly had laid bare a picture of weakness and confusion that conflicted painfully with the vainglorious portrait which the national radio was giving to Nasser's hungry people and to the awakening Arab nationalists of the Middle East.

I was called at eleven o'clock one night by Ahmed Anis of the "Guidance" ministry.

"I'm sorry. I have bad news for you. Our security people want you out of the country in the morning. They asked for your hotel room number and I insisted that it was our right to deal with you. I was afraid, you know, about language problems, about a bad matter being made worse."

The hint that resistance might go badly was plain. It was obvious that "Security" knew exactly which room I occupied.

"I assume I will be given no reason?"

"That's right."

Getting out meant fast moving. The American embassy took official note of the ouster order. The American airline, T.W.A., said they could get me on a plane at 10 A.M., shaving two hours from the implied noon deadline Anis had given. A trip to the office of Colonel Hatem, the ever-cordial director of press relations, was to no avail. His aide said he was in, ducked into his office, and then came out in confusion to say he could not be seen. It took until 3 A.M. to sort through stacks of Egyptian newspapers and notes. There was a hectic 8-A.M. hunt for a tailor to tell him to stop cutting the summer suit I had ordered to meet the 105-degree heat of a March khamsin wind from the Sahara. (The tailor had not arrived at his shop but he sent a full refund to Italy; he had promised to hurry with the suit but had never got to it.) At the airport there was no sign of "Security," no confiscation of notes, and lunch that day was in the blue sky over the Mediterranean homebound to Rome.

Egypt's was a "tumbleweed" government, without roots, "without intellectual humus," a group of army officers around Nasser who argued all night over coffee and then at 5 A.M. pounded the tables with the Eureka cry, "That's the way it will be." That, at least, was a common Western diplomatic analysis those days, at the heart of the Arab revolt. A new world was being born. Nasser and his kind wanted to be free. Western influences over them were still strong. Nasser wore a London-made suit and the Cairo revolutionaries lived in a modern European city whose ousted constructors, it must be said, were getting no thanks. American movies continued to cover the cinema screens of officially un-Western if not anti-Western Cairo. Could there be peace between the Arabs and Europe? Could Europe be sure that the Canal would be open when needed and that tolls would not skyrocket anti-economically? Would the important oil supplies continue to flow at payable prices? The question stayed open as I turned north to report life on another threatening part of Europe's periphery, the Communist bloc from eastern Europe to the Soviet Union.

VIII

EASTERN EUROPE:
GRAY IS THE
COLOR OF COMMUNISM

A Western diplomat chatted one day about the discord in France and the weaknesses in Italy.

"It does seem alarming, but we have at least one consolation," the ambassador said. "Perhaps their troubles are even worse."

The "they" were the fourteen men and one woman in the Soviet communist presidium in the Kremlin.

In another Western ambassador's summary of the European plight the two outside pressures against the continental storehouse of Western traditions could be seen as one: "The Kremlin fears the rise of the colored peoples as much as we do; they are trying to turn them off against us the way they attempted to do with the Nazis when they signed in 1939 with Hitler."

There was no question of the Kremlin's importance as the force that had lifted Nasser from a position as the ex-colonel dictator of one of the poorest and most nearly impotent Arab states to that of a major worry for the West. Even so, it was a mistake to see the problem of the former colonial nations merely as Moscow-concocted. The first part of the diplomat's analysis was important, too. The advance of the "colored peoples" was a capital fact of the mid-twentieth century and one that could threaten the relatively advanced white men of Russia as much as West Europeans and the people of the two Americas.

The solution, it seemed, was for the white men of Russia and of all the West to accept the birth of the independent "colored" nations and to trade and cooperate with them in the hope that increased prices of raw materials from the former colonies would not ruin Europe and the West.

If that was true, however, it was clear that the Soviet communist presidium, bent on world victory, had decided to harness the anti-colonialist force as an aid, however dangerous to all the whites, in destroying the non-communist West.

The answer, then, even to the anti-colonialist pressure on Europe was in part to be found in the communist world.

My first glimpse of communism in control was in Yugoslav-occupied Istria in 1946. The American and British armies advancing up the Italian peninsula had met the ragged guerrillas of the Yugoslav communist, Josip Broz Tito, at Trieste. Tito, a tough labor organizer who had been undeterred by periodic jail sentences, had taken to the plentiful hills of forested and mountainous Yugoslavia at the start of World War II, had harassed the German occupiers so successfully that a substantial Hitler force had been tied up there in the heart of the Balkans, and, finally, at war's end, had descended on the Italian frontier area. Italy had been Fascist and Italy would have to pay with a considerable chunk of her northeastern border area, Tito proclaimed.

Tito's attitude caused one of the first East-West splits in the wake of the world war. The British and Americans, appalled at the way Tito's raiders were seizing middle-class Italians on the streets of the former Austrian seaport of Trieste and killing them cruelly by dropping them into limestone caves, drew a line around Trieste and told the Communists that they would have to wait for a top-level agreement before advancing further. Part of what the Yugoslavs wanted had been Slav-occupied farm land, and there was no doubt but that Mussolini had been brutal in attempting to force "Italianity" on the unfortunate Eastern population inside his frontier. On the other hand, many of the cities and shore-front villages had been Italian since the time of the Venetian merchant princes of the Middle Ages or even since the Roman Empire. The Yugoslav labor rouser of the twenties was reaching far.

An East-West commission was formed to pass judgment on the border quarrel. American troops dug in on the military alert on their side of the temporary border, the chaotically uniformed Tito guerrillas took up positions menacingly in the face of the Americans, and a few of us of the American press corps in Trieste were invited, to my surprise, to tour the area behind Tito's lines. If we could be led to say a few kind words for the Yugoslav communist case, perhaps the top-level commission could be influenced in Belgrade's favor.

We were driven through the lightly-guarded Allied border post and stopped for close scrutiny of our red-star-stamped passes at the Tito side. A wooden pole blocked the road and a grim youth with a submachine gun and a star-marked cap made sure that no one attempted end runs around the barrier. The thin protection at the Allied side reflected a still-lingering attitude that the Communists were colleagues of the just-won anti-Fascist war and friends until proved differently. The humorless Tito Reds, on the other hand, were obviously security minded, with no outsiders trusted, not even the comrades of the day before.

Our guides conversed pleasantly as we drove high onto the barren, cave-pitted ridge that divides the Latin and Slav worlds at Istria. Guerrilla days had been immensely exciting, our Yugoslav hosts told us: many a farmhouse had trap doors near the fireplace where Tito men could hide from the Nazi or Fascist searching parties.

"Will you show some of those hideouts to the border commission? They might interest them. They might impress them."

"Oh, no." The tone was horrified. "We might need those places again."

I was unprepared for the answer. Against whom could the Communists need the refuges? Surely not against prostrate Germany or ravaged Italy. It was my first direct contact with a new communist stream of thought: that the Allies of 1945 might be the battlefield opponents of 1946 or sometime later.

The scrappy Yugoslavs' split with the Soviets was not to come for another five years and was, to me, unthinkable then.

We drove past a factory.

"Can we see in there?"

"Of course. You can see anything. But that wouldn't interest you. It's an industry for making farm machinery."

We insisted anyway. Reluctantly we were taken in. There was not a plow or a tractor in sight, but scores of grimy German prisoners were at work scraping and oiling torpedoes. In Allied-controlled Italy bombs were being dismantled for scrap metal and for fertilizer chemicals; in Communist Yugoslavia war matériel was being moth-balled for a possible new war against a yet-unnamed enemy.

We drove on toward Fiume, the Austrian seaport the Italian writer Gabriele d'Annunzio and other Latin nationalists had captured in defiance of peace treaty terms after World War I. We passed a roadside shrine. A metal cross, concrete clinging to its foot, lay on its side atop a partly gouged stanchion. Someone evidently had wrenched it from its stone base. Another had placed it back on the pillar. No one had touched it after that. Yugoslavia and Istria were Communist now but they were also still religious. An official census of the Communist government later was to give the religious breakdown as 49.53 per cent Orthodox Christian, 36.7 per cent Roman Catholic, 12.52 per cent Moslem, and 1.25 per cent "other creeds," or a totally believing population.

An enormous sign above a Fiume skyscraper proclaimed: *Hocemo Tito* ("We want Tito"). The city had been renamed. It was Rijeka now, a Yugoslav word for *fiume* or river.

"Rescue us, we are Italians," a woman pressed forward to say.

"Quiet!" one of our guides cried at her. "We are happy as we are."

We were taken back out of Fiume-Rijeka to Abbazia ("the Abbey"), now named Opatija. There was a party for us at the Hotel Moskva (Moscow) whose old name could be made out

by the stains where letters had been pried from the wall: the
Hotel Regina. The spirit of the steppes was "queen" there
now. The dance went on far into the night. Officers wore
pistols as they waltzed. Peace had come but Tito was taking
no chances. A few priests attended during the early hours of
the evening but were reticent when I tried to draw them into
conversation. I went into the church across the street. Mass
was said but there was no sermon. Paper bills of the smaller
denominations marked with the red star of communism were
heaped on the collection plate at the offertory.

I asked to see something of the interior of ex-Italian Istria.
My Communist hosts agreed with alacrity. The ethnically
Italian areas were along the coast. In the hills I would see lib-
erated Slavs.

I was driven to a settlement on one of Istria's highest pin-
nacles, the hamlet of Beram. It was in a land so stony a peasant could build his house and still have a field three quarters
rock. The village seemed lifeless as we arrived. I was taken
first to a house whose front door was banked thick with evergreen, like the Tunisian village later for the arrival of Bourguiba. I was told that the young man of the house had been
killed by Italian Fascists. He and others in Beram had laid
an ambush to break up Rome's efforts to get the hillspeople
out to an election they had considered rigged.

There was no explanation of how the doorway happened
to be bordered that moment with green, whether it was an
event of every day, or whether it had been arranged especially
for my visit or for the border commission's. I was invited to
take note of the devotion in which the anti-Fascist martyr was
held, and we moved on.

The woman of one of the stone houses invited us in for a
snack and drinks. She brought sandwiches of fried pork, two
strong Istrian wines, and a powerful plum brandy. The liquor
loosened tongues and the oratory took alcohol itself as the
theme. The peasant hostess refused to join in the drinks, insisting it was not ladylike, but she was ready with a few anti-
Italian stories. Good homemade alcohol like that, she said,

was a hardship to produce under fascism. The revenue collectors were always after home brewers and the tax on Istrian wine was so high it was more economical to import from the Italian peninsula. The lady never had learned the Tuscan-Roman language. Every time she had gone to town with her eggs she had risked a $2.50 fine for speaking Serbo-Croat as she hawked her few wares.

The Italian Fascists had been oppressive in dozens of ways. The Cyrillic letters of a quotation from St. Matthew had been pulled from the façade of the village Catholic church although they had been there almost since antiquity. Family names had been Italianized forcibly, as one could see in the cemetery. The Mrach of 1925 who lay beside Maracci of 1942 was a member of the same family.

Fascism had been rough on the border population. I accepted that and stepped out into the street again. The tiny community was alive. Forty young men and women jiggled in a circle dancing the Yugoslav kolo. One sang as an accompaniment:

"Marshal Tito is our white violet.
Tito! All the youth greet you.
Young and old greet you.
This is our homeland, here where our dead lie.
This is Yugoslavia. Don't let's go back under Italy!"

Beyond the dancers a score of troops stood at attention. They were in the mixed khakis, grays, and blues of the German and Allied armies, but their rifles were well oiled and their faces were hard and uncompromising. Our automobile was buried in evergreen branches, flowers, red stars, pictures of Tito, and placards saying that Istria belonged to Yugoslavia. The moral seemed plain: one could believe, as he chose, whether or not the house of the martyr was kept always as a verdant shrine; one could accept or reject that our hostess had nothing but ill to say about Italy and no doubts to express about the Communists; one could find it normal or extraordinary that an "empty" village should burst into song and dance in midafternoon of a work day; but one had to recognize that Tito had soldiers hidden in Istria's thickets and that they were ready to fight to put down any anti-communism that should show itself. Unless we chose to offend our hosts we should drive out of Beram in our half-buried car as propagandists for Tito. One idea only—Tito—was permitted in totalitarian Beram. We cleaned off the car around a bend.

It was that carefully stage-managed glimpse of communism which I had on that first occasion, in 1946. A decade later I returned to Yugoslavia for a few more looks. By that time no one attempted any longer to present communism as one long array of evergreen-shrouded heroes' homes, kolos, plum brandy, and violets. Tito had fought a new struggle, this one against the Kremlin. He had exposed the fact that communism was no big happy family. A new kind of "national communism" had taken the place of the old international brand. In the words of some diplomats in Belgrade: "It is a system with all the worst features of both communism and capitalism." Local factory committees had been given enough "capitalistic" freedom of decision to put a good dose of chaos into the economy, but the secret police, state control over raw materials, and lack of the profit incentive had kept the nation economically stifled and all the people at least morally imprisoned.

No visits to the homes of Italian-oppressed Slavs in a border zone could conceal the drear facts of Yugoslavia's Red totalitarian life a dozen years after World War II.

"How do you find it?" an ambassador asked me.

"Gray," I said.

"Then you've come in from the West and you've never been farther east," he surmised correctly. "Yugoslavia is gray if all you know are the free countries of the West. But it is rather colorful and cheerful if you come from the east. To the east is where it is really drab."

To the east were the Soviet "satellites," Moscow's direct captives. Farther east was the Soviet Union itself. The brighter tints in Yugoslavia were something I was to recognize only in retrospect after seeing the Soviet East.

For the first of several trips to Yugoslavia in 1956 I boarded the Turkey-bound Orient Express in Venice, the legendary, mysterious Balkan special. If it was a train of intrigue, it was also a limping local. We stopped after a few score miles, just outside Trieste, at the border which finally had been drawn after a decade of wrangling at approximately the same position as that of the Allied-Yugoslav troop line at the end of the war. Tito had kept what he had. The Americans and British gave Italy theirs. Thanks to the Tito revolt against the Soviet Presidium, the Latin-Slav border was calm and the red tape slow but relatively reasonable.

While we waited, a few of us in the compartment peered at what communism had meant for that former corner of northeast Italy. The countryside behind us was still marked with poverty, some of it the grave, invisible kind represented by inadequate factory facilities; but the shiny marble counters, gleaming chrome machines, neon lights, and cheerful colors of the coffee bars of Venice and Trieste seemed like luxurious dreams compared with the squalor inside Yugoslavia's new expanded border. A railroad hand shuffled by in canvas shoes. A red star marked his grimy blue cap. Windows of the railroad station were cracked. A discolored shade behind one pane was no doubt Fascist in origin. It seemed a safe bet that it would be a long while before a neat communist roller replaced it.

Women in red bandannas and blue coveralls dragged hoses for the Orient Express's water supply.

"Pure Russian!" a Turk sniffed beside me. "In my country we'd have women working in offices, yes, but never doing a job like that."

Turkey, for all its ardent anti-Russianism, was no country to deride another's poverty. I made no effort to carry on with my neighbor from Istanbul a discussion of whether or not there was a difference between Tito's and the Kremlin's communism.

In Belgrade, on the broad Danube, the same impression of indigence struck me again. The flag in front of the parliament building was red, pink, and blue. The middle color was supposed to be white, but the red had run. As a symbol there was something appropriate in the "fluidity" of Yugoslav redness, but another thing was clear. Communism in Yugoslavia had not been able to afford good-quality dyes for the national banner.

Perhaps Americans are too plumbing minded but I could not help notice that toilets were working neither at the Foreign Office nor at Tito's headquarters.

I drove north along the "Highway of Brotherhood and Unity" from Belgrade to Zagreb. Communist youth brigades had built it just after the war. The Yugoslavia over which Tito had taken control was a primitive Balkan rural kingdom with scarcely any roads. With an admirable will to progress and an enviable ability to capture the hearts of youths of many countries, the Yugoslav Communists had organized teams of young men and women to put in a broad road connecting the two main cities. Political fervor, however, was evidently not enough. The engineering know-how of a stable Western economy would have helped, too. The Red youths had mounted the bridges firmly but had put too little underpinning beneath the road. The result was that the highway was sinking and, relatively speaking, the bridges rising. We had to slow down for each bridge to avoid striking its raised lips with a tire-crushing thud.

We had the road to ourselves. We passed only eight cars in eighty miles. If the modified Communist system of Yugoslavia was producing anything, it was not vehicles for Tito's people. I heard talk about this at lunch.

"A secondhand American car is worth $5,000 to $10,000," one meal companion commented.

"Oh, good, I'll sell mine, and import another duty free," a diplomat's wife exclaimed.

"Don't even think of it," the lady was advised. "That would be a jail offense."

To protect Yugoslavia's young industry and artificially valued currency there were tight controls on imports. A Westerner who brought in a car had to take it out again. The same was true of many other consumer goods. One Westerner whose camera was stolen had to buy another before he could leave. It was said in Zagreb that if a man could smuggle in from Italy seven or eight portable typewriters (worth $75.00 in Trieste and offered for sale in Yugoslav shopwindows for $1,000 each) he could support himself by renting them. To buy a bicycle, a Yugoslav told me, "would take twenty years' savings."

Yugoslavia's slightly attenuated communism had not yielded consumer goods. It also had not produced Communists.

A priest whispered his grievances.

"Unless you live here," he said, "you have no idea of our difficulties."

Crowds were at church services but it was desperately difficult to finance seminaries, and sermons were controlled.

When Tito had told farmers they could quit the Communist collectives, "there was the biggest exodus since Moses," an ambassador said.

It would take at least another generation and maybe longer to make Communists of Yugoslavia's land-loving peasants, Vladimir Bakaric, president of the "Republic" of Croatia, one of Yugoslavia's six subdivisions, and Tito's farm expert, admitted.

Bakaric let me visit a few collectives and I could see for myself why it was slow work making the peasants Communists. A sturdy youth of sixteen at one collective was in patched pants and shoeless. A pharmacy and a store had been built to lure the peasants away from living in their own self-contained economies and into the habit of using stores. The temptation of the shops had not been enough, however, to woo the farmers from their faith in their own soil. Inside the collectives the poor who were in the majority had voted low-rent payments for farmers who had brought to the agricultural pools most of their land. As soon as Tito, in his revolt against Moscow and in an effort to win the good will of his people, had opened the

collectives' exit doors, all the rich had withdrawn and many of
the rest had followed. Farmers, whether out of selfishness or
out of love for the soil or for their own families, had seen no
reason why they should work hard in collectives to feed drones
and to yield the cream of production to Red bureaucrats and
to workers in the swiftly built but scantily productive new
heavy industry. Communization of the farmers, at least for the
moment, was a failure. Since farmers made up the bulk of the
population, the significance of the setback was great.

"Will it take a hundred years to make Communists of the
farmers?" I asked the engagingly frank Mr. Bakaric.

"Oh, no, surely less than that," he insisted, but he gave no
reason for optimism.

Churchmen and farmers were not the only ones with laments.
Even a Party member was disconsolate.

"It isn't easy being in the Party," he said. "You always have
to set a good example. You work the whole day like everyone
else and then when others take off you have to start on Party
matters."

The man was well read and a linguist. He had a grievance
against the United States.

"I was a Communist even before we won; I have been ever
since I grew up. I flatter myself I am a man of some culture,
but I know what some of your senators think: that I'm a
'dirty Communist,' that I should not be allowed into the
United States as a visitor. I think my culture is greater than
some of theirs."

As a Communist the man had had to approve the savage
bands which did summary justice on Trieste street strollers
at the end of World War II. But it was "culture" he had on
his mind now. Class warfare and the building of heavy industry for an anti-Western war were no longer enough to
satisfy his mind.

A man whose work made him an expert on Yugoslav youth
gave a local university as an example of what he considered
important.

"Only 10 per cent of the law students are in the Party.

That's the most politically minded faculty, and of that 10 per cent some are mere opportunists thinking of jobs after graduation. The students were asked to write a theme on 'What I Would Do with 1,000,000 Dinars.'[1] All of them answered the same way: 'I'd try to get a car.' They are interested only in self-satisfaction. They have renounced communism. I don't know what they are groping toward but I have confidence they will find an alternative."

The youth were not yet for "capitalism." They had heard it damned too often. Perhaps it was back toward a capitalism without the name that they were going.

It was a weary, disillusioned Yugoslavia that I saw ten years after the kolo, the evergreens, and the anti-Fascist talk of little Beram. But it was not a Yugoslavia in collapse. There were fine qualities in the country which had stood up to the Soviet Union at a time when the rest of the world quailed. It was a national boast that Yugoslavia with its 15,000,000 population had given nearly ten times as many war dead as the United States in the 1939–45 war, five times as many as Britain, and three times as many as France. Ten per cent of the population had been killed. The war death rate was nearly one hundred times higher than that of the United States.

It was a Yugoslavia accustomed to adversity. I was told in Belgrade that it was a nation with *seven* other countries on its borders (Albania, Greece, Romania, Bulgaria, Hungary, Austria, and Italy), that it was broken down into *six* "republics" (Croatia, Serbia, Slovenia, Montenegro, Macedonia, and Bosnia-Herzegovina), that it encompassed *five* "nationalities" (the people of each of the republics except for Bosnia-Herzegovina), that it had *four* main religious divisions (the Orthodox Christians, Catholics, Moslems, and others of scattered faiths), *three* languages (Serb-Croat, Slovenian, and Macedonian), and *two* alphabets (Latin and Cyrillic), but that there was "just *one* Fatherland."

With such a variety of potential enemies on the borders and

[1] $2,500.

such appalling racial, religious, and language divisions inside, it was clear how the Yugoslavs had learned to live with trouble.

Communism had little popularity, but Tito helped keep it afloat by his personal prestige as a two-time national hero. He had led the little nation against the German and Italian invaders, and later had stood up to the Russians. Even the anti-Communists among the nationalistic Yugoslavs thanked Tito for the latter.

That did not mean that Tito was flawless from anyone's point of view. I attended a party he gave for Nasser in Belgrade, visited his summer residence on Brioni Island in the Adriatic, and was present for the trial of Milovan Djilas, author of the blistering attack against Tito's Communist associates as "the New Class."

The party for Nasser was most distinctive for the invitations. Those in Serbo-Croatian, for Yugoslavs, specified "black tie"; those for foreigners, in French, "white tie." It was a far cry from 1945–46 when the lack of any tie had been the badge of Tito and his ragged Communists.

Tito and Nasser were served at the edge of a reflecting pool behind which a ballet troupe in stiff white classical costumes danced prettily in the frozen forty-years-out-of-date style of the Moscow Bolshoi theater. The party was held in the gardens of the ousted Prince Paul. The villa and grounds were a miniature reproduction of the vast French royal palace of Versailles. We were 1,000 guests. We drank Yugoslav "champagne" and only infrequently noticed the dictator's bodyguard in the lights illuminating the treetops at the edge of the garden.

The palace was only one of many fine establishments at Tito's disposal. The fruits of the labor leader's victory had been sweet. At Brioni, a few of us of the press were ferried out past Tito's shiny yacht to his broad island estate. Deer, hare, and pheasants rustled in the bushes. A bird beneath the leader's terrace called a two-note cry that sounded like "Tito, Tito." A little fleet of new American cars stood outside Tito's door—about as many vehicles as we had seen in nearly half the country's length, from Belgrade to Zagreb. Behind the dictator's thick doors was the same kind of flamboyant middle-class luxury Claretta Petacci had favored in her hideaway for Mussolini in Rome. The floors were of marble. As in the Roman hilltop house of Petacci, which became a postwar public restaurant, the walls were lined with cages of chirping, bright-feathered birds. In still another parallel to the Petacci-Mussolini house there were archaeological treasures, scores of Etruscan figurines found in Brioni's ancient soil.

Mediterranean dictators who rose from peasant poverty had the same ideas of household beauty, it seemed.

"Isn't it pretty?" Tito asked us.

The Yugoslav strong man had walked into his living room on that sweltering afternoon of July 1956 wearing white gloves, an ice-cream suit, a Panama hat, and white shoes. Nasser had grinned boyishly, shyly, beside him. It was one of Nasser's first trips out of the Nile Valley, but the impression he gave of being a mere apprentice dictator was to be short-lived. Within a week Nasser was to seize the Suez Canal and propel himself higher than Tito in the notoriety of the world's headlines.

Photographers spoiled the idyll.

"Please remove your hat," they asked Tito.

The miffed president did, but within moments he strode huffily away.

The Djilas trial took place in a Belgrade courtroom beneath a huge picture of Tito. Djilas had written that communism, instead of creating the longed-for "classless society," had merely set up a "new class," a few former proletarians who had moved into the villas and palaces of the kings and princes and had left the overwhelming mass of the population in its original misery, if not worse. The prosecutor pronounced the charges against the rigid but unretracting Djilas. Then a list of those permitted to remain in the trial room was read. The list omitted the names of all Western newsmen. Djilas spoke his defense in the privacy of an almost-empty courtroom and was hustled off to jail.

Djilas had been the brain of Tito's national communism. He had explained why Moscow-run world communism could not work, had gone further and concluded that communism was a failure, a system hard fisted in smashing its opponents but incapable, because of its ill adaptation to human nature, of setting a worthy ideal of its own.

Yugoslavia, in a common opinion among Westerners in Belgrade, would stay out of Moscow's grip while Tito lived. "He would not want to be a small fish in the Soviet pond," said one diplomat. But some thought Yugoslavia could fall to the Soviets after the dictator's death. "The shoemakers and butchers who became Party bosses are determined, no matter what, not to go back to where they were, and they are likely to feel that there is more future for them under Moscow communism than under the Western freedom which might become the sole alternative," one Yugoslav anti-Communist said.

The Yugoslav experiment in national communism might fail, but it had served a precious purpose, exposing profound divisions and discontent inside the Red world. The myth that the 1,000,000,000 under communism were content with their lot was proved a typical falsehood. The threat to Europe was at least a little less than it seemed.

Tito's Yugoslavia was not the only eastern European communist satellite seething with anti-Sovietism and even anti-Marxism. Impressions gained in Yugoslavia were confirmed and deepened during a month's trip through Poland at the time of the parliamentary elections in the first months of 1957. Perhaps it was no surprise in Yugoslavia that the dictator should be honored for his break with the Kremlin, but that was no preparation for a Poland which was headquarters of the "Warsaw Pact," the military alliance of the Soviet bloc. I had not been many hours in the Polish capital before I was sure that of all the cities of the earth, it was one of the fiercest foes of the "agreement" of Warsaw. Poland's people, in those first months of 1957, were officially "anti-Stalinist" since that was the Kremlin-blessed Red fad of the moment, but in fact they were anti-Russian and anti-Communist with a passion that no propaganda and no oppression could eradicate.

I had a long conversation with one Pole. Our talk wandered from one confidence to another until I wondered whether I had been mistaken about his identity. I asked cautiously and he confirmed what I had first understood. The man with the violent anti-Russian views was the local spokesman for the Communist party.

The disaffection was at every social level.

"There's the Soviet embassy," a chauffeur said contemptuously. "Notice the tall spikes on the fence. To protect them against us Poles!"

Another driver grunted as we drove into a village.

"Look, a jail. That's this country for you—the first thing you see in any town is the jail."

The comment was exaggerated but the anti-regime sentiments were limpid. I had not been many hours in Poland before I heard the national expression: "Ours is a country like Christ—crucified between two thieves." The two crooks, it was evident, included not only the officially-hated Germans but the "mother country of socialism"—the Soviet Union.

A story circulated about what happened in one of the few Warsaw night clubs to one of our group, a journalist from neutral Sweden. One of Poland's many drunks had swayed up to him and slapped him violently.

"You're a German," the Pole accused him.

The Swede reeled back.

"I'm not," he objected.

The Pole braced himself and hit the Swedish reporter again. "You're not a German? Then you're Russian!"

Either was good for a swing.

The anti-Sovietism and the corresponding sympathy for the West showed itself in dozens of ways. In a hotel I was disturbed to see that every dining table had a Red country's flag and that the only two places free were marked by the banners of the Soviet Union and Red China. I hesitated while a waiter watched and then sat down at the Soviet table. The waiter was instantly at my side. With his right hand he gave me the menu, with his left he palmed the Russian flag. I had handed in my American passport as required when I had registered, and perhaps that or some giveaway American mannerism in clothes or behavior had identified me.

At the next meal the empty table in the middle of the room displayed America's Old Glory.

I hated to be difficult, but I saw no reason why I or anyone else had to make a proclamation on international politics every time he sat down to eat. I skipped the "American" table and took one that had no flag. Perhaps it was all a coincidence, but at the next meal and for the rest of my stay there were no more flags on any table.

The flag game may have been the fruit of chance, but there was no accident in the Warsaw jokes about the "Stalin Palace of Culture" skyscraper. It was forty stories tall and dominated the capital. A dozen square blocks of homes and office buildings had been razed so that the building would be noticed from everywhere. If you were up close you would see it across the broad park around it. At a distance it stood alone far above the low horizon. It was of the heavy, ornate style I was to see later in Moscow.

"Lots of palace, not much culture," was one remark from Poles who felt that they had a charming national tradition of architecture of their own and no need for the Eastern proletarian version of how to erect a building.

Poles amused one another bitterly with the text of a mythical advertisement: "Will swap apartments; mine has beautiful view of Palace of Culture."

The Russians could have put up a town for 80,000 with all usual comforts, including a motion-picture theater, for the money they poured into the gift eyesore, Poles said. And as for its being a "gift," they added, it was a trifling repayment for the mountains of coal the Russians had looted from vanquished Poland by juggling the ruble-zloty exchange rates.

The ruble had been ludicrously overvalued and Poland had been bled economically to the edge of collapse.

Poland had opened its doors to a few dozen Western newspapermen to let us see its parliamentary election. The people would turn out solidly at the polls and resounding support would be given to Wladislaw Gomulka's new national Communist regime. The government was sure of that and was contented that a few of us should see it for ourselves and inform the people of the West.

It was my first experience with a Communist election. There was only one slate of candidates, all of them approved by the Polish Communist party but, unlike most other Red elections, there was a slim sporting chance of opposition. If enough voters canceled the top one third of the slate, some of the lower third would be elected. They were regime-authorized, too, but at least the most favored communist candidates would lose and a moral defeat would be inflicted.

Gomulka had taken power a few months before. The Kremlin evidently had become alarmed by the way "anti-Stalinism" had degenerated into anti-Moscowism, and had made concessions. Gomulka, who had tasted Stalin cruelty because of his Polish patriotism, was called back from disgrace and put in charge of an experiment in mildly nationalistic communism, a brand halfway between Tito's condemned anti-Kremlin kind and the subservient Moscow-following type the Soviet presidium preferred.

Gomulka's final radio appeal was simple.

Poland, he said, would vote for him, or Poland would be wiped from the map of "free nations."

The use of the word "free" to apply to Russian-occupied Poland was gratuitous, but no Poles missed the point. Even the half-liberated Poland of Gomulka's national communism would be destroyed unless the people said "yes" to Gomulka.

Signs just outside polling places and even occasionally inside them told voters what was wanted. They were asked to cast "clean ballots." That meant that no candidates were to be scratched. There was to be a "voluntary" renunciation of the one opportunity for protest which had been given.

We toured the polls. At many the voters went directly from the desk to the ballot box, ignoring the booths. At one place the potted plants and velvet drapes over the booth hid it completely. Where the booth stood looked like a blank wall.

The poll manager noticed our astonishment.

"They're allowed to use the booth," he assured us. "You," he called to an old woman who was making a beeline for the ballot box, "use the booth!"

The woman was frightened. She stared at us with wide eyes, hesitated, ducked behind the curtain for an instant, pushed out again abruptly, flung in her ballot, and fled. She had at least managed to stay in the box too short a time to cancel any of the top two thirds. Her ballot was clean, as the many watchers could testify, if need be, in her behalf.

The woman behind her used a different tactic. She ignored the order to use the booth, dashed to the ballot box, and escaped in seconds.

Gomulka had a ringing victory to announce. Merely 5.86 per cent of the Poles had neglected to vote, and only 1.6 per cent had said "no" to the complete Gomulka slate, running a line through the whole list, the top two thirds and the bottom third as well. In one district no one had been elected. That was Nowy Sącz on the Czech border. By contrast with the percentages high in the nineties which were reported for most of those on the ticket's upper two thirds, in this district the preferred candidate, Jan Antoniszczak, had collected an inglorious 45.8 per cent even with each "clean ballot" working for him. What was wrong in Nowy Sącz had been indicated in *Po Prostu (Plain Talk)*, a Gomulka communist youth publication which had justified its name. In line with "anti-Stalinism," *Po Prostu* had sent a team to Nowy Sącz and had published an exposé: the average weekly family income was 250 zlotys (about $10.00); the usual diet was lard on bread, vegetable soup, potatoes, and, rarely, some cheap meat. Winter frost got into every nook and cranny of a schoolteacher's home which had been investigated as an example of typical living conditions. The local communist town council "of course did not like it" when they found people living in their own privately owned homes, and had evicted them. What with bribery, bureaucracy, injustice, and fear of speaking freely about troubles, the people of Nowy Sącz were "cursing the past twelve years" of communism, the *Po Prostu* reported.

Papers such as *Po Prostu* soon were to draw the Kremlin's wrath, but like the Tito revolt in Yugoslavia they had revealed enough to the world to destroy forever the propaganda-fostered picture of happiness and unity under the red star of the Soviet bloc.

I crisscrossed Poland from the Soviet border at Terespol on the east to the Oder-Neisse boundary with Germany on the west, and then dipped south to the steel area around Krakow.

Terespol, on the Soviet border, was a portrait of misery. Its main street was rutted and muddy. The principal attraction, so far as I was concerned, was a forlorn collection of shacks through which Poles were being repatriated from the Soviet Union. The trickle of arriving Poles, fruit of a new peace gesture from the Kremlin, were treated as if they were reaching freedom.

"Speak up," a young man told the cowering returned men and women. "You are in Poland now. What you say will help those who are still back there."

It had taken him two months to travel three miles, one man said. Her cow and house had brought only a handful of rubles because "everyone else wants to come," said a widow. "They" had told her that in Poland she would be even worse off, "starving in the lee of a wall," another woman said. "But I told them 'All right, at least I'll be in Poland!' "

It was hard to realize that the border was so deep inside the Soviet world.

On the other side of Poland, at Wrocław, the prewar German town of Breslau, I was amazed by the ruins. A dozen years after the war and after arrival of the "people's power" there was a half-mile-wide sea of rubble still separating the

airfield from the center of town. Walls teetered precariously
just as the last desperate German-Russian battles had left
them. A busy corner of town was an iron market in an empty
lot, where nails, hinges, and every other type of metal junk
were sold. The second-hand market was a prime local source
of hardware. A razor-blade salesman warned me against buying
what he had for sale, and later as I slashed my face I wished
I had taken his advice. In Legnica (prewar Liegnitz), near
the new Polish-German line, Soviet troops led by sergeants
with red traffic-control flags sang as they marched past decade-
old, pulverized ruins spilling from abandoned doorways.

At a steel mill workers told gleefully how they had pulled
down huge portraits of Poland's "Stalinist" Communist leaders, including that of the Soviet Marshal Rokossovski, who had
been defense minister in Warsaw until Gomulka took
over. The steel workers decried the low quality of the Soviet
ore they had to use. When, they wanted to know, would the
United States begin to help?

To that I had no answer. Postwar agreements had turned
Catholic and anti-Communist Poland over to Moscow as its
sphere of influence. Liberating Poland militarily was impossible without risking World War III. For the moment one
fact besides the crucifixion of Poland was plain: the Soviets
were shunned, as I saw symbolized by their pathetic telephone-
repair crews, little bands of armed servicemen working alone
back and forth across Poland taking care of the communica-
tion lines connecting the Kremlin and occupied East Germany.
A lot of Russia's strength was going to keep Eastern Europe
captive. In a showdown enemies of the Kremlin would rise in
many places beneath the red star.

IX

REVOLUTION:
HUNGARY'S MOMENT OF TRUTH

How great was the misery and protest under communism I could not have realized without seeing the Hungarian revolution in October and November of 1956.

The revolt started when Communist police and Soviet troops fired into a mildly demonstrating crowd in front of the cathedral-like government and puppet-parliament building on the banks of the Danube in Budapest. The throng had not been very excited; Hungarians knew they were hopelessly imprisoned by the twenty-times-larger Soviet Union. The crowd, in rather a holiday mood, had let off only the slightest steam. The sudden slaughter had sent the Budapest people berserk. The crowd had reassembled, received reinforcements from the automobile factory at Csepel, and had begun attacking Communist party strongholds. Five days later, when I reached the Austro-Hungarian frontier, a red, white and green national flag flapped stringily inside the Red line. Its communist star had been cut out, so that it no longer could snap but could only jab thin fingers nervously in the breeze. The revolution had disintegrated the communist power structure out to the very edges of the country.

The uniforms of the frontier guards were discolored where communist red stars had been torn away. Even the bright tiles of a mural on the customhouse were dotted with bits of brown paper pasted on to cover the communist symbol.

A few civilians with tommy guns mingled with the uniformed frontier watchers. They, like the others, wore the badge of insurrection, an armband with the three colors of Hungary but without the star.

How detested was the star was indicated when a Yugoslav diplomat arrived from Budapest. His country, as the first to rebel against Moscow, was the most honored of the Soviet bloc nations, but the diplomat felt unsafe even at that. Yugoslavia, after all, was still Communist. The attaché traveled with a cover over his license plate's star.

The post was at the "iron curtain." That was clear from the gallowslike, thirty-foot-tall wooden lookout towers which could be seen strung along the border in either direction. From them members of the hand-picked frontier patrol peered to keep back or kill any of the 1,000,000,000 people of the Soviet bloc who tried to flee to Austria and to freedom. But the towers were now empty and the rest of the frontier guard was of a new timbre, even though many were the same men who had done an efficient job only a week earlier. Anyone who wanted to cross in or out of Hungary was welcome to do so with or without a visa. If he wanted a sign in his passport, the rebel frontier squad would give it—with last week's carefully guarded and rarely used stamp, now, of course, minus the star which had been one of its main features.

I returned to Vienna for the night and next day drove thirty miles inside Hungary to Győr, one of the many revolutionary "capitals." It was there that I began to suspect the tragic worst about the destiny of the freedom uprising. Disorganization was complete. Moscow was to claim quickly that "foreign agents," "reactionaries," landlords, and rich men of the feudal Hungarian past had created a "counterrevolutionary" machine; but the truth was that there was no leadership, no guidance, and no cohesion of any sort. There was nothing but the chaotic fruits of an explosion that had leaped simultaneously from 10,000,000 Hungarian hearts, even those of Communist party leaders.

Two hundred men milled in the wintry midafternoon dusk before the city hall, which had been captured as revolution headquarters. The men were buoyed up by what they had accomplished. They had sacked the barracks of the secret police and had torn three agents literally limb from limb. They had moved up against the Soviet barracks and had been secretly relieved when the Russians had offered to evacuate the community if allowed to leave quietly. The Soviet tanks had pulled out, and Györ's people had been so uplifted by hope that a delegation had gone after the Russians to say that their women and children should return, that they would be warmer in their own homes in town, and that the townspeople pledged that they would be safe. The Soviets dryly had refused. The good-willed villagers had met the rebuff by setting up a service of fresh milk and vegetables instead. It all seemed to be going fairly well, except for the fact that the place in the woods chosen by the Russians gave them control of the strategic Vienna–Budapest highway, the road through which Western help would have to come.

Perhaps the Russian choice of their place of "retreat" was a reason, but whatever the cause, there was uneasiness in the crowd. The success of the revolution was still not assured. The loud-speaker on the balcony blatted down news about what the town committee and the government of Premier Imre Nagy in Budapest were doing, and each time the crowd shouted back dissatisfied suggestions for new and quicker measures.

The crowd's demands revealed what life had been under Soviet communist control. The townspeople cried up for:

An end to night work for women and children;

Extra pay for those on heavy, dangerous, and unhealthy jobs;

A general increase in wages and reduction of work hours;

The right to strike;

Permission for citizens to travel freely abroad.

And, for Hungary, they demanded:

Neutrality guaranteed by the United Nations;

Repudiation of the Warsaw Pact, which gave Soviet troops the right to use Hungarian soil;

Immediate withdrawal of the Soviet armed forces;

The right of Hungary to accept loans from outside the Soviet bloc;

Permission for Hungary to exploit her own uranium instead of having to hand it over to the Soviets.

The workers' condition was as poor as under early nineteenth-century capitalism, or even worse. Hungary was in Russian chains.

A few things had changed in rebel Györ, but too much was still the same. The portly blond man with the soup-strainer mustache who was presiding over the insurrectionary destinies was the same who had been number-two chief of local communism only a week before. No one in the streets could be sure that the right leaders were guiding Hungary swiftly enough on the road of liberation.

We returned to our car for the drive back to Vienna.

"Are you really Americans?" some leaned in through our windows to ask. "What help will the United States send? When will it be here? Is the new Free Hungary government already waiting on the Austrian border? When will it come?"

The questions about aid were the same I was to hear the following year in the Polish steel mill. It occurred to no one that for fear of World War III the United States and the West would do nothing.

Next day we tagged behind a United States legation courier and drove into Budapest a week to the day after the start of the uprising. It was like the war in the Pacific in the sense that so much was unexpectedly peaceful and handsome. The blue-green Danube was as placid as the Marne or the Mississippi, the one wry note the watchtowers on the opposite bank in Czechoslovakia. As I was to see on the Polish-Soviet border at Terespol, the national cells in the Soviet prison bloc were as tightly sealed off against one another as the Communist world itself was iron-curtained off from the zone of democracy and freedom.

Two men fished in the river Raab. A well-lipsticked, pretty young woman pushed a baby carriage. A dozen boys kicked a soccer ball on a town athletic field. I noticed, though, that all players were under ten. The latter was unspoken draft age for the "free Hungarian army."

Nearer Budapest clearer signs of revolt appeared. The starless national flag waved defiantly from chimney tops and from the roofs of Communist-built housing developments. I remembered the wake of World War II in Trieste and other parts of Western Europe when Communist banners had been posted on factory ridge poles and when it had been so hard to judge whether or not Communist strong-arm squads really spoke for "the people" as they claimed. With their fine organization and brutal methods the Communist minority pretended successfully, sometimes, that they were the majority. Here in Budapest's outskirts all was in reverse. Individuals, unguided, had scaled chimneys in acts of anti-Communist revolution which they knew were the will of all. No one feared that he would be betrayed by Red sympathizers; none hesitated because of the chance that the Soviets and the Communists might return. The heroic and spontaneous revolt was sweeping every corner of Hungary.

At Komárom, two thirds of the way to Budapest, we saw troops with the red star for the first time. They were Russians. They looked at the large American flags on each of our cars, hesitated, and then waved us through. The Soviets were still pursuing a hands-off policy. They were provoking the Hungarians no more than they needed. But they were in position to seize power again in a matter of hours.

On the heights above Budapest there was a last ring of Soviet tanks and then a long descent into the city straddling the river.

The revolution until then had been for me a series of symbols and stories. In Budapest it became more real. Streetcars lay on their sides as barricades. For blocks every store window had been smashed. Holes had been drilled through buildings by tanks' shells. Thirty-three Russian tanks clustered side by side around the government and legislature building, their cannon covering the long Danube bridge across which we had to drive. The Russians watched but let us pass. We parted company with the legation car and drove to the dreary Duna Hotel, which was unofficial headquarters for the Western press.

Conversation at the hotel was excited. There had been a new tank attack and two of the press were among the casualties. Tim Foote of *Time-Life* had a bullet hole through the hand, and the photographer of *Paris-Match,* the French picture magazine, had been creased across the abdomen by machine-gun fire. He was dying.

I was awakened that night by the harsh song of tank treads. Dozens of armored cars were rolling, but whether they were Soviets going out or reinforcements coming in I could not judge. Tanks moved in both directions. Only in the morning did I get the news. The Soviets had evacuated Budapest.

That began the Hungarian capital's five hopeful, pitiful days of freedom. Were the Russians really going? No one seemed so pessimistic, so cynical, or so callous as to deny it. All Budapest set to work as if it were sure that Hungary in the future could keep its own uranium, that it could be out of the Warsaw Pact and neutral, that Hungary's old and ill were to have better pensions, that workmen again would have the right to strike. A dozen papers were started, a half-dozen parties formed. All Budapest was jubilantly awake, but all were dreaming.

I went for some macabre sight-seeing. Half of one street was blocked by the contents of a Soviet bookstore which had been scooped out into the gutter and set afire to burn for the whole five days of liberty. A throng filled the street in front of the radio station. The building was riddled with hundreds of gunshots. Across it was a great sign: "Budapest Free Radio." I remembered the moment when the rebels had taken it. I was driving through Austria toward the border when my Hungarian-speaking companion had gasped. He was listening to Radio Budapest, doing his best to comb out nuggets of fact from the mass of exaggerations, understatements, lies, and propaganda.

"Oh, no," he had exclaimed. "Even they can't do that. One hour ago they were saying that a few 'hooligans' and 'looters' were in the streets. Now they are calling them 'glorious freedom fighters' who have restored Hungarian honor."

My companion had assumed that the Hungarian party had switched tactics, pretending to go over to the insurgents in order better to lead them back to submission, using flattery where threats had failed. It had not occurred to him that in Soviet-garrisoned Hungary insurgents even momentarily could capture an instrument of such key Communist importance as a radio station.

Down the street from the station women in bandannas were helping one another onto burned-out Russian tanks, to peer into their charred interiors. Ten-year-old boys played atop an anti-tank gun. Perhaps it was one they had wrecked themselves. Children, using guerrilla tactics the Russians themselves had taught, had burned out Soviet armored cars with no other weapon than a bottle of gasoline.

The worst wreckage was at the Killian barracks. A brave young Hungarian colonel, Pal Maleter, had held out there against a massed tank attack. The thick castle walls of the barracks were gnawed open like a mouse-eaten cheese, and the fronts of dozens of nearby homes had been shot away, but the little Hungarian garrison had held out. A dozen Soviet tanks, burned out, stood outside. A half-dozen Russian corpses lay on the sidewalk beside them. Four days dead, they still lay unattended.

"Greetings, Americans," one in the crowd called into our car. Our American flag had identified us.

"Communism is finished," another said as if merely speaking the words could eliminate doubt.

Above his head I noticed that a church steeple had been shot away.

I visited the government and Parliament headquarters. High on its pinnacle, twenty stories above the ground, a man was at work dismantling another of the Soviet bloc's Red Stars, this one twenty feet tall. About half the big job was finished.

At the government building I asked to see Janos Kadar, head of the Hungarian Communists. There was a moment's confusion and then one young soldier volunteered that he had seen the number-one Communist and would guide me. He led me to a vast, high-ceilinged room overlooking the river. The woman secretary seemed surprised at my request, went into the room behind her, and then returned to say: "Premier Nagy is busy on matters of utmost international importance. You may come back tomorrow."

The well-intentioned young soldier had taken me to the office of Premier Nagy, who was in conference with Kadar. The secretary had assumed that it was the premier, not his visitor, I had come to see. I left with no attempt at an explanation and only later realized how close I had come to one of satellite Europe's saddest and most dramatic moments. The matter of "utmost international importance" was the proclamation of Hungary's withdrawal from the Soviet alliance and the declaration of her neutrality under U.N. safeguard. The man I had sought in the wrong office was the one who was indeed to be premier there within a week, the Soviet's new puppet. The Nagy I nearly met was the martyr who was to be executed a year and a half later by the Soviets for his Hungarian patriotism.

I never went back to claim the proffered interview with Nagy. Another event dominated journalistic attention next day: the freeing of the spiritual leader of most of Hungary's population, Cardinal Mindszenty.

There were no taxicabs and one of my companions had gone back with our hired car to Vienna, so I walked to the Cardinal's hilltop residence. In the square beside the Duna Hotel a monument to the Soviet victory of 1945 lay shattered into hundreds of pieces. Written across the pedestal were four digits: "1956." No longer text was needed to express Hungarian fury and vengeance.

At the edge of the square Russian wives and children pushed against one another in their hurry to get onto the gangplank of a river steamer which would carry them eastward to safety. One little boy had a rudely manufactured cardboard game box strapped in a net bag to his back. It was easy to see why the Györ villagers had taken pity on the families of the tank crews. Hungarians leaned over a railing, jeering softly, but none moved to do the Russian women and children violence.

I wondered why the Russians were getting their families out, but in the exertion of the steep climb to the top of the heights on the far side of the Danube I gave no further thought to it.

Two "Free Hungarian" tanks protected the Cardinal's residence. A sniper on duty on a garden wall watched from the rear. One of the rebels' first acts had been to free the prince of the Church who had been a Communist captive for eight years.

I had interviewed the primate of Hungary's Catholics in Rome ten years before. He had been gaunt and piercing-eyed even then, but his appearance was more haggard and haunted now.

The prelate was the last of the thirty-two new Cardinals to arrive in Rome for the 1946 conclave. The Russians had interfered with his departure, but an American general had intervened and had lent him his plane. The Budapest prelate had been taciturn. He had resisted Nazi oppression and if need arose under the new Red regime would do the same again, he told me gravely. The churchman had refused to talk ill of the Communists, insisting that events would have to speak for themselves.

This time the Cardinal was more communicative. One of our group was delegated to speak to him privately.

During the eight years in Red hands, the Cardinal said, he had been "tortured in body and soul in ways no decent mind would imagine." "Hellish devices" had been used. He did not elaborate.

Besides the more intimate one-man talk there was a group interview. The Cardinal received us in a small room of faded elegance. The gilded chairs were threadbare. The copy of the Vatican annual on a table was twelve years out of date. It still listed the primate merely as an Archbishop, not as a Cardinal.

"I will carry on my work where I was compelled to stop eight years ago," said the prelate.

Would there be a Catholic party? Would it be in opposition? Not if it were in a coalition, the Cardinal said cautiously, implying that a pro-Hungary pact with national Communists or at least native socialists might be possible. Had Pope Pius XII been in touch with him? Only by telegram to send a "blessing—no more than that."

Photographers pushed in. The Cardinal was a major news picture. He was the first of the four Cardinals of the Red world to regain freedom in his country, just as he had been the first seized. When he was arrested, his had been a unique case. Church historians in Rome had gone back to the tumult of the ninth century, more than a millennium earlier, to find a parallel. Napoleon had arrested Pope Pius VII a century and a half before, but it had not been the French emperor's intention to eradicate religion itself. England had decapitated Saint Cardinal John Fisher in 1535, but the prelate had not become a Cardinal until after his sentencing.

Like the well-intentioned people of Györ, the Cardinal wanted to forget fury over the past and to look forward, instead, to the rebuilding of a free and religious Hungary. On that note we left, but outside in the rest of Budapest the drama rushed forward toward a different climax.

A colleague told me of an interview with Joszef Dudas, head of the revolutionary committee. The burly man sobbed suddenly as he asked the reporter: "Did you see that swatch of blond hair at the Astoria Hotel? It was a young girl who lay down under a Soviet tank to blow it up."

Even with that horrible memory, Dudas' aides were not malicious against the pro-Soviets. Should the Communists be given newsprint so that they could resume publication? Yes, a Dudas assistant decided, "that's democracy."

Government spokesmen told us that negotiations were under way for the evacuation of the Russians. Speaking for Hungary were Nagy and Maleter. The latter was by then a general and minister of defense in the constantly reshuffled and progressively less Communist Nagy cabinet.

The optimistic thought they saw signs for hope and one reporter offered to share a scoop: "The Russians have agreed to leave Hungary." I chose to pass up the "exclusive" and hours later had that omission as one of the few things about which I could be content.

The revolution took an ugly turn. Five days of freedom had gone by, yet the manhunts for Communist political policemen and other major offenders kept up. A boy told me why he was joining the search squads: "The police caught a small child and what do you think they did when he refused to inform? They cut off his tongue." It was like the war in the Pacific and in French North Africa, atrocity stories encouraging the very cruelties the relater deplored; the crimes the same, the victims different. I watched crowds dropping grenades down subway shafts in front of the government building where quick-triggered Communists had started it all. Reds, I was told, were reported hiding in the underground. Another downtown Budapest street echoed with an attack against a building identified as a stronghold of Red defenders. Some in the crowd urged me to follow to a park where Communist police had been strung up dead by the heels. There was the same cold glee I had seen when the man was burned alive in the sultan's compound in Morocco. Revolted, I refused. A young vigilante rolled by in an automobile, a fat pistol poking over his sill. Woe to any "Communists" he saw. The story spread that the crowds were finding "secret police" by means of their telltale brown shoes. I glanced at my own feet and was sorry I had not worn black instead. I let dust scuff up my shoes to be sure they had no nice, shiny, police look about them. The freedom revolt was degenerating into chaos.

That night the Nagy government made an appeal. Busses should go back into service as a step toward normal life. Disorder must not give the Russians an excuse for returning. By late evening the strange new insurrectionary gesture was made. Busses stood emptily at downtown corners waiting for patrons who were far too prudent to be abroad. The light of the public cars poured odd pools of brilliance into dull streets where every shop and café was closed.

Hundreds of tanks, we learned from Hungarian intelligence, were pouring in from Poland, Romania, and directly from the Soviet Ukraine. The determined optimists managed an explanation. They might be fresh troops to protect the Russian withdrawal. Perhaps the thousands of tanks that had been on duty in Budapest, at Györ, at Komáron, and at dozens of similar places were so demoralized that they needed new men to shield them as they left. There was no conviction in the words and military experts dismissed it as nonsense. The ocean of tanks the Russians retained after the first lost round was well able to cover a retreat. The military authorities had another unpleasant bit of information. Those who had trailed the Russian tanks out of Budapest five days earlier had seen all armored cars taking up new positions in a tight circle around the capital. A few reportedly had rolled into the Budapest airport under white flags. The Hungarian air force had accepted the signals in good faith and had allowed the Russians to advance. As soon as they reached the field the Russians, according to anti-Soviet military information, had pulled down the white banners, had "buttoned up" (sealing their turrets), and since then had commanded the airfield. No planes would be able to take off to help the rest of the Hungarian forces if fighting resumed. The noose we had seen in the Györ woods, at Komáron, and on the Budapest heights was tightening.

The correspondents were in confusion. Some still talked about what they had seen. It was a lie that the throngs had been looters; even diamonds had been left inside broken jewelry store windows, one said. Others concentrated on the present. It was time to leave, a few argued. Though it was night at the end of the fifth day of freedom some took off toward Austria. Rebel chaos was better than taking a chance with Russian "order," some flung back over their shoulders.

Uncertainty lasted little longer. I was awakened next day at dawn by cannonading on the outskirts. I was to learn later in Moscow what had happened. The top Kremlin leadership had been uncertain what to do. Neutral diplomats who had spoken to members of the Presidium and General Staff members slowly had drawn out the story. The Kremlin had feared World War III but had believed that the loss of the Hungarian keystone would destroy the whole of the eastern European satellite structure. They had decided to act. If the West moved in, the Russians would shoot back and take the consequences, even if that meant global war. If the West did not react, the Soviet troops would stop at the regained Austrian border.

I was weary from telephoning my previous day's story until three o'clock that morning. The cannon fire stopped after ten minutes. I rolled over and left the crisis of Hungary for a few hours later, but at eight I got up. Below my window another wave of departing correspondents were tying on bags and getting ready for a dash for Vienna. I joined the stately, elderly John MacCormac of the New York *Times,* the earnest and intense Seymour Friedin of the New York *Post,* and a few others, and drove toward the American legation. The streets were deserted, but at every corner we came upon a Soviet tank cannon. The armored cars were back and Budapest faced its moment of truth.

A large American flag covered the legation entrance. If there was to be an incident, it would be by no accident. A marine checked our passports through a grille and let us in. Seated by the entrance was Cardinal Mindszenty. He was unshaven. He had been so taciturn in interviews that it was hard to be sure what was going on in his mind as he faced the chance of going back into the hands of the Communists. I had had glimpse enough, however, into the horrors of the Cardinal's case to imagine. I recalled the Budapest handwriting expert, Lazslo Sulner, who had come to me in Rome with microfilmed proof of how he had forged the Cardinal's name to incriminating documents nearly a decade earlier at the Mindszenty trial. Sulner had agreed to publish the story to get a small fund with which to flee farther westward, but he had told me he wanted no career as a professional anti-Communist. His dream was to get as far from European Red politics as he could go. His idea, however impractical for a central European city man, was to farm in central Australia. A few days after his series began he died of a strange fever in Paris. The Budapest graphologist never had left the Continent. It was that Sulner-described Red Budapest the Cardinal must have had in mind as he sat near the legation doorway. The deep eyes were more anguished than ever.

Edward Wales, the new American minister, received us graciously. Only the faintest tension hinted strain. He and his aides told us the rules of our stay. There were some blankets but we would have to sleep on desk tops or the floor. Meals would be served in the snack bar. We were asked to report promptly when Mrs. Wales and a few other legation wives got the food ready, but to avoid overcrowding. The legation canteen had been designed for no more than twenty; we were more than sixty. We could move in and out of the building as we pleased and we could make use of the telephone while service lasted.

We organized a news pool. Those who could speak Hungarian tuned in recaptured Radio Budapest and typed summaries of its bulletins. Others who had friends in Budapest telephoned to the different corners of the city asking what was happening. It was like local news work back in New York. Soon incoming calls supplied another stream of information. The Hungarians still believed that the arrival of American aid was imminent, and dozens were anxious that the first troops be diverted to their neighborhoods. It was the bitter task of the next few days to discourage such hopes.

The several-hour lull after the dawn cannonading ended as the arriving Russians met centers of resistance. The Hungarians were determined to go down fighting. One in our legation group had seen two boys of twelve carrying old rifles as big as themselves.

"Where are you going?" he had asked.

The children were surprised at the question but were respectful in the answer.

"To fight the Russians."

Shelling began. First there was a reverberating bang like the pounding of a giant oil drum, then, moments later, the crash of the shell in another part of the city. Rifle and machine-gun fire chattered everywhere. The Russians must have decided that resistance was general, for shelling spread to the whole city. Tanks on one bank of the Danube fired at buildings on the far side, as we were to see later written in the angles of shell holes through houses. Five embassies and legations were hit, whether in the accident of a wholesale attack or with deliberate attempt at intimidating the diplomats it was impossible to learn. The reporters' own Duna Hotel took a machine-gun raking through the kitchen and two tank cannon shots through the bedrooms. A young man was thrown from a window opposite the Duna and lay dead on the sidewalk for days afterward, a reminder to newspapermen that punished Budapest was a dangerous place.

Hour after hour cannonading went on. Mrs. Wales's disciplined pet dog trembled from the strain. Pigeons in front of the American legation took off and wheeled at every shot until it was a marvel they could still keep flying.

Silvery MiGs streaked overhead. Inside the legation word was passed that a Soviet ultimatum had been reported. Budapest might be bombed at 4 P.M. We of the press were free to do as we chose, but the legation staff would go to the cellar. There were strong arches which would withstand direct hits from moderate-sized bombs. I noticed that the military attachés decided to pass 4 P.M. under the basement roof supports, so I joined them there for scotch in a water-fountain paper cup.

The air raid did not come off. We had another "for the road" and went upstairs. Pitiful calls were coming in. A group at a motion-picture theater was under attack by tanks and could hold out only for another two hours. If the United States were to help it would have to do it instantly. Another band, the phone told us, was under assault from tanks, mortars, and medium-sized artillery. They needed "flame throwers and those so-called tank breakers." A youth at the legation door passed a note through the grille. His friends, the message said, were in "death throes" the world could not see. "If you can help us, do so by one o'clock. We will be back for an answer. Otherwise we are going to die." The young man was told gently that he could spare himself the trouble of a return trip.

It was possible some of the callers were Soviet agents. A gray-haired man drove up in an ambulance. The car was white with a red cross. The man begged for a pistol "to blow my brains out." He said he had been freed from jail "three days ago, after eight years in prison," and "could not stand it." The details paralleled those of Cardinal Mindszenty so exactly as to parody them. The marine captain at a desk inside was unimpressed.

"Tell him if he wants to commit suicide to slap one of those Russian officers out there."

If it were a plant and if the Soviets wanted a telescopic photo of the American legation passing out guns, they would not get it. The man left silently. His use of the ambulance was no surprise. Each side appeared to be making ample misuse of the international symbols of neutrality, destroying them for those who had a legitimate claim.

The second day began with no letup in the barrage against the Soviet Union's Warsaw Pact "ally." Cardinal Mindszenty celebrated mass at the American minister's desk, using a teacup for the chalice, napkins as sacred cloths, and a bedsheet as the altar cover. The sound of gunfire mixed with the murmured Latin. The Cardinal's secretary-altar boy, Monsignor Egon Turchanyi, watched as the Americans went to their knees at the Consecration and burst into tears. Days later, as the outcome of an unsuccessful flight toward the frontier, the monsignor ended in Budapest prison.

The radio monitors had a report. The re-communized Budapest station, stripped no doubt of its "Free Radio" sign, was lying even with music. Most of its transmissions were light opera. Anyone listening from outside the Hungarian capital might believe that Communist happiness had re-embraced the stricken city. Inside Budapest, to hear simultaneously both the sweet music and the guns, was to be stunned by the cynicism.

The Soviets were not stopping at falsehood by rhythm. The radio was pouring out messages, some of them in an awkward Hungarian no native could have written. The Russians were doing their own translations themselves.

"We are soldiers of freedom and of international friendship! Don't believe slanderers who try to drive a wedge between us and the Hungarian people. We are your selfless friends. . . . The Kadar government has asked us to re-establish peace and quiet. . . . We have not come to conquer your country. We don't need the land of others nor the fruits of their labors. We have sufficient land and natural treasures of our own. . . . We soldiers and officers are working people the same as you are. . . . We fight for a just and common cause. . . ."

A British Communist who lost his faith as a Red during the Budapest cannonading told me a day or two later that he followed the "fantastic" communiqués with astonishment. "There isn't anyone in Budapest who believes them."

What was not staggering for its insolent disregard of truths well known in Budapest was easily answered by argument. The Soviets, it was true, should have been content with the unexploited riches of their own half-continent, but the fact was that they had looted the fruits of Poland's coal mines and of the labor of many other nations. Service in the Red Army was a strange kind of "work" by Marxist standards. And the "Kadar government"! Whence had that come? The last words from the Budapest Free Radio had been a desperate plea for help for Nagy in perfect Hungarian, quite good French, fair English, and badly broken German. The station obviously had grabbed anyone near at hand who had a smattering of Western languages to translate and broadcast the final cry.

But the Russians did not need arguments. They had guns.

Life in the legation settled down for a siege. One of the last to arrive before the Soviet attack had been an army doctor from Germany. He looked over the stocks of canned goods in the basement and told Mrs. Wales: "Cut the ration in half; Americans eat too much anyway." A typical meal after that was meat, lima beans, asparagus tips, no bread, and a choice of beer, Coca-Cola, or coffee. No one left a speck, and even the meal at Nandron's in food-revering Lyon tasted no better.

The Cardinal ate in what had been the minister's office. Mr. Wales had turned it over to the prelate as part of a small suite. Luckily the legation had been larger than needed. The Cardinal, too, learned the rules of the strange stay. I was talking to him at a window when Mr. Wales approached.

"I beg your pardon, Your Eminence," the legation chief said, "but a Soviet tank has just moved into position across the way. We may be cut by flying glass if it should fire."

The Cardinal and I, with dignity but with no delay, moved from the windows.

Soviet interest in the legation neighborhood increased. We watched from behind the curtains as patrols of a tank and a half-dozen rifle-armed infantrymen began house-to-house searches along Szabadsag Ter (Liberty Square), the ironically-named plaza on which all Budapest knew the American mission was located. The tank would take up a position in front of a building as the foot soldiers combed through it. It was a case of a "building for a bullet." If so much as a single sniper shot was heard the tanks might reply with a cannon shell. Language difficulties were causing no problems. The Soviet soldiers would slash a hand down in a short, harsh gesture and Hungarian pedestrians would stop instantly. Russia was talking with syllables her satellite bitterly well could understand.

In small groups we began sorties out of the legation. Food already was scarce and there were half-block lines in front of stores. Queues dissolved when cars approached. Sometimes it proved to be only an ambulance, although even ambulances were equivocal. It was better to take the minimum of chances, all on the sidewalks agreed.

I paused to look at a new proclamation. A cultured-mannered man of late middle age saw my American-flag armband and offered to translate. The declaration, he said, was a glorious one from students who pledged to fight until the departure of the last Russian. A crowd of twenty collected but the elderly man talked on. Every home was armed, he assured me. It was a repetition of what I had observed indirectly in the case of the chimney-top rebel emblem. The man talked freely, giving apparently not a moment's thought to the possibility that at least one of the twenty might be a Communist spy and might turn him in if the tide were to go against Hungary.

A man ducked into a doorway to escape a combined Hungarian-Russian infantry-and-tank patrol. Hungarians were reappearing in the Soviet service.

"Tell the world," the man whispered, "that we hate the Russians but that it is not true that we are Fascists."

He had begun to worry about the Communist line: "Non-Communists are Fascists." What the Communists said and did once again were getting the upper hand in Budapest.

Word reached us that Mr. Wales wanted all Americans to return at once. Moscow Radio reportedly had said that Soviet troops had taken Cardinal Mindszenty from the American legation. No such attempt had been made, but the broadcast might be an instance of events casting a shadow before. Just possibly the source of the report had been at the origin of an order now filtering through Russian military ranks.

The legation was a-bustle when we returned. The Cardinal would not be surrendered on request. The Russians would have to break in to take him. A large American flag was placed inside the entrance and newsreel cameramen set up machines behind packing cases to portray the expectedly violent scene. The flag would leave no doubt of where it had been filmed. The pictures might never reach the West but that was a problem for another day.

It was a false alarm, just as when all the legation had braced themselves as twelve Soviet tanks rolled into position opposite in Szabadsag Ter. The tanks had stopped, waited a few moments, swung into a slow loop, and then gone off the way they had come.

None came for the Cardinal and, over two years later, he was still there. For the United States and the Catholic

Church the situation was without precedent. Except where men were in imminent extreme danger the United States, unlike much more open-armed South American republics, refused diplomatic asylum to fugitives. For the Soviets the Cardinal's use of legation asylum was the first variation to a rule which had provided for only two alternatives: departure of Church leaders such as Cardinal Thomas Tien of Red China for exile, where they could have little or no further influence on their flocks, or the battering and cajoling of remaining clergymen into submission or silence. In Rome the impression was strong that the Pope wanted each priest, bishop, or cardinal to stay in his own area in contact with his flock until Communist violence made it no longer possible.

For no one, whether for the United States, for the Soviets, or for the Church, was the situation of the tormented prelate desirable. The Cardinal was still inside his country's limits but he was cut off from contact with his flock. The scandal of the churchman's suffering stayed alive as one more outrage to the account of the Soviets; but outside the legation the Reds went back to the work they did everywhere behind the Curtain, trying to set up an anti-papal, national Catholic church, attempting to make pro-Communist "patriots" of priests, and working eternally to channel religious sentiment temporarily into Kremlin service and then to destroy it.

It was in line with what one of Gomulka's chief aides, the Education Minister Wladislaw Bienkowski, had told me in Warsaw. I asked him whether the partial freedom restored to Cardinal Stephen Wyszinski and to other jailed bishops in late 1956 and 1957 was not an abandonment of an essential Communist objective. He answered that the move was merely one of tactics. For the moment the people were still religious, but they would change, he said. When they took a new view the Church would tag along and the problem would be solved. But would the people change and would the Church alter, in any case? The answer in Rome was that the Church would change in "nonessentials," as in the postwar grant of permission for evening instead of exclusively morning masses, but that nothing "basic" would be altered or surrendered. The Church would accept regional extinction first. Extermination of the Church in Red China, as one example, was widely forecast. The Church could die in the Hungary outside the Szabadsag Ter windows, but the shame of the treatment of the tortured-eyed Cardinal would live. That was sure, even as the cannonading of the four-day Soviet assault kept on.

On the fifth day, as a half-joke, we decided to phone the Soviet embassy for permission to leave Hungary. We had pictures and stories enough. Only a trickle of what we had seen and recorded had got out.

The Soviet embassy, to our surprise, treated our call as in order.

"The ambassador is sorry he cannot give you an immediate answer. It is up to the Soviet military commander. Call back in ten minutes."

In a quarter of an hour, with a wholly different attitude, we phoned a second time.

"The commander regrets that he cannot guarantee your safety on the roads for another twenty-four hours. But you can go two days from now."

Our mood changed. Perhaps, after all, we would be back in the West in another few hours with the enormous story to tell. Behind us we would be leaving people whose plight would never cease to haunt us, those, for instance, who had phoned the day after the American elections, the fourth day of the Soviet assault, to express polite and apparently sincere congratulations on President Eisenhower's reconfirmation; or the recently liberated couple who asked whether I found their two pre-teen aged daughters quiet and well behaved. I had said they were and could not forget the reply of the two who had been sent to jail as friends of the West:

"Yes, when we were both in prison that's what we heard from the people we left them with; we do think it's true."

Now that a light ray shone for us in the Western press corps gloom settled on the little family.

"We had a week of hope and now we see that it cannot be,"

the newly freed mother said. "We can't go on. If it were only that life were gray it would be bearable. But this grayness plus terror! It's too much."

It was the same color used again to describe life behind the Curtain. I had seen now why Belgrade, with a few neon lights and some American motion pictures, seemed less drab than the rest of the Communist world. Hungary was a much deeper gray. For most Hungarians the ending of the story was a sad one. Sometimes, as in the case of the brave Maleter and Nagy, there was execution. For the couple with the well-behaved daughters it finished well. They and their small girls were among the more than one hundred thousand who fled west as the Austrian border gapped open for another month.

The radio kept up its bizarre interpretation of what was happening and reports continued to flow in. The radio said happily that other satellites were rushing supplies of glass to fix the broken windows of Hungary. Something else in addition to tank shells and machine-gun bullets was to be given! But far more than new windows were needed to fill the new ditch of detestation which had been dug and would be carved even deeper during the coming reprisals.

We prepared to go. The Hungarian Foreign Office, communist stars back in its official stamp, gave us the visas for departure which are as important in Communist countries as those for entering. The approval from the nominally sovereign Kadar regime needed Soviet countersigning, but there was delay when we applied at the Russian military command in its neighborhood of shot-off shade trees, fallen telephone poles, tangled wires, and massed tanks.

We decided to try a dash for it without Soviet approval. With our Kadar passes we set out in a column of thirty cars flying the flags of our dozen Western nations.

A few Hungarians ran up to us as we drove toward the city's edge. For the first time there was resentment.

"Why did America let us down? What was shot up here was the reputation of the United Nations."

We passed the broken wheels and shattered metal parts of what had evidently been a Hungarian Army defense position.

The little satellite force had turned its guns against the Soviet master and had paid a terrible price. At regular 100-foot intervals shell holes were drilled through rows of houses and factory walls. The two-foot-wide punctures had not been there when we had reached Budapest the eternity of ten days before. The tanks in that dawn barrage must have rolled forward blasting holes through everything as fast as they could reload.

At the city's edge a Soviet tank, promptly re-enforced by a second, turned us back. The Foreign Ministry approval was not enough. We must have Russian passes, too. Behind the Soviet tanks as they blocked our way was a great wall scrawl, freshly painted: "Russkis, go home!" Like the Molotov cocktails which had burned out tanks, the signs were another tool of subversion taught by Moscow and, in the end, used against it. We stalled for two hours, hoping for a change of heart, and watched horses and wagons trudging into the Russian strong point, delivering captured or surrendered rifles. The stage was being set for the next act, a new man hunt, this one for Hungarians who had tried to be free.

We turned back. Again, just as at our arrival not quite a fortnight earlier, we were greeted by cheers. The Budapest people thought we were the spearhead of a United Nations relief column. It was about all the Western Communist newspaperman in the car with us could stand. Others had refused him a ride so we had opened our car to him.

"Surely it can't be as pitiful as it seems," he said. "Certainly some of these people must have seen us go out. Some of them must know we are only newspapermen who couldn't leave."

The Communist asked whether I had my stories written. I shook my head.

"I haven't either," he said. "I find this very difficult to write."

He must have noticed a wry expression, for he went on:

"I mean to put it down just the way I saw it and if my paper won't print it I'll quit. But I won't leave the Party. I've been in it since I was fifteen and my wife's in it, too. I'll stay and fight from within. If they expel me, of course that will be another matter."

I was skeptical about the leopard and his spots, but weeks later I regretted the doubt. Events happened as the reporter promised. His Party expelled him. He wrote an account of the crushing of Budapest little different from that of any of the rest of us. A non-Party publisher put it in print.

Next day we tried it again and this time we made it. We told the Soviets we hoped for an 8 A.M. start in order to get to the Austrian border before dark, but they answered curtly that they could not see us before ten. We went at eight anyway, and two hours later watched the Soviets taking lunch. Issuing of passes had begun as we had arrived. A grandfather clock in the main hall said 10 A.M. when our watches showed eight, and noon when we had ten. Ours had been an argument over something on which we had not differed. The Soviets literally were running Hungary on Moscow time.

Narrow-eyed Mongolians were on sentry duty outside the shattered command villa. They stared blankly, as if uncomprehending. Asia, I thought, had flowed into Europe. When the crowd had seized the radio station a woman had helped turn the tide by calling out to the rebel throng not to retreat in front of the Hungarian Army tanks which threatened them: "They won't hurt us. I know. My brother and my father are in the army and they would never shoot Hungarians." She had been right. The tanks had backed off and the revolution had accomplished one of its great victories. It would not be the same with these strangers from Mongolia. When Russians ordered them to fire, they did so, as new ruins everywhere testified. Budapest's typically Western tree-lined streets and the women and children behind its apartment-house walls aroused no sympathy among the men from farthest Asia.

There was one familiar face at the *komandatura*. The silver-haired agent who had asked the American legation for a pistol to "blow my brains out" was bustling about as if he were in charge. Around him were dozens of the officer faces the American had told him to slap if he were tired of living.

Before getting exit permits each of us was grilled:

What did you think of what you saw here?

What did you see? Tell me whom you saw and we may let you go!

The words must have been partially a bluff, for all got visas.

Outside, Hungarian courage still persisted. Almost in the komandatura doorway we were stopped with notes for relatives in the United States. Whatever would be the cost in new suffering the Hungarians were still speaking out. In the choice between America and Russia their desires were clear.

We ducked back to the Duna to settle accounts. A squad of timid-mannered, Soviet-commanded soldiers filed into the lobby.

"Are there any arms, Fascists, or counterrevolutionaries here?" they asked politely.

A half-dozen hastily assured them that there were none. The squad trooped out again. The first visit from the new authorities had gone easily enough, but Soviet interest in the correspondents' hotel was plain. In the dining room a dozen ate glumly. There was no choice on the menu. Since the kitchen had been machine-gunned there was only one fixed meal for all.

We drove out past the American legation. It, too, was different from what it had been before. I remembered the evening when hopes sank lowest and the windows looking into the inner courtyard had glowed orange for more than an hour while a sooty-faced marine burned all but a few confidential documents. The last handful could be destroyed in a few moments. Those last key papers presumably still sat in the thinned-out safe.

We had our last look at the Hungarian government building. Half a red star still balanced on the highest pinnacle. The demolisher never had finished his work.

At Nickelsdorf on the Austrian border our party of three, the reforming Communist, the correspondent driver, and I, had a liberation celebration as we drove: sandwiches of Swiss cheese we had hoarded against an emergency, bites of chocolate, and shots of cognac.

The village was the border community which was becoming

famous among Hungarian refugees as the doorway to freedom. They had a joke about it: "What is the most beautiful sight in the world? Venice? Rio de Janeiro? No, Nickelsdorf!"

With its mud, its geese, and its roaming pig herds Nickelsdorf could never win acclaim as a beauty spot, but it was liberty's portal, and no sight was lovelier to escaping Hungarians.

For another month I covered Hungary's border, watching it from the far side as more than 1 per cent of the population abandoned their homes and fled the retaliation the Soviet Union and the Communists were certain to inflict on those who stayed behind.

Night after night the men, women, and children of the martyred nation fled by the thousands. Fortunately, what had evidently been a new bit of Red propaganda served the fugitives. The ten-foot-wide minefield along the border had been plowed up a few months before in what served as a mute gesture to Austrians to believe that communism was not so dreadful as it seemed and that the Vienna government safely could slide from official neutrality into a position as a satellite or at least as a collaborator with communism. The Austrians had been too canny to be taken in by the gesture, but the fleeing tens of thousands were able, as a result, to walk through the plowed earth without the horrible mutilations that otherwise would have been certain.

I watched on many nights. First there would be a cluster of tiny red dots in the distance as an oncoming throng puffed on cigarettes. Then in the silvery light of the moon on snow a smudge would appear. The group was nearer. Minutes later vertical black lines would be seen and then the crunch of snow could be heard. Another one to two hundred would be free. Volunteers served tea and schnapps at a border shack.

"How good it tasted," a fleeing Evangelical minister told us about the gin as we drove him to Vienna one dawn.

The throng was so big and so endless that the refugees lost their identity for us as people until chance encounters brought their personalities and individual plights into understandable perspective. I drove up to the border one frosty morning with General William ("Wild Bill") Donovan, wartime intelligence chief for the United States, and Pierce Gerety, American refugee commissioner. They wanted to judge the problem on the scene, but they became wholly absorbed in a mere five of the refugees instead. It was a quintet between the ages of eight and twelve, mostly girls. The two eldest were dragging a suitcase by a strap. The valise trailed over the slippery ground like a sled. The eyes of one child were red-rimmed as if tears had been recent. Their cheeks fortunately were still red, not yet blue. It was twenty above zero, but so far their exposure in the night had not caused freezing. The five said a crowded truck had taken their parents into Andau, three miles ahead, and that the grownups had promised to come back promptly.

The two officials looked at the children with shock. They visited the border for a few minutes and then hurried back to drive the five to Andau.

Chances were that the children quickly found their parents, but the incident was only one of many border horrors that month. A man arrived at Andau, remembered the wife he had left in his panic in Budapest, went back to the capital on the Danube to tell the woman it was safe to come, and reached there to find that she, too, had left in the meantime. He arrived back at the makeshift Andau collection center, hunting madly. His wife was not there. No one stayed at the little collection center in a dance hall at Andau more than a dozen hours, he was told. The man wanted to go back to Hungary for another search but was urged to take his chances first with the rather haphazard refugee registration service deeper inside Austria.

Even Communists fled. A man in what looked like an American military uniform approached me at my Vienna hotel. He said he was John Santo, director of Hungarian meat supply, who had sat in the top councils of the Kadar government until two days before. He had been head of the bus drivers' union in New York and had tied up Fifth Avenue once in a strike which had alarmed American officials about growing Red power. He had been deported as a Communist alien and Hungary, in a fanfare of propaganda, had given him asylum and a top job.

Santo wanted, he told me, to go back to "my country," the United States. His disillusion with communism, he said, was complete. He had risen high enough to get on the private telephone circuit shared by the upper couple of hundred, but he and his American-citizen wife had slept each night with a traveling bag beside them. When the terror used by the regime as the main impulse for the Communist society of Hungary had worn down, Laszlo Rajk, the country's number-two Communist, had been executed on the ludicrous charge of "spying for the Americans." The purpose, Santo said, had been to say threateningly to the people that if this could happen to one so high it could happen to them also. Who could be better accused next of being an "American spy" than himself, who had lived in the United States and had served as a sergeant in its army, Santo and his wife wondered.

Communism had cruelly exploited the workers, he said, tricking them into spurts and then setting the record as a norm which all were required to reach regularly. Workers had lost interest in their jobs and the products were shoddy. "In my field, for example, if they had to let the blood of a slaughtered animal run for five minutes, they'd stop it at one or two."

I grilled Santo all one day and had others talk to him. He was reluctant to inform on old friends in the American communist movement, but promised at last to take his chances with the demands of American justice if he could go back to the States. He convinced me that he was telling the truth but months later American authorities still hesitated to give him the waivers he needed as a "permanent deportee."

All Hungary had repudiated the Red faith. I went to the border one night with Robert Kleiman, Paris correspondent of *United States News and World Report*. We asked the Austrian border guard where the Hungarian frontier watchers were.

"Behind us," they said.

Our idea had been to be cautious about trigger-happy Red border patrollers, but the Austrians explained that the Iron-

Curtain men had been chilled and had come over to warm up at the Westerners' stove. There was no heater on the Red side.

We went back a hundred yards to the Austrians' shed. Inside were the five Hungarian frontier patrolmen. It was nearly a month since the Soviets had reseized Budapest, but the young border soldiers assured us that "none in our company; none, that is, except the lieutenant," were for the new puppet premier, Kadar. In the six weeks since the start of the revolution not one of the patrolmen had mounted the watch tower. "It's twice as cold up there," one soldier said. The group had made no effort to interfere with fugitives, and had even been knocking off without waiting for reliefs. "We were never permitted to do that before," they commented. Even now they thought it wisest not to tell which hours saw the border wholly exposed.

But even the Russians, they said, did not seem interested in stopping fugitives. "They're a mile behind us, but their guns are pointing this way. If they wanted to stop the people, they'd be aiming the other way, don't you think?"

It was one more confirmation that the Russians' first worry had been to brace themselves against a possible Western attempt to help the crushed Hungarians.

We asked whether the border guards would flee, too.

"Well, no, not for the moment," their eldest answered for the others. "We have homes and farms. We'd lose all that. We feel that when you start to flee you pass your whole life in flight. We figure the Russians are sure to go. It's impossible for them to stay against the will of everyone. Of course we could be wrong and if we are we'll leave, too."

The guards were picked men, chosen for special loyalty to communism. The collapse of the Red dream had been complete. Russia stayed in Hungary by brute force. Soviet communism had won that battle with the forces of freedom, but would it end by conquering the world? I could not believe it, and a three-month look inside the Soviet Union confirmed the opinion.

X

RUSSIA: NATIONALISM, TYRANNY, AND "HOWEVER"

A three-month assignment to Moscow in the late winter and early spring of 1958 was a climax, a coveted opportunity to study the Soviet threat at its source.

I went in through miserable Terespol, the Polish frontier village of the dazed and ragged repatriates of a year earlier. A good-natured Polish frontier guard asked to see the money in my wallet. He counted it haphazardly, took my word for the total, and then gaped at the picture of Benjamin Franklin on a $100 bill.

"Who's this, Lincoln?" he asked. "One hundred dollars! What I could do with that!"

The Russians were polite but much more businesslike. An English-speaking guard pored through my pile of books and stiffened.

"Djilas' *The New Class!*" He looked up with a nervous smile as if we shared a naughty secret. "Have you read it?"

He seemed to want to ask something more about the book and its charge that communism had created a new clique of exploiters, the Party presidium and a few favorites around it, but he put the volume down and said no more. A young soldier was busy on his knees and then on his toes as he flashed a light under the seats and up into the recesses of the baggage rack. With one exception it was the most thorough border search I had seen. The other was on Communist Czechoslovakia's section of the Iron Curtain facing Austria. There, beside the electrified barbed wire of the frontier, soldiers combed under cars while comrades stood back thirty feet with machine guns ready to spray flushed-out fugitives.

A few minutes later, inside the Soviet border station, a stern buxom woman of middle age approached.

"You have a copy of Djilas' book?" she said. "Don't you know you're not allowed to bring that into the Soviet Union? You'll have to leave it here."

A tense little English-speaking guide from the Soviet tourist bureau, Intourist, intervened. He had met me at the compartment.

"It's all right," he said. "He can put it through customs in Moscow."

The Intourist man evidently had the upper hand, for the customs woman, after a moment's hesitation, left. In Moscow there was no customs and the book stayed with me. The rule, other correspondents told me, was that foreign reporters were allowed to have any documents they wanted but were forbidden to pass them to Russians. One correspondent had been expelled on a double charge: handing an American news magazine to a Soviet citizen (and thus exposing him to non-Communist journalism) and selling a few clothes in one of the bustling Soviet secondhand stores (thus evading the currency control laws with their fictitiously high evaluation of the ruble). Presumably Soviet disapproval of the reporter's dispatches was the true reason for the expulsion, but if so it was not mentioned.

Living standards had sunk lower and lower as I rode from once-prosperous Prague, with its unrepaired World War II ruins, eastward through the Czechoslovak and Polish countrysides. Roofing turned to humble thatch until finally in eastern Poland even that had tumbled in. Moscow-ordered emphasis on heavy industry, on military production, had left little room for consumer goods, even for roofing. From Prague to Terespol, a twenty-four-hour ride on one of the main Czechoslovak-Russian sleepers, there had been no dining car. I would have been famished indeed if the porters in our car had not brewed me occasional tea served in a finger-burning glass. With that I washed down sandwiches fortunately carried from Rome.

I wondered how much worse conditions would get as we

moved beyond Terespol, but on the Soviet side the trend was reversed. A dining car was put on. It had cracked windows, but there were several dozen choices on the menu, and the tea glasses were in comfortable metal holders. There was even a slice of lemon in the tea, a tropical luxury Poland had not offered the previous winter. Across the aisle a Soviet officer solemnly fed a child on his knee. Russia's people were not living in luxury, but they were better off than in the Soviet satellites.

It was already well after dark. Next morning we were still rolling toward Moscow. The houses were of logs. The one note of bright color in some of the tree-brown villages was the red flag in front of what was presumably the mayor's office. It was a scene from the American frontier of a century earlier, but with an exception. There were television antennas on the roofs, and as we got nearer the capital there were ever more of them. It was evidently in large part a primitive country but one with its own power, not dependent on the West.

My first impression of Moscow was divided. Gray again was the word for it, the gray of stone buildings and street pavements, but above all the dreariness of a whole population dressed in the same sensible dark clothes, all turned out by the same few factories where "frivolous" Western ideas of style and variety penetrated but little. There was gloom, the mood of a people tired of the oddly puritanical official ideas about music and dancing; bored with a press which included "not a single interesting newspaper," as one journalist colleague told me, and depressed by the mixture of terror and twisted propaganda which life had been for four decades.

It was a divided reaction, for my second thought, almost as quick, was how surprisingly familiar so much was. However innocent that may have been, I was not prepared for the sight of traffic stopping on red. Even in the land of the Reds, their own color meant what it did to the free world, danger and the forbidden. The traffic lights, the curbstones, the sidewalks, the plate-glass windows of shops, the apartment houses, and even a dozen or two proud and strategically placed forty-story

skyscrapers, were all lifted bodily from a score of neighborhoods in my own New York.

The similarity was no accident. Many pirated Western in-
ventions had been copied, down to the very label on which
the original manufacturer in the United States or elsewhere in
the free world had had his brand name.

"They crave to be like you," a non-American Westerner
told me. "The pity is that in the process so much of the charm
of Old Russia is being lost."

It was no uniquely Russian failing. Mussolini in Rome had
done much the same, destroying delightful medieval quarters
in order to replace them with dull, broad streets. An exception to the modernization trend in the Moscow of early 1958
was the gilding of the domes of the Orthodox churches inside
the walls of the Kremlin fortress and through the rest of the
city and countryside. After years of desecrating churches as
part of the godless campaign, they had "suddenly come to
realize that those churches are the only things of beauty here,"
as one Moscow resident said.

Another favorable surprise was my freedom of movement. I
could hail any cab, tell the driver in carefully memorized
Russian phrases where I wanted to go in Moscow, and set off
with no police car trailing. I could walk, take the bus, or use
the metro—the subway. Some parts of the city were out of
bounds, but I never learned which they were, and my travels
never took me toward them.

At about that point my attention was drawn back to unpleasant facts about Moscow. With one or two exceptions
every known non-communist foreigner was required to live
either in a hotel or in one of four special apartment houses.
At the entrance of each was a fur-hatted policeman in a sentry
box. At his elbow was a telephone. The policeman saluted as
each of us came and went, and at first the experience was en-
joyable. It was more gentility than a Paris janitress ever
showed. But the comfort was short-lived, for on second thought
it was plain that each greeting was in effect the jailer's authorization to pass. All but specially authorized Russians were

strained out at the door. The Soviet Union was taking no chances on foreigners' having many unsupervised relationships with its citizens.

Each of the four residences had several staircases, and at the bottom of each one sat a janitress. Like characters out of the French Revolution, they seemed usually to be knitting. The janitresses double-checked the work of the policeman.

The same close watch was kept at hotels. On each floor a woman at a reception desk had a clear view of the staircase, of the elevator, and of all who stepped onto the floor.

The observation of foreigners went further. All maids, chauffeurs, interpreters, and secretaries had to be hired from the same government agency. It was common belief that all of them had an organization to which they were summoned for periodic pep talks about their duties with regard to the glimpses they had into what the foreigners were doing.

Foreigners spoke cautiously or not at all in the presence of their employees. Even in the servants' absence the diplomats and journalists were careful. One embassy attaché set up a system of loud-speakers throughout his apartment so that he could play loud music wherever he had a conversation with a guest.

Even at that, neither the attaché nor any other foreigner ever had a feeling of privacy. One newly-arrived foreign woman told her husband's secretary chattily, "I'd like to go across town today, but I'm afraid I'll get lost."

"Don't worry," the other blurted, "we'll know where you are all the time."

Whether it would be the policeman at the door, with his telephone at his elbow, or some other who would magically track the woman was not explained.

I tried to approach the Soviet Union with an open mind. The ideal of the American liberal newspaper is "objectivity," a goal many Europeans consider unattainable and not even desirable. In the American news view, a reporter's duty is to get as many facts as he can and to present them fairly, letting the reader in his democratic sovereignty form the judgments which become votes and, finally, national policy. In a commonly held European view, no man can divorce himself utterly from his prejudices, and in any case, this theory holds, any writer ought to judge and to pass on his counsels as best he can.

It was an embassy wife with perhaps that view who upbraided me one night at a cocktail party.

"Do you have an open mind?" she asked. "Well, I don't, and I don't think anyone should."

So far as she was concerned it was too late in Soviet history for any diplomat, politician, journalist, or thinking person to refuse to draw conclusions. It was no longer a matter of "prejudice."

"Do you know what my servants tell me?" the woman asked with a choke of frustration. "They see these pretty clothes and tell me: 'They're not yours. They belong to your government. When you are through with this assignment you will have to give them back.' "

If it was psychological warfare against the woman's nerves and, through her, against her already distraught husband, it was successful. The woman was ill with fury.

Her case was similar to that of another foreigner whose assistant, otherwise a perfect employee, would interrupt periodically to say: "Please, about the war in Korea, it's really true, you know, that it was South Korea that attacked North Korea."

The words had been used so often that they had a striking effect. The Western victim would jump to his feet.

"Say all you want, but I'll be outside the room. When you've finished, let me know and I'll come back."

All the old arguments that Communist North Korea could never have counterattacked so quickly and effectively had been used and reused by the Westerner until he found them savorless. The Westerner began having physical disturbances a doctor diagnosed as imaginary.

I had expected to find many Soviet sympathizers among Moscow's foreigners. It had been that way in every other capi-

tal I had known. Familiarity, despite the old saw to the contrary, breeds understanding. It was not so in the Soviet city.
If there were any who saw Russia's side they kept the secret
to themselves.

The Soviets seemed to take enmity for granted and to make
scant effort to win friends among the foreigners. When Mary
joined me for two weeks we threw a cocktail party, mostly
for Western journalists and diplomats, but we asked a Russian or two as well. When the Soviets came, other reporters
expressed astonishment and even admiration: "What a good
idea, to ask Russians!" It was a rare chance to probe what the
Soviets were thinking.

Up to the last moment the Russian guests had told us: "We
don't know whether we can make it, but we will if we can."

One proved a problem. He said he would drink whatever
most of the others were taking (scotch and water) and later
that he would switch to what I considered most American (a
very dry martini). I begged him for his sake not to mix
whisky and gin, but he insisted. He weaved his gay but uncertain way to the door an hour or so later.

The wall between the foreigners and Soviets had many
forms.

"I've been here eighteen months and I've been inside the
Foreign Ministry just three times," the number-two man of
one Western embassy told me. "And on each of those a policeman met me at the door, took me where I wanted to go, and
then led me out again. There's just no way to make contact."

Newsmen were as disaffected as the diplomats, although
they are usually more easy-going. I remembered once calling
on Italy's Premier De Gasperi in a delegation of three representing the one hundred fifty foreign correspondents in Italy.
In our group were our association president, Antonio Scan-
ziani, a Swiss; and two vice-presidents, Alexander Vishnevski
of Tass, the Soviet agency, and I, an American.

"Swiss, American, Russian!" the premier said with a small
smile. "You've done what we politicians have failed to do."

With exception made for the sprinkling of men from the official Communist press, the fifteen Americans and seventy other foreign correspondents scarcely could have been more hostile to the regime. Even some of the Reds seemed to have doubts. What they were dealing with in Moscow, after all, was not merely communism in theory, as they had learned or imagined it in their homelands, but communism in practice and, importantly and repulsively, Russian imperialism. No foreign Communist, as Tito had revealed in Yugoslavia, liked that.

"Here's the censor's office," one journalistic colleague told me. "You will pass most of your time here and you will learn to hate everything about it."

The bureau was in the main telegraph building. Correspondents, "like schoolchildren" as they said, had to submit every word for approval. Usually there was a half-hour wait but sometimes, at key moments, such as when Nikita Khrushchev seized all power as combined head of the Party and government, six or seven hours might elapse before mangled copy was returned. Words, phrases, paragraphs, and occasionally whole stories would be suppressed. The experience was more unnerving the more often it was repeated.

"You feel as if you were back in school. 'Teacher! Is it all right?'" one said.

The normally scoop-conscious reporters reacted by pooling everything they could comb from between-the-lines reading of the Soviet press, their main source of information. If copy came back from the censor in good shape, the lucky reporter spread the word: "The easy one's on tonight!" It was usually only a manner of speaking, however, for others who tried to slip through long-hoarded choice items found promptly that even the "easy one" was hard.

The art of reading the papers was one the others taught me.

"Look for the word *adnaka* [however]," one advised. "All editorials are the same. The first one third says that everything's fine. Then you come to the adnaka. After that you find what's wrong and what the article is all about. Sometimes when I'm in a hurry I ask my translator right off, 'Where's the adnaka?' "

Some even recommended that outgoing articles be written the same way in order to get them through the censor.

"You make a great mistake trying to put the news in the first paragraph," a European told me seriously. "They're not used to that. You should start off by saying, 'Everything's going well, the weather is nice, and nothing much is happening,' and then you can put in what you want."

In the leisurely style of his continental paper, the system worked well enough. That reporter was publishing some of the most penetrating exposés of Soviet life.

With so few correspondents permitted in Moscow, the Soviets had an opportunity to get to know each intimately. At least one had a "tail." That journalist had managed to see a substantial number of Russians, and police were watching him.

"They're behind us now," he told me one evening as we drove in his car. "I see them through the rear-view mirror. Now they've ducked behind a car; now they're out again."

The trailing car backed swiftly into a taxi rack across the street as we parked at the censor's office. Its heavy, distinctive design stood out from the cabs on either side.

My own dossier must have expanded after one luncheon conversation with a Soviet guest. We had caviar and vodka but I refused to follow his example as he swallowed six vodkas, each at a gulp.

"It's worse if you sip it," he warned.

I decided to risk it.

Suddenly my companion's manner changed. In a few minutes he blurted out a string of questions which reminded me of nothing so much as the cross-questioning at the Budapest *komandatura*.

"Where were you born? What was your father's occupation? Was he in business for himself? How would you grade his profits: large, medium-sized, small? Who has the real control inside your newspaper?"

The questions aimed neatly to classify me and my probable political opinions on the basis of economic conditions in my childhood home in Brooklyn. They would also help to pry a bit into the mysteries of the important American paper I represented. I answered with reserve. As quickly as it had begun the catechism ended. "Excuse the questions!"

Although the foreigners in Moscow were shut off from the Soviets, a rather complete picture of life inside the homeland of communism gradually unfolded. It was an existence of fear, bureaucracy, brutality, Russian nationalism, frustration, inefficiency, lies, cynicism, ignorance, poverty, and the same human aspirations people have everywhere. Slowly in Moscow's streets, restaurants, and hotels, in the homes of foreigners, in talks in the embassies, in visits to a factory and a farm in a two-hundred-and-fifty-mile round trip into the countryside along the trans-Siberian railroad I pieced together an impression.

The lies were in every day's papers. The West was loaded with insults and the truth about the free world was so persistently distorted that it was painful to read.

"Every time you run across the phrase 'as is well known,' you can be sure," one journalist told me, "that what follows will be a lie."

There were signs that some of the people saw through at least a few of the falsehoods and omissions. Sometimes they got information through the fiercely jammed Western radio broadcasts. One diplomat who made a practice of attending lectures and their question-and-answer periods was impressed when one man in an audience three days after the Russian suppression of the Poznan, Poland, uprising in 1956 asked to have the "truth" on it. Not a word about the riots had been given inside the Soviet Union.

Another diplomat, on a trip to the Pacific, was impressed by a chance acquaintance who challenged him with the Kremlin version of a current controversy. The foreigner was convinced by the manner of the man that what he really wanted was to draw out the Western view of the issue.

I saw a reflection of the Soviet public's hunger for the "other side of the story" on a visit to one of the hundreds of thousands of *agitpunkts,* literally "agitation points," which were set up throughout the Soviet Union early in 1958 for the first national elections in five years. The agitpunkt was a well-lit clubroom with propaganda photographs, wall proclamations, and a television set. All twenty visitors were at the TV, but since that was thick with propaganda, too, they had no real escape from indoctrination.

My Western journalist companion baited the "agitators." Why were there only 1,378 candidates for 1,378 parliament seats? What choice did a voter have? Were write-in candidates permitted? Could they be elected?

The agitators smiled with good enough spirit. A critical, even hostile, attitude was so unusual they were not prepared for it as irascible Communists would have been in the West. The propaganda, as we knew from reading *Pravda,* had answers for each of the points, and the Party agents mechanically ticked them off: "Rival candidates are not necessary because we have no conflicting classes; we under communism have unity. Our voters have a different psychology. Write-in candidates are permitted, but votes for them are not counted, and in our district we have never had a case of the sort."

The defensive was not to the agitators' liking. They showed signs of being nettled. They took the initiative themselves.

"The poor can't vote in the United States! There are no workers in the American Congress!"

"How can you say that?" my friend demanded. "The poor can't vote! No workers in Congress! The congressmen work twelve hours a day for their constituents. How can they work more than that?"

"For the capitalists, those are the ones for whom they work!" The agitators were pleased with their comeback. "If Roosevelt had been against Rockefeller he couldn't have been elected."

My interpreter pulled at my sleeve. Soviet agitpunkts were no place for American political speeches. It was time to leave.

I passed the word to my friend. By that time the TV set had lost a good share of its watchers. There had been more interest in that discussion than in any the agitators had arranged in a long time.

"Anyway," the correspondent said, "I had half of them on my side."

He probably had. Every ear, even the agitators', had been open when the Westerner spoke.

Officials mentioned gently next day that the episode had been noted. It was not to be repeated; that was made clear.

Other hints of dissatisfaction with the mendacious, totalitarian regime were everywhere. In the restaurants, Moscow's only night spots (closed at 1 A.M.), young couples formed tight circles around the few daring innovators who tried the latest jubilant and extroverted dance steps from the West, those of the "rock 'n' roll." The bands swung out with American jazz in a stylized and stiff version, the closest to the admired United States original the Muscovites could come. There was a flavor of the conspiratorial. The Kremlin often had condemned jazz as decadent. The young were bored with the gray life painted for them by the Kremlin puritans and were breaking through toward a rosier and more Western life of their yearnings.

What might be called the musical and dancing rebellion was paralleled by others in the worlds of phonograph records, perfumes, and even that of the formal theater. There was a lively black market in old X-ray plates on which forbidden songs had been registered. In a typical case the music was that of a popular old singer who had spoken or acted against some Communist slogan and had been put under a ban. The square-corner X-ray films worked about fifty times before the needle pricked through.

The perfume insurrection was a peaceful one accomplished by women shoppers. Communist officials had used even names of perfumes for propaganda. One scent was called "Fifth All-Union Railway Men's Day." The railroad hands of the Soviet Union for the fifth time had been honored with a "day," and some grim bureaucrat had felt that that made a good name for a perfume. The few department stores of Moscow were still selling such unlikely fragrances as "My Moscow," "Kremlin," "May Day" (International Workers' Day), "The Eighth of May" (Communist International Women's Day), "Friendship Among the Peoples" and "Fortieth Anniversary of the Soviet Army," but at least there was no more of the old "Fifth All-Union Railway Men's Day" and there was a selection of such slightly less forbidding new brands as "Spring," "White Night," "Carmen," "Diamond," "Happy New Year," "Queen of Spades," "Starting to Fly," and even "Ecstasy."

A hint that even the Bolshoi ("Grand") Theater felt the need for something new came from its most accomplished ballet director, Igor Moiseyev. The Bolshoi ranked so high in the scale of Soviet prides that Stalin had reserved the royal box in the center at the back and his Kremlin successors had moved to a box on the left above the stage. One official loge outdid the other in good views of the long, high, and floating leaps of the theater's ballet dancers. The Bolshoi ballet was to a great extent where the revolution had found it in 1917 and needed change, Moiseyev admitted to me. He had already begun modifications. In place of frozen classic formalisms he was bringing in a more relaxed, intimate style. No doubt it was a mistake to conclude much from so little, but I was encouraged to believe that the strait jacket in which the Kremlin Communists had attempted to bind all life could not forever resist, and that the same human instincts which had gone to make the free West eventually would reform the imprisoned East.

Although there were heartening signs of resistance and of change, there were still appalling evidences of totalitarian domination. Little was not secret. Even telephone lists seemed to be classified information. Moscow had had no new telephone book in seven years. Copies even of that were hard to find.

As reluctant as the Soviets were about letting out their phone lists, so were they anxious to get those of other countries. Diplomats told me that one of the first requests Soviet

spy rings made of prospective new agents in the West was to
get a few telephone directories. With their long lists of names
and addresses they were full of data, however banal. Westerners found the request innocent enough, but as soon as they
had fulfilled it felt compromised. What seemed in retrospect
like the fatal first step had been taken.

The lack of phone books was far from all. One Western
journalist looked on with astonishment, on the eve of the
"World Youth Festival" in 1957, as wooden shields were put
up around the sentry boxes at the prison camp opposite his
dom diplomat ("diplomatic house," one of the residences for
foreigners). The additions did not match the old wall so that
they stood out sharply when you knew about them, though a
Youth Festival guest would have been most unlikely to notice. The shields were left permanently in place, but the
sentries could be seen behind them from upper floors of the
dom diplomat.

Another resident of the same building told me of her shock
one day when she and her three-year-old son strolled beside
the unmarked jail. A hand reached from a window slot. The
child waved back and instantly dozens of other arms stretched
out in a pitiful greeting. The sentries were furious. "Get out
of there!" one bawled from behind his screen.

The woman and child fled. The boy's nerves were on edge
for two nights afterward.

"The guard was wild because it was a demonstration," the
woman said.

The Soviets were understandably anxious that no opposi-
tions unite, not even hand-wavers at a prison.

Guards on walls and behind barbed wire were no uncom-
mon sight even in the selected parts of the Soviet Union I
was allowed to visit, but I came on few other buildings I knew
to be jails. Fear, however, was easy to find. I asked a policeman to help hail a cab. Obligingly he waved his night stick
in the same harsh gesture which had stopped pedestrians in
the Hungarian revolution. A cab braked abruptly. The cabby
giggled nervously for moments afterward.

"I was sure I had done nothing wrong," he kept repeating.

The Soviets let me inspect a child's nursery, a factory, and a farm, and raised no objection when I told them I wanted to make a thirty-six-hour round trip to two of Russia's capitals of the Middle Ages, Suzdal and Vladimir, on the trans-Siberian railroad. Each cast further light on the severe, relentlessly propagandized life of the often likable Soviet people.

The factory was the former Kaganovich Ball-bearing Works on the edge of Moscow. It must have been specially declassified for visits by foreigners, for the American ambassador, studious, soft-spoken Llewellyn Thompson, and a few other diplomats, were permitted to go there a week later. Perhaps my visit was a practice run for theirs.

The assistant manager received me at a desk decorated with four telephones which were replicas of the one-piece type used in the West. Above his head, despite a half decade of attacks which had followed Stalin's death, was a picture of the late dictator in uniform and, beside him, Lenin in civilian clothes. "De-Stalinization" had not removed the accused madman and murderer from the large, museumlike glass case he shared with Lenin in Moscow's central Red Square, and each week brought new evidence that nothing about Stalin had been repudiated. "De-Stalinization" had been merely a step in replacing the Stalin dictatorship with one by Khrushchev.

The factory's number-two man told us with satisfaction that his plant was the largest of its kind in Europe. The assistant manager added amiably that the 10,000-person work staff was about equally divided between men and women, that pay was $25.00 to $50.00 a week, and that so little could be saved for such major expenses as household furnishings that the factory management dipped into a plant fund, when it had money enough, to equip the small new apartments of their newlywed employees. It was a hard-strapped kind of paternalism, just what Communists in Western labor movements were quickest to deplore.

The official made no comment on the change in the factory name. Kaganovich had been one of the top figures in the

Red hierarchy, but he had quarreled with Khrushchev and the latter had won. Kaganovich and three others had been run out of the Communist Presidium with the charge that they were an "anti-Party group," a clumsy euphemism for "anti-Khrushchev." The factory was now known as "Ball-bearing Plant Number One."

Not all elimination of Khrushchev rivals had been as easy. In the plant's yard were a dozen "Molotov" trucks. The former premier had been expelled as "anti-Party" at the same time as Kaganovich, but his name by then was irrevocably stamped into the metal of vehicles all over the Soviet Union. Heavy transportation continued to be done in his name.

Sour-featured police checked us in and out. Factories, in the Communist view, were prime targets for saboteurs.

A few travel-photo displays lined the corridors. One showed wonders of France. A chart reported how each department stood in relation to its "plan." A few were just ahead, some behind, none very far from the goal of the moment. Around and above were the Party's slogans for the workers of all nations.

The guide seemed most anxious to show off an all-automatic room.

"It was our workers' gift to the Central Committee on the occasion of the Twentieth Party Congress," he said.

I listened without comment. According to the Moscow press of those days there was severe resistance to "automation," with waiters in partly-mechanized restaurants, for instance, letting food machines stand empty despite Central Committee demands that machinery replace workers so far as possible. With all power in the hands of the 125-man Central Committee, it was ironic to hear that "workers" anywhere had decided what they would do for the Party committee.

Women in their early twenties were lifting red-hot ingots with the help of long pincers.

"How long does a woman last at the job?" I asked.

"Two or three years," was the answer.

"And after that?"

"Oh, she qualifies for another job."

Presumably ruined health went with her. I remembered the demands at Györ during the Hungarian revolution: no more night jobs for women and better pay for all in heavy, dangerous work.

The nursery was for children of women of the factory. They stayed from 7 A.M to 7 P.M. and did not want to go home, the matronly school director said convincingly. There were tiny chairs and tables, closet space for each child in frail but brightly painted wooden cabinets, a little garden with sprouting beans, and a miniature menagerie with a hedgehog and a turtle. The children were having an after-lunch nap. Two or three of the five-year-olds opened one eye to look at us but the other thirty made a good show of being asleep.

The nursery of Ball-bearing Plant Number One made a good appearance, I thought, but I wondered which of two reasons explained the children's reluctance to go home. Was it because of the quality of the preschool institution or, instead, because of hardships in a home with a mother exhausted by factory work? All in Moscow agreed that the doubling and tripling up in apartments were so bad that Muscovites happily strolled outdoors on winter Sundays at twenty degrees below freezing, as I saw them doing, rather than face the cramped life in their homes.

I asked about indoctrination. It started as quickly as tots could take it, the nursery mistress answered. The bald, bearded, never-smiling Lenin looked down at the children from every wall; the little ones learned special songs for occasions such as the approaching International Women's Day (Communist version of Mother's Day); and, even on walks outdoors, the belated and admittedly still inadequate Soviet housing construction program was called to the children's attention with approving remarks such as "Those are homes in which you will someday live." If another generation was not well rooted in devotion to the Soviet state it would not be because the Party had not started soon enough. Only by chance did I hear from a Russian mother that even Communists did not consider nursery raising desirable. The institutions, with their dialectics, were good only as an unavoidable substitute for the mother, for a grandmother, for some other member of the family, or for a private servant, the Communist woman said.

The farm the Soviets permitted me to see was another to which a stream of foreigners was directed. It was a vegetable and dairy collective, named for "Ilyich," at Tarasovka, fifteen miles from Moscow. Ilyich, I was reminded by the heroic-sized statue in front of the farm's shabby wood office building, was the middle name of Lenin. So many institutions had been given the last name of the dictator that the Soviets had begun using the man's first and middle names for variety.

The importance of the farm was indicated by the decoration, the Order of Lenin, propped up like an icon in a glass case on the wall behind the desk of the deputy director, Semyen Romanyuk. The collective was relatively prosperous, Mr. Romanyuk told us with pleasure. It was near Moscow and so was able to sell its products at a 50 to 100 per cent markup. Shoppers, foreigners, and others, were willing to pay for freshness and quality.

In a gesture to relieve discontent and to encourage needed production Khrushchev was permitting farmers such as those at Tarasovka to keep a one-acre farmhouse plot for their own exploitation. Some were earning as much from that as they were from the common farm. The collective was doing so well that workers at the wholly Communistic state farm, or *sovkhoz*, nearby, wished they could switch to the semi-free, only semi-Communistic Ilyich *kolkhoz*, or collective.

But what did it mean in income for the kolkhoz's four hundred families? Each family, Mr. Romanyuk said, hoped to earn $23.00 a week from the collective during the coming year, double what they got before the Khrushchev relaxation.

And what did that imply in terms of creature comforts? Many had television, but only one family in the four hundred had an automobile. A few had motorcycles. A family in relatively fortunate circumstances was still living in the frame building it had had before the 1917 revolution.

The trip to Suzdal and Vladimir, the old Russian capitals, was one the Soviets freely permitted to Moscow foreigners. There were no great war secrets to expose and there were a score of handsome medieval churches the Russians considered a legitimate goal for an art pilgrimage.

Even so there were formalities. A letter had to be handed in forty-eight hours ahead of time to the Foreign Office, setting forth the itinerary, departure times, and even the numbers of the trains we would use. With the help of the railroad station my Russian-speaking companion, Michel Tatu, of *Le Monde* of Paris, got the train numbers, and shortly after midnight one morning we took off on the trans-Siberian.

We reached Vladimir at 5 A.M. To our pleased surprise a hotel took us in for the final two or three hours of the night.

"You are not our first foreigners," the woman clerk told us good-humoredly. "We had some last year."

An assistant showed us to a plain but adequate room. I noticed that as we started up the stairs a militiaman, one of the few persons abroad at that hour, walked into the lobby and poked his head into the registration window. It was not yet dawn but our presence evidently already had been noted. Our passports were at the registration desk. They presumably answered the policeman's questions for us.

For the thirty-mile ride from Vladimir to Suzdal we used a taxi. It was a Volga, a small new Soviet car with the lines and general appearance of one of America's "low-priced three" of a decade earlier. The driver was so pleased with such frills as the reindeer on the radiator cap and with how the vehicle had performed in its first one thousand miles of life that we found ourselves in trouble within ten minutes. We asked to walk off the road one hundred yards to examine an abandoned, centuries-old Orthodox church, and the driver assured us his Volga could carry us all the way. The snow was a foot deep. We were mired in for a half-hour.

Farther down the road we steered around what appeared to be a pile of rags.

"Drunk," the driver said with an expert air. "I saw a woman like that, too, this morning."

He drove past. A dozen workers were in the road about one hundred yards from the fallen man. Presumably they would succor him in time. In any case the cabby considered it no problem of his.

It was one of many glimpses at the problem of alcoholism bedeviling Russia's rulers.

Suzdal proved of interest for two reasons. It was a community of log houses, horse-drawn sleds, and a cluster of some of Russia's most graceful churches, relics of days a half millennium earlier when the Russian court was there. A smokestack poked through the fine, pointed-arch window of one six-hundred-year-old church converted into a power station. What interested me was the attitude both toward the churches and toward the United States.

The community's feeling about the places of worship seemed neatly summed up by one woman in her late forties. We asked her the name of one especially noble structure.

"Ask the old," she answered, and went on.

The United States was reflected in the dark little bookshop and on placards throughout the town. In the shop my eye was caught by a title: *American Aggression in Korea*. With titles like that so widely distributed, perhaps the correspondent's assistant in Moscow really believed, after all, that South Korea had attacked the communist North. The slogans on the billboards repeated a single theme: the Soviet Union must overtake the United States in the production of meat, milk, and butter. How the horses and sleds of Suzdal were to match the agricultural machines of the American Middle West no imagination could suggest, but the villagers clearly knew so little about the truth of the United States that they were not discouraged.

What the country people felt about America was indicated a few hours later in Vladimir when Michel and I looked at a pre-1917 monastery turned into civilian housing. A resident cheerfully told us its story and then paused.

"I know you're not Soviets; who are you—democrats?" he asked.

We knew enough of *Pravda's* jargon to know what he meant.

"We're not from the 'Popular democracies,'" Tatu answered. "I'm from France."

The Vladimir resident stiffened slightly but nodded.

"And he?"

Tatu braced himself. "He's from the United States."

The man's eyes widened and kept widening. We shook hands and left.

"It was all right," Tatu said. "He thought we were Communists anyway."

The idea that an American non-Communist might be encountered on one's own street was clearly more than our acquaintance could conceive. That Americans might look like any other people also was evidently far from his mind.

Ignorance was profound.

"We know more about them than they know about themselves," one journalist had told me. "One asked me if it were really true that the Soviets had launched a sputnik. He couldn't believe his own papers."

"And I challenged a high official about whether he knew the contents of the latest Khrushchev-Eisenhower exchange," a diplomat added. "He said he didn't but that it wasn't his particular field. I told him that any literate person in the West could pick it up on a newsstand."

We returned to Moscow after three more Vladimir experiences: a visit to a "working church," i.e., one still in use; supper at the hotel; and another ride on the trans-Asiatic train.

The church, a splendid one built in the early Middle Ages, was uphill from a Communist clubroom where International Women's Day was being celebrated. Loud-speakers blared the speech out of the official building into the park below the shrine. The revolution had produced a "new Soviet woman," the amplifiers roared. The words came through the crisp air

over the shawl-covered heads of elderly women trudging up
toward a service in the ancient place of worship. It was another case, like Hungary, of propaganda and fact in collision.
Very many "new Soviet women" still clung to the pieties of
old.

At the church a half-dozen aged begged with outstretched
hands.

"Christ bless you," they murmured after an offering.

Mendicants, too, we could see, were still part of the Soviet
scene four decades after the Marxist insurrection.

The church, like a scattering of others I visited, was
crowded. A tall, long-haired priest in his forties led the service. The frescoes had been recently and competently restored.
A plaque on the rear wall quoted two telegrams from Stalin
thanking the "believers" of the parish for wartime aid to Red
Army sufferers. A sprinkling of the congregation were in their
twenties. There were a few children. Most were past forty.
Religion, it was plain, was still surviving, still vigorous, but as
the Metropolitan Nikolai, number-two prelate of the Russian
church, told me in an interview, the number of faithful had
shrunk in proportion at least by half. The Moscow archbishop
said 25 per cent of the Soviet people were still Christian. The
Stalin telegrams in the Vladimir place of worship seemed a bit
too much like "safe-conduct passes" put up by the congregation in a last-ditch self-defense. They implied uncomfortably,
too, that the Kremlin atheists slowly were harnessing the Orthodox Church to their own Communist and, in the long run,
anti-religious purposes. I could not forget what one young
Russian had told me when I asked whether a long-winded
editorial in *Red Star,* the army paper, meant, in short, that
religion was "bad for the Soviet armed forces."

"Religion," I was told with eyes large with astonishment at
such a question, "is bad for all the Soviet people."

Supper at the Vladimir hotel before returning to Moscow
pointed up the way the ever-vigilant regime imposed isolation
on its people. The waitress was gentle and attractive. She
recommended turkey. We took her advice and ate well, but

twice when others asked to share our table they were summoned from the room and we saw them return, red-faced, to
other tables. An officer and his pretty but plump wife came
last. We did our best not to laugh when he, too, requested
places. We shrugged agreement. The army official had swallowed several vodkas, his wife declining to join him, and the
two had gone through *zakouskis* (hors d'oeuvres) of herring
and into the meat course before an offer of a cigarette from
Tatu opened a conversation.

The officer was cautious and hostile to what seemed an
absurd degree. Slowly he expressed several opinions and reported a few autobiographical facts. We told him who we
were. He said that his home town and that of his wife had
been destroyed by the Germans and that he had volunteered
to serve until the threat to the Soviet homeland was over. He
seemed to feel that that meant a lifetime career. He asked un-
pleasantly and pointedly what country was responsible for
Germany's revival.

Tatu, the one who had fluency in Russian, was doing the
talking. He refused to answer "the United States." Before the
conversation could take any new awkward turn, the officer
got his call from outside the room. We looked at the half-
finished meat on his plate, took pity, gulped down our coffee,
and left. The officer, who could not have done a better job
of voicing the official line, need not suffer the indignity of
having to change tables to avoid Western infection.

The ride back to Moscow was remarkable for the way in
which we were awakened. The Soviets had a method of their
own. A half-hour before we were due to arrive, the radio in
our compartment began to play softly. Volume increased each
five minutes until ten minutes before the station, when an
expressionless though rather pretty young woman snatched
away the bed sheets and even the towels. As we descended
either the radio or a public-address system was declaring:
"This is Moscow, capital of our beautiful country."

One of our first assignments back in Moscow was to cover
the elections for which the *agitpunkts* were preparing. Once

again there was not only a landslide for the single ticket of
unopposed candidates, with no slipups such as the one Gomulka had had at desperate Nowy Sącz; but all but a few
thousand of the eligible voters reportedly turned out at the
polls. I toured Moscow voting places on election day with an
official American observer team, the first the Soviets had permitted. The team was unimpressed. There was no sign that
Khrushchev was using the fear which was the latter-day Stalin's
sole instrument for government, but, the Americans decided,
the mere memory of terror was enough only five years after the
dread ruler's death. Those against the regime could do no
good by denying votes to the single slate and they could save
themselves more securely for another day if they had made
no such gesture.

The next big assignment was to cover the opening session of
the new "parliament" which was to serve until 1963. The
meeting was an insult to the forms of democracy. All speeches
approved the doings of the 125-man Communist Central Committee, or rather those of the 15-man presidium or even more
narrowly those of the tiny clique around Khrushchev. It was
a far cry from Western parliaments where the pro-Moscow
minority's violent disrespect for the majority had reached its
culmination for me one day when a new Communist deputy
in the Italian chamber of deputies had used dip pens as darts
to attack Christian Democratic opponents on the far side of
the hall.

"Why did you do that?" the indignant chairman had demanded.

"Because they were punching back at one of my Communist
colleagues and I couldn't get over in time," the new "Hon-
orable" had replied.

All the votes in the Red "parliament" were unanimous, but
the new session was no dull one all the same. It proved to be
the occasion on which Khrushchev seized public total control
as the third in the totalitarian line of Lenin and Stalin.

By then I had seen the number-one man of the 1958 Communist world several times. He showed up at a few cocktail

parties where I could study him in groups of a dozen or two, and at public rallies where I watched through glasses. Through the Soviet papers and through conversations with Western diplomats I had followed the Party leader's maneuvers for two and one-half months. My impression had solidified: Khrushchev was a vain, cruel, cynical, cunning little man, hagridden by complexes because of his humble origins and his unprepossessing physique, and capable of almost any violence in his fight for Russian imperialist objectives and in behalf of his harsh philosophy of life.

A gambler, was one diplomatic appraisal of the Soviet ruler. An old man, already sixty-three, in a hurry to make his mark before the death which he felt approaching, said another. A third called him a man appalled at the possibility of accidental atomic war and anxious to avoid it, but one who might miscalculate as he walked close to the edge, and might slip over.

Like the Arabs' young Nasser, the far more significant Khrushchev was a man of strong masculine charm. A grin split his round bald head from ear to ear as he peered up at tall diplomats at a celebration of the Indian national holiday one evening soon after my arrival in Moscow. It was hard not to smile in return. "Mr. K." carried his vast power lightly. His stocky, rather too fat figure suggested personal strength. His laugh hinted that the distortions and falsehoods of his propaganda, which so exasperated and infuriated Westerners, were something above which he could rise in pleasant company.

An instant later, when attention turned to the other member of the Soviet pair of early 1958, Premier Nikolai Bulganin, Khrushchev's appearance was transformed. All eyes turned to the relatively handsome, tall, white-goateed Bulganin, a man whose alcohol-reddened cheeks could be mistaken for signs of ruddy health. Bulganin went into the speech of the evening. As head of the government he technically outranked Party leader Khrushchev. Bulganin spun through the expected niceties and even embroidered a little with a rustic version of what might have been an English gentleman's manner in such a situation. He said that the decoration India

had just given her Moscow ambassador ought to be duplicated
by an award as well to the envoy's gracious wife.

Khrushchev's little eyes seemed to retreat under his forehead. The thin-lipped mouth curled down at the edges in
a hard, narrow line.

The diminutive Party leader's spirits were restored a few
minutes later when Bulganin stopped and the ambassadors
went back into a huddle around Khrushchev. Why not start sincere disarmament talks in the special United Nations subcom-
mittee, the tall, patrician, rosy-haired British ambassador, Sir
Patrick Reilly, urged.

"Aren't you sick of that, after six years of talk?" Khrushchev
answered with a laugh that shook him.

After a while Khrushchev beckoned to olive-skinned, hook-
nosed, bemustached Vice-Premier Anastas Mikoyan to join
him.

The Soviets' number-three man bent his shoulders and
glided forward.

"I was going to join you but I saw you were doing fine just
as you were," Mikoyan fawned. "I am sure that all these
ambassadors would agree with you except for the fact that
they do not yet 'have authorization from their governments.'"

Mikoyan doubled under the force of laughter at his own
joke. He glanced fleetingly at his audience, Khrushchev. The
latter, lordly, smiled. The tableau could not have made plainer
how extreme was the personal dictatorship the scrappy, crude-
minded former coal miner Khrushchev had imposed. Even
number three was light-years beneath number one. Bulganin,
the premier, signer of the peremptory invitations to a "summit conference" which were alarming the free world that
winter, officially number one or two, grinned wordlessly at the
edge of the group. It seemed to me that by his manner he was
begging the little Khrushchev for good will. Khrushchev ignored him.

I studied Khrushchev again at his one campaign speech
for election to Parliament. He and his immediate aides had
picked each of the 1,378 candidates and Khrushchev had been
nominated two hundred times. With a grand gesture Mr. K.

had refused one hundred and ninety-nine offers and "modestly" had accepted the last, one of the prize Moscow city seats. Bulganin, too, had been put up, but he had been switched out of Moscow, which he had represented in the previous parliament, and had been nominated only a dozen times. By such subtleties were trends revealed in the totalitarian Soviet Union. Whoever had rigged the nominations—and it was proper to assume that it was Mr. K.—had given a rousing vote of approval to Khrushchev and the slimmest acceptance to the other member of what had been the "B. and K." team.

Three hundred who shared the platform with the Party leader for his combined maiden and windup speech of the campaign walked on in a body. Khrushchev, his head bowed boyishly, followed. The expected applause thundered toward him with discipline. All was as foreseen, until a half-hour later the former representative of Moscow, Premier Bulganin, came in. There was electrified attention. The fine art of reading between the lines is well developed under the Soviet red star. All knew by then what Khrushchev was doing to his former partner. Bulganin strode to his former teammate and embraced him. The audience cheered, this time with passion. Was it possible that the wound at the nation's top might heal, that the joint leadership might not disintegrate into another one-man dictatorship? "How can you account for it?" a Westerner whispered. " 'Rehabilitation' before the 'execution.' " He referred to what was by then the well-known practice of killing men and then exonerating them after the funeral. This time, however, the "rehabilitation" seemed to be Bulganin's sole doing, for a moment later, as attention shifted back to the speaker's rostrum, I noticed that Khrushchev's broad back was turned squarely on his old associate.

What was going on irresistibly was the process of elimination of rivalry and consolidation of one-man totalitarianism. It was being managed with the rhythm of a dance, two steps forward, one back. The one to the rear disarmed reaction which might have been feared from the premier's allies after forty years in top revolutionary circles. The emphasis was again on the "one step back" when I asked a Communist editor about three editorials which had appeared simultaneously in different parts of the Soviet Union, praising the caliber of candidates and listing fourteen names as examples. The fourteen were Khrushchev, of course, and all the rest of the Presidium with one exception: Premier Bulganin.

"It's impossible," the editor said. "They were typographical errors."

Next day, as if to prove good faith, the editor in his paper praised the Presidium and mentioned Bulganin.

But the Khrushchev cat was about ready for the Bulganin mouse. It happened swiftly as the new parliament convened. Marshal Kliment E. Voroshilov, Soviet "president," rose to the accompaniment of an energetic burst of hand clapping from Khrushchev. The president sprang the surprise. The 125-man Communist Central Committee, he said, had decided that the vigorous little extrovert who guided Party destinies should run the government, too, and should keep both jobs. Khrushchev's pate shone as his bald head bowed in a repetition of the show of youthful modesty the master of the Soviet Communists had offered to the audience at the campaign speech. Then the new successor of the czars looked up with a smile and clapped, too. It was Soviet fashion for all to applaud, even the one who was cheered. Bulganin, his pink cheeks redder than ever, struck his palms together, too.

"That's what's worst: even the victim has to approve," a Western reporter murmured as we stared.

With an admirable technique for reducing excitement, Khrushchev stood up for a two-hour speech on the need for more manure and similar improvements on the farms. If there was any danger of protest in the handpicked parliament at the spectacle of the discarding of the so recently extolled "collective leadership" and the revival of the reviled one-man dictatorship, it was buried under Khrushchev's drone.

"Why the long speech on farming?" I asked a Soviet official in the corridors.

"It's not that others don't know about agriculture and, for that matter, about industry and all the other things," the man replied with embarrassment. "It's just that Khrushchev knows more."

The vacant throne, the altar of Lenin and Stalin, was empty no longer. It was a moment of history. It had gone so easily —but had it really been managed that well? A Western reporter asked his Moscow cabdriver that night whether he had heard the news that there was a new premier.

"Who?" asked the cabby, "Kirichenko?"

"No, Khrushchev."

"Khrushchev?" The man was stunned. "Then who is the new head of the Party, Suslov?"

"No, it's still Khrushchev."

The cabdriver was shaken.

"Impossible! Well, if not impossible, at least it's just temporary. The two jobs are incompatible."

He was to learn differently. Another Soviet myth had been dissipated. "Collective leadership" no longer was necessary, one-person dictatorship was no longer bad. The Party line had doubled back on itself. The cabby surely uttered no such sentiments again, but he could never forget. There must have been millions like him.

There were faults in the heavy, pretentious skyscraper of the Communist ideology, but it still dominated Russia, Asia, and much of the world, just as the "Stalin Culture Palace" brooded over imprisoned Warsaw. Many were searching for truth, but too many were like one Russian who told me that he had known a Western naval attaché who had been "P.N.G.'d" (declared *persona non grata*) as a hooligan.

"Really a perfect gentleman," the Russian said. "But maybe you can explain it to me. Whatever could have got into him to make him act like a hooligan?"

Even a Soviet citizen who had known the slandered man's character had been taken in by the official lie.

"I argued a good part of the way from Moscow to Leningrad to try to convince one Russian that you don't need a passport from Brooklyn to Manhattan, but he wouldn't believe it," said a Westerner. " 'Town-to-town passports here are nothing unusual, because the world has them everywhere,' the Russian kept saying."

For every one who saw through the falsehoods of the regime ten or a hundred believed them.

Bolstering the regime, too, was nationalism. The Soviet conscience was shaken when word spread that Russian troops had shot down Hungarian workers, but nationalism finally dominated, one Western correspondent recalled. He had been in Moscow while I was in Budapest.

"They said that, after all, the Hungarians had slain Russians and then they asked: 'Who do they think they are? Hungarians, doing that to us great Russians!' "

Even the very many who were anti-Communist, one diplomat told me, "can't help being pleased when a country like Guatemala goes Red—it's one more ally for Russia." The significant word was "Russia." It was not "the Soviets" or "communism."

More and more pictures of Khrushchev appeared in public places. The wart on the left side of the dictator's nose faded in progressively handsomer portraits. But all was not well with the new tyranny. It was clear that not merely the Eastern European satellites were rebelling. At Moscow University, another forty-story skyscraper, where pampered students lunched on fifteen-cent caviar sandwiches, things were far from perfect from a Presidium point of view. It was not just a question of black-market jazz and rock 'n' roll; students were refusing to volunteer for the desolate "virgin lands" which the Soviets were trying to build up along the borders of the demographically explosive Chinese ally. College youth had gone East, but under compulsion. University teachers had protested against the massacre in Hungary. Diplomats saw trouble almost everywhere; in the army where generals could not forget the way the Party had purged the top leadership in the thirties and the manner in which Khrushchev did the same to Marshal Zhukov late in 1957; on the farms like the one at Tarasovka, where Khrushchev had to scrap Communist theory and allow a return of some private enterprise, with the glib remark that "what works is what is really Communist"; among the artists who hated the ban on "art for its own sake"; among the general public who longed for an easier life and felt more and more the influence of music, clothing styles, and all the other comforts of the West.

No multiplication of prettied-up pictures of Khrushchev could ease the discontent. Diplomats had a variety of forecasts. Some were sure that Khrushchev or his successors would have to revive terror as a way of ruling. Some predicted that unless there was more relaxation the Soviet Union within five years, by 1963, would see revolution. Writers, musicians, scientists, intellectuals of all sorts, could not keep swallowing ignorant edicts from Khrushchev and the few around him, these foreigners argued. If revolution came in the satellites, in Poland for instance, "we would have a real go here in the Soviet Union," such Westerners forecast. Forty per cent of the Soviet population were second-class citizens like the Ukrainians, and ever restive under the heel of the language, culture, and dominance of the Great Russians. At the very least today's twenty-year-olds would make it a different, less revolutionary Russia when they replaced the sexagenarian Bolsheviks, still others thought.

Countering them were those who emphasized another point: no matter what happened to communism, the virile Russian people would be an important world factor at least until well into the seventies. To hear some such Westerners talk, continentals among them, Europe and even Britain were well into decadence, with sturdy Russia and a still virile America the sole real international contestants.

I flew out of the Soviet Union on its jet airline to Denmark. Ice floated in the Baltic Sea, cold still gripping the northern waters although it was already well into spring. Moscow, we saw, was not many dozens of jet minutes from the thin slice of West Eurasia which was "the Continent." The menace from Moscow was enormous. There was no sign in those early months of 1958 that the Kremlin fortress, sitting as it does on the bull's-eye of the great target of concentric circular highways which is Moscow, would soon give up its missionary determination to make the world Communist; would turn its energies peacefully in on the great ill-exploited land mass the Presidium already controls; or would give up whispering belligerently to diplomats, "We can hit you with rockets, even with airplanes."

The reason for fear was great, but cause for hope was large, too. Even foreign Communists were troubled if not repelled when they saw at first hand the disillusioning truth the Moscow cabby and so many others were learning. A Westerner who had become a Soviet agent because he had thought at the time of the Berlin blockade that the free world was threatening to "impose its way of life" on reluctant Easterners had swallowed the crushing of Hungary only by deciding, "If you're tough enough you can take it." Life under the Soviets' red star made sense only by a double standard. Surely that could not go on forever.

With relief I turned my back on the plane of the world's first anti-economic jet airline. I stepped into the colorful and relaxed waiting room of the airport of free Denmark. I could not believe that the West, for all its exhaustion, its discouragement, its temptations to neutralism, its scant discipline, its disunity, and its thirst for high-cost pleasures, would fall to the Soviet Presidium and its dictator, to the toadying Mikoyan and the brutal Khrushchev, to the mere 4 per cent of the Soviets who are their country's Communist party. Friends of the West were everywhere, behind the curtain in the satellites, among the intellectuals and youth of the Soviet Union, perhaps even among wiser Russian nationalists in the Soviet communist upper reaches.

If the West—the Continent, America, and all the free world —kept faith in itself, preserved the willingness to pay for its precious freedom and human values, and harbored a self-sacrificing missionary spirit toward the wavering new nations on communism's edge, there was no reason why the future should belong to the Kremlin Presidium.

XI

CONFIDENCE
IN EUROPE

Midsummer 1958 saw a new assignment, another trip back to French North Africa. The army had revolted against the Parliament and against the government in Paris and had imposed General De Gaulle as a more authoritarian new leader.

I followed De Gaulle as he made two successive one-thousand-mile tours of Algeria in a month, hunting a formula that would satisfy the "humiliated" Arab natives and would keep the rest of independence-minded French Africa bound even loosely to Paris. I watched as the earnest, dedicated World War II hero groped for something even more important, a device for bringing some sort of unity and patriotic devotion to the France of tired premiers and white nights, the France which had sent no draftees to save Indo-China, the France which was still torn about how to preserve or even whether to cling to its rich holdings in the Dark Continent.

They were strange journeys, for none could work miracles, not even the proud and dedicated De Gaulle. Some volunteers in the premier's entourage tried, even with a strong seasoning of cynicism, to help the new leader with the same sort of propaganda the Communists had used successfully against them in Indo-China. Practically all the Moslems, they lied, were with the general, happy to change sides and choose the French as soon as they recognized "strength" in that camp. The Moslem women, too, said the volunteer propagandists, wanted to put aside the veils which helped make them second-class people and to take a new and better place in the modern world France represented. There was no doubt that liberal France exerted a strong attraction for the natives of French

North Africa, but the self-chosen press agents exaggerated it and ignored the opposing influence exerted by Egypt. It was summed up for me by two bearded Moslem patriarchs at the rally at Mostaganem where De Gaulle finished his first Algerian tour. Each looked a good deal like the aged Mahometan who had used his silver-mounted rifle, fortunately ineffectively, against our little party at Oued Zem.

The two men, surely illiterate, thrust up a banner in French under De Gaulle's eyes. It had been meant to be carried by a pair of veiled women who might have underlined its significance by whipping off their face kerchiefs at the climax. But hard-pressed propagandists must have had no time for niceties, and the first sets of hands had received the banners.

"We want to be like our French sisters," read the grizzled pair's sign.

It was a changed North Africa from the one I had seen in the first months of the Algerian war four years earlier. Officials had assured me cheerfully in 1954 that all would soon be over if there were a few expected good breaks, and that the rebel force was so slight that I should be careful not even to use the word "war" in my dispatches. But there had been no good breaks and even a steady build-up of the French force to an army of a half a million, including many draftees this time, had won no peace by mid-1958. Officers were then wearing chains on their pistols so that Arab passers-by could not snatch the weapons. Screens against hand grenades protected the windows of busses and restaurants. Shoppers were frisked for bombs at the doors of large department stores. Both of my main French and Arab contacts were gone: Aly Chekkal, a white-cloaked and spool-turbaned Moslem member of the Algerian parliament who had ticked off for me on my last visit a long list of French concessions he considered necessary if there was to be peace between his Arab and French friends; and Amédée Frogier, head of the French Mayors' Association, one of the most intransigent of the European settlers. Frogier had been cool to me at first because he shared European resentments against what was regarded as the anti-colonialist

United States, but he had warmed up as one who was an ally at heart and had agreed to introduce me on my next trip to what he considered a typical settler family. I would be able to describe its hopes and fears, its satisfactions and sufferings, perhaps even its casualties. It had been little more than a year since my last trip to Algeria, but I saw neither Chekkal nor Frogier, for both had been assassinated. The war between the well-armed men of France and the primitively equipped, Egyptian-backed native slayers, killers at one moment and apparently peaceful members of the teeming Arab civil community the next, was largely invisible, but it was taking a steady toll, just as had the lost Indo-China war against Asia's Communists.

The trend in Algeria that summer seemed to be toward independence for all France's Africans. It was less clear whether France could keep some ties to the old territories, as Britain to some extent had managed in the Commonwealth. Whether France would reform her liberties enough to give her the minimum of discipline needed for peace and prosperity was also unsure. For a forecast I would fall back on what Italy's foreign minister, Count Carlo Sforza, had told us of the international press in Rome on the eve of the dramatic elections in 1948 in which his country chose between the Communist and anti-Communist alternatives.

"You want to know what will happen?" the wise old professor-statesman and anti-Fascist democrat asked us. "Well, I'll tell you. Nothing will occur. Nothing ever happens in Italy."

Others were delighted with the quip. I was at first offended. It seemed to me that everything had happened in the Italian peninsula, from Hannibal's elephants and Julius Caesar to the Vatican, the Renaissance, and Fascism. But in a way Sforza was right. The Italians voted down the Communists and an undramatic but effective recovery continued. And the France of Sorbonne brilliance, of the wit of the Paris theater, of the armies of Napoleon, of the audacity of the eighteenth-century philosophers, of the cult of Joan of Arc, and of the natural wealth of the homeland, could not die. New leaves would sprout on the old trunk. Life in France would help preserve it in tired, crowded Italy, too.

Perhaps it seemed only an act of faith in the Continent but there were many, however often tenuous, reasons for it. When the emotional and bitter Nasser received me, he was wearing a suit of English wool. He spoke almost perfect English. When Nasser wanted to justify his neutralism he had asked the American embassy to send him a copy of George Washington's Farewell Address with its warning against "foreign entanglements." Even as he cut ties with America the Egyptian dictator had thought in United States historical and philosophical terms. It was at least mildly reassuring evidence of Western and even specifically American intellectual penetration.

Even the often rather brutish Khrushchev seemed to me uncertain as he marshaled forces against free Europe and the West. I remembered one of his speeches while I was in Moscow. He recalled petulantly that Western critics saw Soviet minorities as enslaved. If the Liberals were to dine on the "slavish pilaff" those minorities ate they would find it not so bad, the Soviets' master said. The words had been cocky enough, but somehow I was convinced that even the crude Khrushchev realized secretly that "pilaff" was not enough.

Many diplomats thought that Egypt, at the core of the Middle Eastern Arab revolt, was not lost to the free world despite all the infantility and even viciousness of so much it typified. Perhaps even the Soviet bloc, as the greater of the external threats, was a somewhat less formidable foe than it seemed.

I remembered the statue of the Bolshevik secret policeman the Russians had erected in Warsaw after World War II. He was Felix Dzerzinsky, a Pole who had gone to Moscow at the time of the 1917 revolution to help direct the CEKA, the dread terrorist organization which slaughtered so many, Communists and non-Communists alike. Few love a secret policeman, but no hot-tempered Pole had damaged the monument. Perhaps that was because of the word which had spread about it: "It honors a Pole who went to Russia to kill Russians."

I recalled the policeman at the Soviet Patriarch's door in Moscow, a sign that four decades after the atheist revolution the Kremlin had to tolerate and exercise surveillance over a representative of religion.

I thought back on the word which was on the lips of every Soviet citizen: *kulturny* (culture), an all-embracing though vague summary of the spiritual qualities even the most materialistic and amoral of the Marxists longed to possess, so much so that the most terrible rebuke to hurl at someone grabbing a Moscow taxi out of turn was to cry: *"ni kulturny!"* ("lacking in culture!"). Where kulturny so much mattered, surely some of the civil values of the West still exerted an influence.

Still another memory was what every Hungarian had heard in Budapest at the time of the rape of the satellite capital: "These soldiers think the Danube is the Nile!" The troops, from what Budapest understood, had been groomed for action in Egypt, and had been kept in such ignorance that they thought captive Hungary was the land of the pyramids. Armies always preserve secrets from the troops, but there was something uniquely obscurantist about the Soviets. Surely no modernizing society long could endure such mental serfdom.

North Africa posed new questions, but at least the visit to Moscow had given answers to many others. For me it had closed a book I had opened in college. At my university (Fordham), in New York in 1935, I had been swamped, as editor of the college newspaper, by pamphlets "against war and Fascism," for the "students' league," and in franker moments, for the Young Communist League. For an editor of a Catholic college newspaper, with the university's heavy emphasis on religious values, there was scant likelihood even then, at the end of a depression and on the eve of a new world war, that I should join the Communists, but other college editors did. There was something plausible about the opinion of certain students at Oxford that the way to end wars was for all, individually, to refuse arms even in his own nation's frontier defense. It seemed at least a partial truth that wars were the creation of arms manufacturers. There was something exciting also about youths remaking feudal China in a new (Communist) image. It had been easy then to take guidance from the Kremlin dictator. A generation and a long glimpse of Russia later it was unthinkable.

It did not mean that the struggle was over. A young Chinese in a seat next to Mary and me one night in the Stanislavsky ballet theater in the Soviet capital started up a conversation to say that he had just finished eight years of university engineering studies in the United States and had decided to go to the Red China he had never seen. By his account he was the son of an upper-class anti-Communist family, had felt himself an Oriental outsider in America, and finally, after seeing the Jewish nationalist as well as religious De Mille motion picture *The Ten Commandments,* decided that his place was "like Moses" with "my people." Red Chinese he had met in Communist Czechoslovakia on his way into the Soviet bloc had assured him he was doing the right thing, and Russians in Moscow had been amiable.

"I'm convinced there is heavy propaganda on both sides. Eisenhower has no hooked nose and claws, the way you see him on the posters of Communist China, but communism is not warlike the way you Western newspapermen paint it, either."

I hoped for his sake that he was right, but the Hungarian-American Santo's experience promised the opposite.

There was still bitter emotion on levels far below that of the violent Khrushchev. I remembered what one American consulate attaché had told me in Zagreb in Yugoslavia. The four-year-old from next door, using fistfuls of sand, patiently had rubbed the paint from the back of the diplomat's automobile.

"Why are you doing that?" the attaché had demanded in the newly-acquired Serbo-Croat of which he was proud.

"You Americans," the child told him calmly, "have everything."

The fact that Americans were sharing a good deal of their

substance with the tot's country made him no more grateful
than I had found Egypt's President Nasser in similar circumstances.

Western wealth, even shared, was making enemies. It would
not be easy to live even as benefactors with the array of new
nations of Africa and Asia and with the changing countries of
Latin America.

It would not be simple, but it had to be done. All the material and spiritual resources of Europe would be needed, and
however distressing the thought, young America would have
to lead. I recalled what one retired American ambassador had
told me: "In my last post there was never any question as to
who was number one in the diplomatic corps. It was not the
Britisher and it was not the Russian. It was I as the American."

Another prominent American diplomat, this one an am-
bassador-to-be, had reacted quickly when I had asked whether
the United States still took its lead quietly from the more experienced and skilled foreign-policy officials of England.

"Not for little apples," he assured me in the language of
his Midwest birthplace.

For an American there was nationalistic satisfaction in that,
but there was appalling responsibility, too.

Americans in effect were electing the president of the whole
Western federation. Others with no say in his choice had to
accept him as their guide, too: a sort of leadership without
representation, something all too embarrassingly similar to
what caused the thirteen colonies' eighteenth-century revolt
against England.

It was a dismayingly great deal to ask of Americans: that
they be ever-ready soldiers to form the core of free-world de-
fenses; that they be unselfish economic missionaries, sharing
know-how; that they be linguists and philosophers, worthy
representatives of the Western tradition; that they be masters
of tact as they shaped an alliance in which proud and brilliant
Europe could give its best willingly and without resentment
against the Americans who "have everything." It demanded an

immense amount from Americans and from long-dominant Europe, too, from continental nationalists and ex-imperialists who faced bitter change and at least temporary setbacks. To be mere auxiliaries under Washington leadership was repugnant to peoples who had been so great. It was their very qualities of magnanimity, however, their very achievements of the past, and their still-full reservoirs of thought and capabilities, which gave me confidence that they would join effectively in the common defense of the generous, liberal West. The anticolonialist and Western struggle was still far from its conclusion, but after a decade in and around the Continent which I had longed to see I was heartened with what I had found and was sure that the beneficent contribution of Europe and the West was far from finished.